THE HIDDEN PLOT

Notes on Theatre and the State

Edward Bond

THE HIDDEN PLOT

Notes on Theatre and the State

Edward Bond

Methuen

Published by Methuen 2000

1 3 5 7 9 10 8 6 4 2

First published in Great Britain in 2000 by Methuen Publishing Limited
215 Vauxhall Bridge Road, London SW1V 1EJ

Copyright © Edward Bond 2000

The author has asserted his rights under the Copyright, Designs
and Patents Act, 1988, to be identified as the author of this work

Methuen Publishing Limited Reg. No. 3543167

A CIP catalogue record for this book is available from the British Library

ISBN 0 413 72550 2

Typeset by Deltatype Ltd, Birkenhead, Merseyside

Printed and bound in Great Britain by
Creative Print and Design (Wales), Ebbw Vale

For Ian Stuart

Contents

Letter to Tom Erhardt

Tom Erhardt
Casarotto Ramsay
60–66 Wardour Street
London W1

3 November 98

Dear Tom

Thanks for sending me the list of plays the Royal National Theatre intend to use to mark the end of the century. *Saved* is on the list. Do not give them a licence to use the play.

If today *Saved* were offered to the Royal National Theatre as a new play it would refuse it as certainly as it refused *Coffee* and *The Crime of the Twenty-first Century*. I am content that these plays should be performed abroad in other languages. This is not to spare myself complicity in hypocrisy. My motive is more serious.

We are made not by our ability to reason but by our need to dramatize ourselves and our situations. In drama reason and imagination elucidate each other. This enables us to understand ourselves and what we do. Dramatization in all its forms is the one means we have of creating this knowledge and constantly recreating our humanness. The Royal National Theatre trivializes drama and – with a consequence that is so inevitable it is almost the punishment inflicted on error by history – has made itself incompetent to deal with the problems of being human. It is a consequence that is the lesson of drama itself. I am not surprised that the Royal National Theatre has not learnt it.

The dead cannot defend themselves or their works. But no living writer should allow his or her work to be used to celebrate drama in a place which damages it so irresponsibly.

Best wishes

Edward

A Writer's Story

I was born at 8.30 pm on Wednesday the 18th of July 1934
In a thunderstorm
An hour before her labour began my mother scrubbed the stairs to her flat
  to clean them for the midwife to tread on
In the district in which my mother lived medical people were regarded as
  agents of authority
I was first bombed when I was five
The bombing went on till I was eleven
Later the army taught me ten ways to kill my enemy
And the community taught me a hundred ways to kill my neighbour
I saw there was no justice between one part of the community and another
An injustice is like a pebble dropped in the centre of the ocean
When the ripples reach the shores they have turned into tidal waves that
  drown cities
Necessity rules our days by the law of cause-and-effect
Those who govern do not know what a person is
And the governed do not know what a government should be
Instead the evil do evil and because there is no justice the good must also do evil
How else can they govern the prison they live in?
I walked the streets and raged
I wanted the stones in the military cemetery to weep for the dead beneath them
I wanted the skull to dream of justice
And then I remembered the iron kite that flies in the child's mind
And saw the old touch their white hairs as gently as a sparrow nesting on the side
  of an iceberg
So at twenty I wrote a play
The law of plays must be cause-and-use
To break necessity and show how there may be justice
Like all who lived at the midpoint of this century or were born later
I am a citizen of Auschwitz and a citizen of Hiroshima
Of the place where the evil did evil and the place where the good did evil
Till there is justice there are no other places on earth: there are only these two
  places
But I am also a citizen of the just world still to be made

(1997)

Our Story

Ayee

Since the last century the material conditions of most people in the West and some other places have become better. There are more clothes, houses, food. We can't know whether we are now happier, but it's sure that we do not think we are.

In the past people found ways to explain their good and bad times. The explanations were stories because they gave a meaning to what they described. Together the stories made one complete story called a 'culture'. And so the stories became the reality they described. They appeared in language: coloured words, drove idioms, prescribed rational language and evoked poetry. The story was served on plates and eaten. It was worn. It was beaten into weapons. People lived and died for it.

A culture's story is a plot which binds its people to their place and means of existence. It gives life meaning and so it is the source of judgement. It isn't reason that makes us human, it's imagination. Einstein's reason is a more complicated form of the reasoning of a rat. But no rat – no animal – imagines. Animals have no stories.

The child who never told stories would be a human shell. If it did not imagine it could not reason. Stories structure our minds. In fact we are our story, it's what we live. And as it relates us to the world, the imagination that creates the story is logical and disciplined – more so than reason. We used to call this logic fate, and thought the gods owned the story. Really it is our story and we are the storytellers. When stories lose their logic – when things are too chaotic to be shaped by the story – the storytellers go mad.

Stories let us live and create civilizations, but they concern a wound. One reason for this is that we are limited and mortal. But because stories tell of a wound, if we cure the wound we die and civilizations fall. Only madness and discipline are left.

Without the real world there would be no story, but without the story there would be no real world. Always the story placed daily life in a larger frame so that people could find a meaning for all things. Because they told stories they were able to build and farm and escape starvation. But stories were told in a time of scarcity and need (which was another part of the wound). When a story tells of need it must also tell of justice. Justice is the desire of the imagination.

The story told in need must have a Utopia, a heaven in earth or sky.

There could be no stories or human beings without Utopia. But suppose there was no scarcity? Suppose we were so affluent that we could say we were *all* better off (we might even postpone death) – how would the story change? The gods would no longer own it and its plot would not be justice. It would be owned by the administration and its plot would be law and order.

Affluence abolishes need and with it the common-sense 'reason' for discord and crime. Yet these things continue. Why? The wound has stopped being part of the cure and become our disease. More and more we will use criminals, the asocial, the unregimented, as the medieval ages used heretics. They burnt them. The imagination is very logical and that is why step by step, prison by prison, law by law, we return to the age of barbarism.

The story told in our time of affluence concerns not creation but consumption – the frantic consumption we need to maintain the economy. The story no longer relates us to the real world but turns in on itself and shuts out reality. Now there is no Utopia, no heavenly or earthly city of justice. There is no eternity, not even a tomorrow. The story becomes a repeated 'now', and justice mere political convenience. But because the imagination is logical it knows that this 'now' is a living death. That is the present state of our minds. The real world breaks down and we invent a world of fantasy and violence.

We begin to lose our humanity. The affluent Utopia becomes a prison. In earlier times stories of gods and demons related their people to their world in a more human way than our supermarkets and machines relate us to ours. Perhaps we will go on being less cruel but we are no longer the guides to our own existence. Our stories are obsessed with the appearance of justice but not its reality. Justice must always question itself. But the criminal-and-detective ethos of our newspapers, TV, films and stages – the ethos that haunts us – asks only 'who dunnit'. It seeks victims, it does not define justice.

To conceive of justice yet question it – not bind it in fetters of law and conformity – was the story's most vital thread. It civilized us. And we have lost it. Our obsessive stories make justice mechanical and try to galvanize it with violence and sentimentality. The two always go together.

Once the story related the community to the world. But the consumer consumes alone. Our democracy sustains itself by systematically de-democratizing its people. Justice flourishes in communities which know how to question justice and recreate it. If there is no community, no society, there is no justice. The economy grows, the means of material well-being and happiness increase – yet socially we are sicker. Our affluence is a higher form of poverty. In the past the story searched for truth, now we search for lies. And so our angst will turn into terror and escapades of sickening communal violence.

Just as our democracy de-democratizes people, religion becomes the enemy of God. It needs the Devil to explain away 'evil', not a God of justice. The regimentation of education is another part of the dehumanization. Capitalism is a human perversion. It forces the imagination to consent to a world run for the sake of the market. We slip into the past.

Drama is the fullest version of the story because it most directly re-enacts our situation and tensions. Consumer democracy saturates us in drama because it must coerce imagination into creating its fake reality. Once all stories allowed some freedom; consumerism allows less and less. Our drama – our theatre – is part of this corruption, deeply involved in the work of de-democratizing. It takes the great questions and trivializes them.

Those who make the story trivial and false – who do not allow justice to question itself – corrupt justice. But because the imagination is logical, it seeks justice even more when it is denied. The imagination must seek to create the world as it is, not as market democracy wants it to be. That is what makes us human. But often the imagination seeks blindly, reacts without understanding, and the chaos worsens. There is conflict in us and in society. Words change their meanings, crime becomes law, violence becomes policy, and we have no way – no story, no drama – of stopping it. A world of misery opens before us.

The question is not whether in the next hundred years there will be a new Auschwitz and a new Hiroshima. There will be. The question is only what new names will be made infamous and what new horrors will be done there.

This will be because our democracy corrupts drama – makes false the story we need to create ourselves.

(1995)

Language

We are human because we have a human language. Other animals communicate and interact, feel pain and pleasure; but they do not know the difference between, say, force and persuasion. This is because they do not know there is a listener. Our language is human because we know that there is a listener when we speak. We listen to each other when we speak and to ourselves when we speak and think. This gives us our self-consciousness and makes our language human.

Not all the language we speak is human. We speak animal languages too. They are not our most biological but our most rational languages – the pure languages of technology, mathematics and so on. These languages work in the way objects interact. They are complete in themselves even before they are spoken. They do not depend on a listener. If we spoke only such languages we would not be human.

It is the self-consciousness sustained by human language that promotes both change and our ability to respond to change. It is a basic dynamic. It originates in the speaker's sense of his or her right to be, to exist, and that this right ought to be acknowledged by the listener. It is the origin of our desire for justice. It appears first in the child and makes it necessary for it to learn to be human and to speak. Without this dynamic the mind is not coherent and cannot listen to itself. It is autistic or insane.

The conviction of the 'right to be', the desire for justice, entails the conviction that the world is an appropriate place for this right and that the only limit on it is our mortality. But this is true only of the natural world, not of the social world. The social world is owned and therefore it is unjust. All human language is spoken within this horizon of injustice, and to speak even the most trivial thing is to assert justice against injustice.

We use technical languages in doing complex things such as splitting atoms and simple things such as opening doors. But all other languages become metaphors for our human language. It is why, for example, the religious spoke of God as a mathematician. God was also called the source of morality and justice. That is another reason why we cannot speak without asserting the desire for justice. Justice is not an objective effect, a natural relation – it depends on a social relationship, on speaking and listening.

This relationship has been the dynamic of history; it is the way in which we respond to material change. And because this is so, history is the record of our increasing humanity – even now, when the great power of technology has multiplied our diminishing *in*humanity to make this the most *in*human of times.

Human language is implicitly the desire for justice, regardless of what the language is used to say. The desire for justice is the inner-idiom of human language. But the social world is unjust. And so human language has always been a desire for a just future, either a political Utopia or a religious Day of Judgement – a time when the mind could speak justice without the corruptions and distortions that come from adapting to authority. In this way the future was always part of the present. Every day was also the last day, and to struggle for Utopia was to anticipate it. The transcendental was part of the immanent. The simplest words, images and actions were also the most sublime. Art was a sign of God. Because of this we not only experienced the torments of history, we could imagine the torments of hell. Everything – the visual and tactile – became language, image and metaphor – as if the whole world desired justice.

Justice presupposes our right to maintain our life. But society was a place of scarcity. This scarcity had to be administered by authority. And inevitably this led to the creation and protection of privilege. Social institutions administered justice but were themselves corrupt. It was part of the inevitable consequence of scarcity. It resulted in terrible ideological and psychological distortions in which the loudest calls for justice came from the unjust. This is why language needed its sense of future – a just time when sufficiency would replace scarcity. The economy depended on storms at sea, on the rain and sun for harvest – on the things in God's hands. And so the daily sustaining of life depended on the last day, the Day of Judgement, on the Utopian time to come. And now it seems as if technology too were directed to the future – but in fact it abolishes it. We do not depend on God for our economic prosperity and technology does not wait for Utopia. If there are faults, they are technological and technology will solve them. Technology does not work like God – it is in our hands here and now. The difference is fundamental. We speak many of the same words but we listen differently.

This change is multiplied by our economy. It seems as if the economy is so closely interrelated with technology that it must be part of technology and speak its language. That is not so. Our economy is an alchemy. Technology observes natural law but the economy does not. Its own activity produces the phenomena it observes and seeks to control. It arbitrarily produces its own necessity. This makes it fundamentally diverge from the needs of human language. Medieval alchemy sought to turn base metal into precious metal, dross into gold. It failed because it did not observe natural law. Our alchemy succeeds: it turns everything into gold, into money and capital, but it turns all other values – our freedom, democracy and justice – into dross. And so our language ceases to be human.

The alchemy works because it is parasitic on technology. And because alchemy does not depend on natural law it is more protean then technology – and so alchemy and not technology drives the economy. Now the economy has become our moral arbiter: the able and industrious prosper and the idle and feckless are cast out into everlasting poverty. Alchemy has all the corruptions of religion and none of its innocence. Modern capitalism is the 'second coming' – and God has returned to the earth mad.

All this is done with the best intentions. Corruption is not an existential evil, it is the desire for justice distorted by fear. Paradoxically, corruption pursues justice, with all the ideological fervour created by the desire for justice: but of course it can never achieve it. Hence the fury of the pathological mind and reactionary politics. Hence the increasing anomie and violence of our cities. Hence our weapons and prisons. But the alchemy that sustains our lives renames all things, and so we cannot explain ourselves to ourselves. Western democracy has become a secret Culture of Death. Instead of speaking human language we chant alchemical spells and arm our magic with the terrors of gigantesque technology.

The economy needs the poor who will fight to be rich, and the rich who are rich only because they have defeated the poor. This is unjust but we have created justice in our own image, it is inherent in our speaking, and when our need for justice is slighted then – like the ancient gods when they were slighted – we turn to wrath. Our democracy is doing what fascism could not: it combines technology with alchemy, and will produce an age of warlocks armed with nuclear weapons. We see the beginnings of this in post-modernism. What has been called the End of History is really the Vanishing of the Future. Post-modernism means that we have begun to live in the past. The roaring of our media is like the sound of dinosaurs. Every species before it becomes extinct enters into a state of post-modernism.

There are signs that we no longer speak a human language. Our philosophers cannot tell us the meaning of things, our moralists cannot tell us how we should act, we are armed with weapons so powerful that peace brings us the dangers of war, our media tell us of distant disasters to distract us from dealing with our own, our democracy cannot define freedom for us, our politicians do not understand what they are doing, our children walk away from us.

Post-modernism is a turning point not yet an end. It is as if human life were a last dream flickering in the minds of the dead. Soon they will fall asleep for ever. For a while we can still hear the echo of human language. It is not spoken in our courts, legislatures, factories, and seldom in our schools and theatres. But we still hear its echoes on the walls of our prisons, madhouses, children's playgrounds, the derelict ghettos of our cities.

Theatre has only one subject: justice. Our minds are the site of imagination because we listen as well as speak. Imagination creates our world. It is as if each of us were a sculptor who created an image out of the raw stone of the world. The image is either just or corrupt. Theatres are the site of public imagination where the distinction between speaking and listening is dissolved. Neither love nor religion can do that. Yet it is essential to our shared humanity, for how else shall we learn to live justly? But now our alchemy corrupts our imagination, and if it succeeds in this we will lose our human language. No previous culture has achieved that extreme of nihilism.

There is an old legend which says that when Lazarus was raised from the dead he remembered how to live – how to walk, eat, dress, sleep, laugh and cry. He knew his family and friends. He had forgotten only one thing: his language – and so he could not remember or say what had happened to him. Our task is to teach the dead to listen.

(1995)

Modern Drama

'I have discovered something about your plays.
The performance of the small things must be right. *small ideas*
Otherwise the big things are not there.' *Big Ideas*

Alain Françon
in conversation with Edward Bond

Why do we make drama? Why do audiences go to plays? In sport both players and supporters hope their team will win. Winning depends on the players. For actors to create drama and audiences to perceive it, both require the same creativity. Neither sport nor drama can be reduced to aesthetic pleasure. But if the aim of sport is to win, what is the aim of drama?

Drama has many 'sites': the stage, the capital or provincial city where the theatre is, the era, language and culture. How does drama occupy these sites?

A. It conforms to the social sites (city, era, culture, etc), which are self-evident to the audience.
B. It conveys to the audience the play's specific sites. These are equivalents to A but of course may be different.
C. It conveys the play to the audience – the audience *as* site. The audience is social, able to receive only in certain (if sometimes innovative) ways. C must convey A and B to the audience.
D. The audience as site of imagination. A, B and C must be conveyed to this site. D is drama's *specific* site because – through the play – it contains all the other sites and their interrelations. What is D? What is the need for drama? Drama's identity comes from meeting the needs of D.

People might go to a play to celebrate a birthday. But it could be celebrated in other ways. Why should a play (even a tragedy) be suitable for a celebration? D obviously relates to the self. What is the self's need for drama? Drama is always extreme and thorough. There are social conventions about this (A, B and C – not D, though imagination may be partly ideologized) and so drama is extreme within limits allowed or comprehensible. Racine's 'anarchism' is presented in rigid, socially acceptable forms. Is the need for drama social or egotistical? Does the self (to use psychological language) wish to explore the self, or society and others? Specific forms of theatre meet different needs. The allowable and comprehensible change historically.

Contemporary theatre may be divided into three sorts, though the divisions are not absolute.

1. The Theatre of Stanislavsky (TS) is public theatre. What is on stage resembles public life as closely as possible and is credible as being public. Actors base their work on private experiences *within* society. The dramatic processes represent public appearances. TV and most films are based on TS.

2. The Theatre of Performance (TP) is both private and surreal. It is pre-social. Spectacular events exist in their own right. They are not recognizable parts of public life. 'Theatre is theatre', not directly translatable back into society, not pragmatic or socially practical. Everything is extreme. It is often associated with drugs. It is drawn from private and often esoteric imagination. It is also archetypal, quasi-mystical, ritual. It might be cathartic by expressing what society represses and in this way make social life freer. But though everyone might recognize an archetype, it is not socially shared. To be shared it must be translated into other, social, practices – which TP cannot do. TP is a 'dead end' even when its end is 'fuller life'. It cannot free itself from its artistic ghetto – in fact, it creates it by its freedom.

3. The Theatre of Brecht (TB) is public but unlike TS does not rely on private experience, or the private right not just to the political but also to 'sensitivity of self in society'. It is the theatre of alienation. It is epic, it deals with situations that TS avoids. People are public beings. They create tragedies and need not. It deconstructs tragedy. But the Greeks' tragic characters were also public beings. They are not autobiographical as, say, Chekhov's *Three Sisters*. They represent social situations and confront moral and political dilemmas vital to their society. All Brecht's plays are tragedies. (What else *is* there to alienate?) TB aims to create understanding through reason and the removal of emotional persuasions. Rational understanding is decisive. For TB, D is the need to reason, or at least theatre must impose reason on D.

These three forms of theatre are not modern (if modish). Drama cannot be reduced to TP performance, happenings, ritual, shock and so on. TP seeks 'effects' which come directly from the self and is analogous to sport. Personal effects are always a desire to understand the confrontation between freedom and tragedy – and so relate the self to the world of others. This is an inevitable consequence of self-consciousness. TP is circular not revelatory. It is the desire to desire, and this reverses the roles of freedom and tragedy. It cannot relate to the world's present state, its political, military and cultural situations. It is irrelevant 'art'.

Modern theatre cannot be TS. Modern theatre is not entirely public because it cannot be created entirely out of the social. Nor can it be TB because drama is not the occasion of something else: of moments or sequences when it withdraws before reason. Reason can say why it is reasonable to reason, but not why we should – must – be reasonable, what it is in us that needs reason. It is as if we said 'reason wants us to be reasonable'. But why should we be? Philosophy is the *love* of wisdom. Why should we love reason (or anything)? Drama needs extremes because their complexity and implacability are the source of humanness. In Brecht's *Baal* madness is lyrical and not condemned. Madness is excluded from Brecht's later plays – the irrational is in them only as drunkenness and corruption. Alienation prevents the enactment of extremity.

Whatever the specific need for drama, does it follow that theatre should meet it? Theatre might be wiser than the need? D's need for drama must be met because it is necessary to humanness. We do not design our lives abstractly but deal with conflicting yet equally justified demands. Drama must recognize the human limits of being. Humanness means surviving without being corrupted by survival. Drama must be particular *and* general. TB seeks the general but postpones (to other processes) the problem of how to make the general particular within the incompatibilities of existence. But the general can only be perceived through particulars. D is rooted in the self, and is removed from it only in coma (not in madness or psychopathy). But the self faces outwards. We become self-aware by relating to others. If there were no others we could not have a self. We cannot imagine ourselves. It is the only thing we cannot imagine. It would mean imagination imagining itself. If we try to imagine ourselves we imagine an 'other' self. Yet imagination is D, the site of the self. That is the basis of drama. Without imagination's drama we would have no continuing self. Imagination is synonymous with self-consciousness, self-continuity. One cannot exist without the other. Strictly speaking we can never be conscious of the self, just as we cannot imagine our self. Can we even think without imagination or must it accompany thought as if it were a light thrown on an object? If we had no imagination it would be as if 'the world dreamt us': we would have will (as we may in dreams) but could not act. But reality coerces imagination into seeking rational understanding: and so imagination comes to desire reason. Reason gives imagination its autonomy and us our power to act. Perhaps in a final synoptic understanding we would see that we do not think. Instead, the world thinks in us. Thought comes from the objective and collective and passes through us. We are the pivot around which particular thinking and experiences polarize – the self is a point in a situation. We are the totality of our presence in the world. We are in the world and not in ourselves, the world is in us. This acknowledges our finitude but does not deny our autonomy or absolve us of our responsibility. It adds to them, perhaps beyond what we can bear. All we can do is choose humanness or corruption. But society is the site of incompatible but equally justified alternatives. We cannot rationally solve its paradoxes. 'Rationally understanding' a situation is not simply a matter of reason. Reason cannot be isolated from imagination's needs. Imagination must 'deliver' reason. Drama is its 'delivery'.

To exist does not merely mean to solve problems and be happy. Imagination is the need to create, to change situations. Creation is its way of being. It articulates itself only through creation, which is the dramatic process. Pure reason is inert and creates nothing. We desire to reason but reason does not desire. Human affairs are not accountable in the way, say, the stress-functions of bridges are.

Why does the human mind recognize reason at all? Through reason we use the world to survive and prosper. Survival depends on reason, the existential depends on paradox. Self-consciousness requires reason and imagination. Without them we would not be self-conscious. They cannot be isolated from each other – or if they are we lose humanness (the value of the human). That is why drama should not (and in practice cannot) use imagination and *then* at critical moments hand over to 'reason as alienation'. These are just the moments when reason would betray humanness. When we reason we do not *understand* what we do. To ask which is the best of alternative actions means to ask: What are the consequences of the alternatives? How are they evaluated? What is good in a good act can be described. Goodness does not exist as an extra ingredient in an act, like the colour yellow on a canary. (Nor does art.) Humanness must be incorporated in acts. Each alternative act may seek the human, one act achieves it more closely. That act makes not a better person – the act's doer – but a better world. That is what imagination seeks – the practically better world which in the past we corrupted as heaven.

To understand drama, words such as deep and profound should be avoided. The superficial is deep in the sense that a fog is. Words such as primal denote primitiveness. The child is the origin of drama, but a child is not a primitive person. A child is a person who imagines and thinks in a particular way, one which is acute but without worldly wisdom and social skills, though with dramatic skills and a 'practice of the universal'. Drama is not a return to infantile pleasure or infantile language (as in *Finnegans Wake*). It is the sense of the universal combined with living skill, with reasoning intelligence. When drama achieves that it is useful. Is pleasure useful for anything but itself? Yes, and what *that* is cannot be reduced to pleasure. Pleasure must be put in context. It is not good to take pleasure while Rome burns because the world will soon rid itself of you. Useful drama puts situations in a context of total facts and values. Then we recognize humanness by creating it.

Drama is not 'reason', but 'reason through the creativity of drama'. Strictly we cannot be surprised by drama, though drama may have surprises in it. If drama were surprise we would only see *Hamlet* once. What more is to be seen in a play beyond the story? There is the *centre*. The place where the drama is set often represents the centre (Elsinore is stone and rock by sea) but the centre is not a place but the site of a situation. Ibsen's greatest plays are invaded by their centres – *Hedda Gabler* by drunkenness and *Ghosts* by disease: both are forms of corruption, what Hamlet calls the 'rotten'. Ibsen's *Master Builder* has a building site but no centre. The mountains in Ibsen's 'mountain plays' are not centres because they are only symbols not sites. The centre is the site of the drama's paradox.

Drama also occurs on the site of the self (for convenience, the 'self-site'). Self-site is a more useful term than ego. It is free of transcendental clutter and describes not an essence but a 'place' where things meet. The audience transforms, conveys, the play to its self-site. That is how it receives the play. It does not watch or listen to the play's story, that is only the play's vehicle of transmission (what sound waves are to listening). What the audience confronts is the play's centre. It is this which it translates to its self-site. Whatever enters the self-site is self-created and self-creating. The self-site cannot be 'imposed on' but 'receives' in its own autonomy. Another may speak for us but not listen for us. Another may show something to us but not see for us. Least of all could they see our blindness – but blindness does not abolish the self's autonomy of sight, which resorts to the imagination and need not be visual but may be a kinetic analogue of sight.

Surprise comes from discovery, but drama is the practice of the self. It is almost in the way a pianist practises to become perfect, but in reality the perfect does not exist theoretically (in a score) but must be created. That is, it is knowledge. In drama the self-site confronts the world and the world moves into the self-site. This first happens in the child's mind when it becomes self-conscious. The world arrives with the dilemmas and traumas of its relation to the child. This sets the child on a course, a journey. The mind is not imprisoned in this first state, as though pilloried by the world. If that happens the mind is traumatized, autistic, and cannot deal (in any sense) with the world. The experiences the world offers – and impedes – in the child's mind are freedom and happiness, which later in adults have the rational form of justice. Freedom and happiness are necessarily associated with the tragic, with offering and impeding. This freedom-tragic is not abstract. It is the experience created by situations and objects. For the child the objects are small and concrete: existential utensils. This creates a structure of the mind. Lear enacts powerlessness not when he gives up his kingdom but when he loses his house, Oedipus blinds himself with his wife's brooches. Justice is immanent. Bad poets easily rise to the grandiose but cannot reach the small. Although the objects are trivial the response to them is absolute. Justice is total whether it concerns the trivial or the great. Usually in life and drama justice is associated with an 'object-moment', an object made critically consequential or revealing by a situation. The object-moment is the site of the freedom-tragic and its paradoxes, the site of the pleasure of freedom and the suffering of the tragic (frustration, mortality, the loss of freedom or its prospect). This is the structure – created in childhood – of our consciousness of the world. No conscious mind may avoid the apposition of freedom and the tragic any more than the visual mind may avoid seeing in two dimensions. Because we exist in time the self-conscious mind must also imagine. Consciousness has only a moment, self-consciousness has time. Self-consciousness creates a future and so a sense of mortality. Imagination is the knowledge given by time that we live and die. Imagination enables us to live self-consciously in the world but also to distort its reality to meet our desire to live, survive and prosper – and our need for justice. The distortions create the chaos of transcendentalism and social-madness. Our means frustrate our ends. Drama occurs on the boundary between the real and our distortions of it. It is the boundary of history, the frontier of humanness.

Our first apprehensions teach us the experience of the freedom-tragic, and this becomes the self-site. It is a truth about our being in the world, contingent on our being but essential to our self-hood. Society all the time repeats and extends the apposition of freedom and the tragic – the repetition is the consequence of the world containing more than one person. The potentially solipsistic self-site of the freedom-tragic must be extended into the similar but wider structure of social activity. So the self-site may be found anywhere, but it becomes critical in important social and personal conflicts. As the self-site is the site of the world, what is personal is also social: the self is extended into those others who are part of the world – and their agency is not limited to the social propertyness of things and places. The dynamic between self and society is unavoidable. But the self is not isolated from society, because society inaugurates the self – the echo sounds before the voice. A child does not just recognize its parent, it recognizes that its parent has lived. Society cannot function without drama.

Drama is the repetition and extension of freedom-tragic and its paradoxes, because it is always extended in experience. Reason seeks to understand the freedom-tragic, and because of its situation it must make choices and cannot be passive. Drama enacts our relationship to the freedom-tragic. It must discover the freedom-tragic in specific, urgent situations, and then generalize to other freedom-tragic situations the understanding achieved in this way. Strictly the Greeks were right, it is better (or at any rate simpler) not to be born. But they were wrong in saying that once born it is better to die – because imagination seeks life. It seeks it even if it has to kill to get it, either because of ideological persuasion (I die for freedom) or ideological fear (I make a sacrificial offering of a life in place of mine) or through psychological compulsion: either the obsessive need to return to the original confrontation with the freedom-tragic and survive it or simply out of the desire to kill death and for a time be its master. Death is the 'capital' injustice without which there would be no justice or the complications of ethics and morality. If we were not mortal we would not be human.

Every drama which is not trivial has a centre. The centre is the drama-site, the confrontation in the freedom-tragic. The centre then occupies the self-site, but only if the play's direction, staging and acting allow it to do so. A play's centre is always the site of the story's freedom-tragic, of its conflicts and paradoxes, and this relates it to the freedom-tragic of the self-site. Dramatic 'effects' occur at moments when under the pressure of time the conflict of freedom-tragic becomes critical. This creates a need for decision or an understanding that will lead to a later decision. In modern theatre, 'effects' are often spurious, an opportunistic use of lights, music, sensational 'business'. Effects ought to come from the centre, the freedom-tragic – as if splintered from it in the conflict. But, as part of the staging of the play, an effect may be deliberately chosen to enact a meaning, and then it is as if the effect had been 'loosened' from the centre. The centre is the site of the drama's logic, the logic of imagination. Logic turns 'effects' into 'events'. A Theatre Event (TE) is the conscious use of 'theatrical drama' to enact or illustrate the centre. It does not comment on meaning but creates it from the interplay of freedom and the tragic. The solution is guaranteed by the problem: the problem was itself the search for humanness.

In TE time may be experienced as slower, as in a car accident. TE can be understood by comparing it to a whirlwind or cyclone. The centre of the cyclone is calm and quiet. In a TE the spectator stands in this still centre. It is the site of the TE. In it everything is seen with great clarity. It is surrounded by the violently rotating grey walls of wind. There are two things on the wall. The whole of the play's text is written on it. And there are bits and pieces – debris and mementos – swept up from the freedom-tragic conflict. They are held on the wall by its spinning motion, some jut out of it and others are flat against it like pictures pinned to it.

The TE is not a sensory experience (TP) or alienated rational reflection (TB). Without the sensory experience the centre vanishes, without rationality it collapses. But TE is not just the presence of the two, it is the enactment between them.

This changes the centre, the relationship between freedom and tragic. It takes place on the drama-site – but this is also the self-site. So the self is changed, or is shown changed from the far side after it has happened. The self cannot avoid this. But the TE cannot control the self's subsequent, later reactions to it. One person may become more rational, closer to the real. Another – perhaps through fear – may affirm corruption and be forced into defending illusions and so become more corrupt. 'Art' makes some people more human and corrupts others – but so does truth. 'Art' cannot do more, it is not like a chemical that has the same effect on everyone who takes it or comes into contact with it. Drama elucidates and enacts a situation. It is an event in the mind. But there are many ways in which illusions are vulnerable to reality. Freedom does not want to be pleased, entertained or surprised by 'effects' – it wishes to understand because it is caught in the mortality of time.

In drama the self-site, the site of freedom-tragic, seeks to recreate itself in the world which is itself the site of freedom-tragic. Drama is an event on the site of the world and the self-site, not an abstract mind reflecting about the world but the creation of meaning. Creation is possible only when imagination and reason interact in the same moment. Drama dramatizes the audience. The audience are not made its objects because they are creators of meaning. That is the power of drama: it is as if for a moment the world knew itself to be different – and there are practical consequences of this.

The freedom-tragic obviously concerns humanness, our understanding of our situation and the expression of our need for justice in all its manifestations. Trivial centreless drama produces an illusion of freedom-tragic 'effect' which may be exposed by reasoned criticism. Drama depends on the extent and precision of its examination of the freedom-tragic. False effects darken the delineation of the apposition. TE strips it bare. The bareness reveals complexity and consequences. Drama is not a reaction to aesthetic 'effects' – what does not come from the centre is peripheral and arbitrary. Only the centre is creative.

Theatre can only be understood by understanding its sites. The self and the world are sites. They are also the sites of each other. They meet critically in the freedom-tragic. The stage is a site – it is the exact topographical analogue of the self-site. When we stand on the stage we stand on ourselves and the world. The play's story comes from its centre. The centre is the site of the freedom-tragic. All the sites come together in the play's centre and are on the stage. Whatever comes from the centre and elucidates is an event. What does not is an effect. Events enact the centre and are means of change. This creates justice or states its condition in the play and by extension in society. This is the need for drama.

The institutions of theatre should create the humanness that society's other institutions do not because they must make the compromises of administration and cannot enter into the paradoxes of drama. Theatre must do what parliaments and law courts – and schools and universities – cannot. Drama is not 'social' but has to do with the 'reasons for the social'. The level of a society's justice depends on the truthfulness of its drama – that is, on its radicalness. We must become more radical. We must learn to trust drama again. We have become too powerful to go on living with our illusions.

An Example
Olly's Prison was staged by the Berliner Ensemble. At the start of the play a father talks to his daughter for forty-five minutes. He has made her a cup of tea (the object). He seeks pleasure. The daughter will not

drink it. Pleasure is frustrated. As the father talks the cup becomes an 'object-moment': a crisis of freedom-tragic. He uses the cup as a map of his life: his self-site and the world-site. After forty-five minutes he strangles his daughter for not drinking the tea.

The stage directions indicate the events (TEs) in the self-sites of the father and daughter. The production did not use them. Instead from time to time a noisy elevated train passed outside. It interrupted the father's talk. This was an alienation effect intended to show that the father and daughter lived in a poor neighbourhood. It was (partly) because he lived there that the father killed his daughter. The play was written to show something else: why things such as poor housing led him to strangle his daughter – it generalized knowledge, or rather 'knowing'. The train made a noise, but the father spoke from the play's centre. Modern theatre must fill the human gap between cause and effect. The TE is more radical than the Alienation Effect.

The strangling of the daughter was suggested by unemphatic gestures. This alienated the strangling so that it might be thought about. It might be useful to act in this way the killing of someone in a bar brawl or war. It is not useful when someone is killed for not drinking a cup of tea. The play's centre is in the reality of modern life. The strangling must be harsh to enact the modern paradox. The TE in the stage directions describes the killing as if the father's body was giving birth to the daughter.

(1999)

Drama

In a trivial sense all human events are in life. But is theatre about life or *of* life? Is it like learning mathematics, which has no other consequence except when the learner does something or thinks of something other than mathematics? Or is theatre always about *that* something other? It would seem that the logic of mathematics made it more determinant in life than drama could be – but there is also a logic of drama, which combines the logic of, for example, mathematics with the inevitabilities of existence. That is why antiquity could talk of the inevitability of fate. These inevitabilities must practise themselves in both law and anarchy – in existence there is no equivalent to mathematical error, instead there is 'sin', cruelty and violence. We cannot be the victims of God because we create God and so we are the victims of each other. Ultimately, that means of ourself. We are victims because we do not – and as yet, cannot – allow drama to dramatize itself. If we could do that we would be not the victims but the objects of drama. It is not that what was known as 'sin' would vanish so that we would be the objects of cruelty and destruction. We could redefine and recreate humanness in a way we cannot recreate mathematics. This would be possible, but it is as if technology has mined with explosive the human site – the 'world stage' beyond the 'theatre stage'. Really there is no discontinuity between the two stages, and if to the 'theatre stage' we add the 'media studio', then we have to say that the 'world stage' is contained in the 'theatre stage'. This is so because drama is not merely about life but is *of* life. Nor may we ever escape from this stage – as we may escape from our clothes by undressing. When we are dead we have no further life, but of our graves and funerals we make theatres.

What is the connection between the two stages: the T(heatre)-stage and the W(orld)-stage? The W-stage influences directly the T-stage only in a minor way: through theatrical architecture and equipment. It is said that life imitates art, but is it that art creates life? We invent tools but also create gods. Therefore we must create the human. We are formed by our relation to the W-stage: we eat, invent machines. But we have access to the W-stage only because we are imaginers. That is the human paradox. An active volcano is not a drama, it is mathematics and physics. When witnessed by humans it is a drama, they sacrifice to it, they flee it. Imagination is the basis of human materialism.

Imagine an ape discovering a car. It sits in it – because seats invite
sitting. It winces when it sounds the horn. It is terrified when the car
moves. We are in the world, the W-stage is complete and logical in the
way the car is. The human drama is that we are the ape in the W-stage.
But we make the car. Making the car is what changes us from ape to
human. But we invented God who created the world before we (as a
species) invented the scientists and mechanics who made the car – or the
cooking pot or hoe. The car has a mathematical logic. What is the logic
of God? It is the logic of imagination. Imagination creates the real –
without it we could not have God or the car. The car (W-stage) is in
God's world (T-stage, in this connection) until we destroy God. That
means that God is a super-ape – which founding religious texts make
clear. Or you could say, a super-car. But God cannot be a super-human
– because he is about but not *of* the human. God always remains buried
in history – God cannot escape to the present. To believe (even in the
age of faith) is to enter the past.

Then is imagination 'visceral thought'? – and so only illogical
inevitability? – thinking driven and shaped by passion, by emotion? No,
because imagination is not performance but is seeking. It seeks to
understand and exist in situation (which theatre must make the 'site').
Elsewhere I argue that what imagination seeks to understand is the
human – that is, its own situation in the W-stage – and to make (it
becomes performance, then) the W-stage a place in which it may survive
and be itself – that is, a W-stage in which it is innocent. Freud believed
that the self sought escape from tensions, to find quietude (Thanatos).
This is an ideological misconception, because the theory of Thanatos
cannot take in all the phenomena of death, cruelty, destruction. It
reduces death to a banality. But death is an existential drama. It is death
which makes drama logical – not merely death in tragedy but all the
existential phenomena – the structures of social and personal life – which
death elaborates. It is also because of death that drama is not about but is
of life.

If there were no theatre the world would be alone, as a machine shop
or field is alone. We would be objects. To act, we must know. In our age
knowledge becomes mechanical, it overwhelms. Technology has practical
logic but knowledge no longer has authority, because the old authorities
created by imagination lose their authority. Overnight, what was law
becomes anarchy, what was order becomes discipline – logically so, as
practical functions and vices. Human endeavour is always in relation to
site and situation and so the logic of imagination is dialectical. Drama is
dialectical. It is 'visceral mathematics': any concept has practical

consequences, as if logic were not itself sensate but always had sensate consequences. We use W-stage logic (mathematics, physics) but we do not create it – but *our* logic is that we must use W-stage logic, which is why law and anarchy are equally logical for us. Drama constantly assesses logical meaning and the meaning of logic. We experience it, it exists in us. If you invent a devil, as God you must sacrifice your children to him – it is logical. If you wish to create a quasi-human God – he must sacrifice his child to you (and inevitably logic annuls his sacrifice). What is true of God must be true of armies, prisons, torture and power – since they all equally structure force. We create God for the reasons we create armies and prisons. But theatre has no force. Even when drama is propaganda it has none – the propaganda stands aside from the theatre it uses and the theatre stands aside from it. You cannot use theatre as you use a page to write on. That the page holds the print is a fact that the print cannot dispute, or the screen the image. To this degree, what we assume we do is not what we do, it is Platonic shadow. But there is no ideal world beyond what we do – the ape in the pre-human world would never find a car because it cannot seek it; therefore there is no ape car. Plato's cave is the stage.

The T-stage is human. The old authorities of God, hell, law, prison, crucifixion, love – these become impotent and change their purpose. They corrupt. The stigmata of post-modernism is not that thought is unfounded – it is that institutions become corrupt and can no longer even propound the human. When the human diminishes in the W-stage it seeks itself in drama, in the T-stage, in art. The stage is the centre of things but is the place apart. It must be the place apart because the T-stage must contain the W-stage or seek to contain it – otherwise there is religion, the Roman games, triviality or madhouses. When the world is a madhouse the stage is the place where sanity seeks to know itself. Hitherto the T-*world* has always contained the W-*stage*. Religion, codes such as chivalry and humanism, have repressed the T-stage because they wished themselves to contain its drama but within restricted forms. For them the T-stage is too radical because it can express law in the form of anarchy – which society cannot. Instead it needs prisons and executioners to act out its anarchy. These and other institutions dominated and controlled society's productive forces, but they always contained a human dialectic – they were sources of human value (without which the corruption of these values could not be created), they had values beyond themselves. That this is no longer true is a unique historical event. Capitalism has no value beyond itself. It is true that the Church was corrupt but its centre was a value. Capitalism changes value for vacuum.

Its activities may be humanly beneficent but at its centre is a vacuum – the mere mechanics of money creating money, profit. It would be as if the Church sent its saints to hell. Capitalism, of course, frees from ancient institutions – but it is like water: sufficiency is good, excess is more destructive than fire. In the past the W-stage was contained in the T-stage because the institutions sought the value of the T-stage (though in distortions). This is no longer so. The W-stage has the valueless dynamics of capital and the total presence of technology. The W-stage begins to corrupt the T-stage.

The Greek stage was serious, the Roman stage brutal and the boulevard stage is trivial because of the logic of their situations. The first desire – they feel it as a responsibility – of the mad is to understand sanity. Medically they cannot. But society is also mad – it invents gods, demons, paranoid causes, patriotisms, fantasies – all of which are necessary if it is to conduct its serious business and be unjust. We are like the ape in the car – we are 'socially mad', mad collectively not individually. It is even possible for many to see that what they do is mad. But the mad cannot use their madness as learning – and pace Freud, madness is not a search for death but a search for life. Drama is the way the socially mad have sought their sanity. But drama deals with the *socially* mad – it cannot be reduced to psychodrama, which is a superstition of the social. The stage is always public and social, drama is not a cure. (Just as you cannot have a private religion. What use would it be?)

Capitalism turns the T-stage into a product of consumption – it is the aesthetic equivalent of cannibalism. It trivializes and subverts drama's seeking for justice and sanity – which is the seeking for the logic of imagination, not the mere experience of the force of imagination. Imagination and error produce a dynamic different from imagination and reason – the former is the experience of hysteria, the latter of drama, which is the understanding created when the action reveals the site. When theatre is corrupt it serves the same psychological purpose as prison or punishment – though its social form seems the opposite. This is so now. Drama is made trivial – its angst reaction not tragedy, its comedy ludicrous not revolutionary. And curiously, though art may degrade (as must religion when the Gods' days are past) it is also the last outpost of humanity – that is its power, because art clings to the real even when people abandon the real. But now drama ceases to be *of* life and becomes about itself, an escape from the drudgery and fear of life into the trivial or into the fake-aesthetic, into obscurantism of the human spirit. It is as if for the first time – as a species – we have begun to betray humanness. From this, only two things may come – the final catastrophe of destruction and cruelty, or evolution will use the human as a bridge into Total Technology, which in its turn will discard us. The machine does not need its user, only its creator: which may be other machines. Because the machine has no purpose it needs no drama. It needs only activity. We will crumble in the vacuum – at most our skeleton would be a blueprint of a human.

The theory of TE (Theatre Event) rehumanizes drama. In the TE instead of drama being about life it becomes an event – an event *in* life. An event is not about something but *of* something. The TE is an event because it happens on the two stages simultaneously – on the W-stage and the T-stage. It does this by destroying the ghettoizing of the T-stage – so that the W-stage is resited on the T-stage (they become one). In practice it makes an anarchism reveal itself as law. The Greeks could not produce real Gods on their stage – but their stage represented (enacted) the real in its gods. Religion cannot produce its God – it is about God not *of* God (God had to dress up as an actor or become man). But TE theatre can enact the real on its stage; imagination becomes the imaginator – the thing becomes itself on the stage. How is this? Does appearance change? No, only incidentally (at least for the present). What changes is the meaning of what is enacted: it stops being an account and becomes an event, it enacts reality and not its ideological distortions. But the distortion cannot be blotted out – the TE is the act of the distortion changing.

Of course the knower is still limited by the knower's ability to know – the ape building the car. Ultimate revelation is not necessary: in this connection, when corruption is removed ignorance is legitimate – it is innocence. Human innocence has all the extremism of corruption, which believes its knowledge is complete and conforms its practice to it. The TE has meaning because of its place in the story. The meaning of the TE cannot be deduced from the story – the TE gives meaning to the story by the role it plays in it. We cannot understand reason unless we enter into the distortions of insanity. They are there because we have not – could not yet have – understood the situation of humanness. They are there for a purpose: to help us to understand humanness. We have only human problems. It is inhumanly irresponsible to say that our existence is meaningless. The Theatre of the Absurd is corrupt. Drama is logic not reason – but it is rational to be logical. Then we understand the way death is reasoned and the logic of living. If we do not we create destruction, cruelty, triviality and – total death – the human absence.

Understand yourself. This means: understand your situation –

understand the structures of the W-stage. Since the death of God this understanding is essential to drama. Without the logic of imagination science is still-born and technology will perform the abortion of humankind. Understanding reality is not to remove glamour from reality – only a dying culture thinks that. But even if it were, it would not be cause to regret. Tragedy, cruelty, destruction – these things have no glamour, just as pleasure is not itself contentment. Only the innocent understand tragedy – others see only its comedy and filth.

Drama needs these things: an understanding of the logic of imagination, the TE and the 'site'. This guides the writing of plays, acting, directing, designing. The TE is the way the logic of imagination is enacted on the site. The aesthetics and dramaturgy of the past have their uses but are insufficient. The past has always excoriated the past. It is what we must do. To do otherwise – artistically, politically, socially – is reaction. We are hurled not into the world but into the future. It comes to us with the definition we create in our manner of receiving it. It is the way we create our humanness. Without TE drama is play-acting. Art comes from the future – this places a great responsibility on us.

(1999)

Le Théâtre de la Cité

Euripides went into exile and the theatre of Dionysus is ruined
Shakespeare took to drink and his theatre was pulled down
Molière was persecuted and the royal theatres of France are empty
And in our time playwrights and others who work in theatres have been shot
   imprisoned exiled and silenced
But what was first said on their stages is still said in our homes and public
   places
The stage is a footprint made by history
On which are raised kitchens schools temples madhouses courts and cells
Cities and their lands
Where kings and ragged beggars stand in each other's shadows
Oracles seek for answers
And democracy wears the tragic and comic masks turn and turn about: she
   cried only once – long ago but two of the tears stay on her cheeks
The future is uncertain
Theatre is the house of hostages: we go there to fight for our lives – never
   doubt it
Honour the city that founds a theatre
On its stages say what you are forbidden to say when the times are dark

Written for the opening of Le Théâtre de la Cité, Toulouse.

(1998)

Letter on Translation

Brigitte Landes
Hamburg

12 October 97

Dear Brigitte

I am going to write a letter to you about translating – especially translating plays, but what I say is true about translations of any literature though not of purely technical writing (or speaking). There is a lot of literature which can be translated 'one dimensionally' because the original writer has not translated experience into his or her own language but instead has skimmed over experience – generalized it – or has used conventional forms (as in pulp romances).

A play has to be in two places. Firstly, in the psychology of the characters – they speak from their psyches. Secondly, in the world in which the characters are. That world is divided into the natural world, the social world and the particular place (such as the army or school) in which the characters are. The psyche itself has a different aspect in each of these worlds – and together these may be called its first world (the world of social realism, primarily). But the psyche also has another world – the world in which it creates its own meaning and value. In the social world, money has a meaning and value – in the other world money might have a different meaning (miserliness) but it might mean something completely different.

So a sentence or phrase or word has to be simultaneously in all these worlds – if it isnt the actor cant really know where he is and so neither can the audience. Good dramatists place their characters accurately. Shakespeare's plays were written long ago – but you can always say exactly where his characters are in all these worlds. That is why he is still useful. Sometimes Shakespeare doesnt know exactly where they are – he would see the 'places' historically differently – and of course neither, very often, do his characters: but they search desperately to find out where they are – that is the energy of all his characters. And because all these worlds are in change – they are part of the 'river' of history – by finding out where they are his characters create new places, new forms of consciousness. In this sense Hamlet 'knows' more than Shakespeare 'knows'. That is why Hamlet must die, so that Shakespeare may retreat back to his daily ignorance. Ignorance is a luxury we arent allowed any more – if *Coffee* is right.

Inadequate translation merely reproduces the surface reality of the original – in this case, an appropriate, suitable German sentence would be found for an English sentence. 'You say X in English, we say Y in German.' And of course a translation has to do that. But the original line isnt 'suitable' or 'appropriate' except in a special sense: it is a map reference which is exact not merely for one world but all the worlds I've listed. This is necessary in drama because drama is an action in these worlds: it takes place in all these worlds at once. Drama's *use* is that it does that – it's why audiences go to drama, to be shown the real relationship between these worlds or – they often hope – to be lied to. If the world changes, what world is the fish in? – sometimes in the sea, sometimes in a net. The audience will like to be told that the net is made of water. That's what we now use theatre for. Theatre wants audiences and so it should sell lies. There are only two reasons why it shouldnt – one is that people arent fish and they fundamentally want to know their situation. Another is, plays should deal with important matters and so writers should not lie about them. If we cannot tell the truth in theatres we should leave them.

I think that directors and actors are being destroyed by a culture of lies. They learn the wrong skills, the wrong techniques. They learn to survive and the art of survival is destructive. That means that we work in a crisis – ultimately it means asking the audience 'Which of the various worlds do you want to survive in? Which worlds must you survive in if you are not to be dead in the others? – and remember: the living dead always kill and destroy.'

We cant begin to do this unless we are aware of the various worlds. Theatre is a social structure invented in order to do precisely that: describe in a way that may be experienced the relationship between the worlds. This is so clearly what happens in Greek theatre and in all good theatre that has followed. The Greeks structured their drama formally – as formally as their temples – because they needed to segmentize their experience in order to understand it: there were, for instance, humans and divinities – in the world they were apart, but not on the stage: the gods were summoned to the stage to speak and even vote. Greek drama had other structures – dance, song, speaking – and the relations between these things were also rigidly structured (in the movements of the chorus, for example). This wasnt an arbitrary aestheticism: it was an attempt to find a map reference in the multiple worlds in which the Greeks, like us, lived. Their problem is: how to be human when the geography of the psyche is schizoid? If we used their structures we would turn them into empty aestheticisms – as we would if we used Shakespeare's or Ibsen's structures: we cannot use princes and trolls.

In us the worlds are closer together and infiltrate each other more persistently. The epiphanies that for the Greeks occurred – as if segregated – only in the temple, the battlefield, the Dionysic rite – for us may occur anywhere: on the street corner, in the kitchen, at work, in the shop – all these places may be the temple, the battlefield, the site of the rite. Our wounds and our recoveries take new shapes.

When the dramatist said to Oedipus: sing *here* and speak *there* – the differences were clear, the map references precise. The precision in a modern text is different – but if the text pursues the same objective as the Greek text (how to be human?) then the map references must be as precise. That is why in a modern text situations are repeated and developed – why one speech is repeated, modified, extended, passed from character to character – as the situations become more precise, closer to the 'total' situation. So patterns of developing imagery become important, contrasts become important, combinations become important, the uses of grammatical tenses and changes in them become important: because the worlds are in struggle, shaking each other, hiding in each other, driving each other. In a way there is necessary chaos. The prison of society-and-self is shaken (in Euripides' last play the God comes from his prison by way of an earthquake: it is paradigm). But there is also order – which is why I'm against the 'mess' of the absurd. Chaos is structure we do not yet know how to read.

Imagine that I witness an earthquake. I see total chaos, confusion, wreck. Why do I see that? – because in my veins there is blood. But suppose that in my veins I had a liquid called 'gravity-fluid' – it was structurally part of me so that I 'read' gravity closely, understood it and didnt merely react to it (or, as an object, myself represent it). Then I would see absolute order in the earthquake: the earthquake is merely obeying the laws of gravity – and so (if I were 'gravity-veined' or so to say, 'gravity-minded') I would regard the earthquake as a perfect example of order: to 'gravity-people' the chaos would be serenely decorous. Of course, to be human we have to learn to see the order in the chaos of our psyches and our world. Gravity-man would not need map references, he would know from his nature – and if a stone had a mind it would of course have a gravity-mind. The human mind acts in history as the stone acts in space: we are 'gravitas' in the presence of history. But the stone has no mind and no freedom – we have an area of freedom but ultimately we must act in a law-bound way in the material world – but we have in some form or other to choose to act in this way. Freedom means this: you must be able to destroy yourself. The stone can be destroyed but cannot destroy itself because it is not free. There is one further burden on us: if we do not recreate ourselves we destroy ourselves – we cannot slumber like the stone. We use the gravity of history to create our humanness or to destroy ourselves – we cannot exist long as inhumans when the material world requires a new humanness. I say 'we have to' – because it isnt a passive process – history will not crush us but we may use history to crush ourselves. If this isnt to happen we have to understand the relationship between the various worlds – and live that relationship in new ways. Technology is impatient and doesnt wait long for us to catch up – we have always caught up in the end, but now we must move more quickly.

So the play says: I am a map of the world – and I must be precise.

I will at last try to give a practical example! It comes from *Coffee*. On page 44 the Sergeant begins a long description of a cigarette case. He describes it as if it were magically gifted; its contents are carefully placed in different sections; he uses imagery of butterflies and smoke, of vomit and shit and piss; he refers to ancient lineages and to supreme craftsmanship and to drunkenness, masturbation, crime, gypsies, fate; he also uses strange, exotic words – 'chamfered', 'chased' in the jeweller's sense, 'engraved escutcheon', the 'echelons of wealth'. In fact it's almost as if the speech maniacally contrasts language – it mentions 'hobnails' and four words later it mentions 'silk'. Whenever there's a grandiose sentiment it's followed by an obscenity. A strange element of the 'chronicler' is used: he doesnt say 'the next afternoon' but 'afternoon of the day following'. All this is in the suitable, appropriate language I mentioned at the beginning – the Sergeant uses English exactly as an English sergeant of his sort would. But he would normally say: 'the next afternoon' – if he were in another situation, *if* the map reference were different. Perhaps you cant say in German something which reflects 'the afternoon of the following day' (it could be a phrase from the Bible or used by a working-class policeman trying to be formal when he spoke in a courtroom witness box: with God it means one thing, with the policeman another, with the Sergeant another – and each of them echoes the other). But if you cant say it you need to know why it appears as it does in the original – because then you will understand how the language works and compensate in some other way, perhaps elsewhere, for the inability to reproduce this particular multi-meaning. I tried to explain this to an earlier translator in connection with the way the Girl in *Coffee* handles a glass. This had been translated into the normal appropriate German sentence and 'had to be right' because that was German usage: but I had not used the appropriate, right, English usage – I had slightly distorted it. The phrase the German translator wanted to use was the appropriate, right, translation of the *normal* English phrase – which I had *not* used.

It is not easier to mistranslate this passage than it is to translate it: but the latter is the greater creative pleasure for the translator. It is as if the text itself asked the translator questions. If the translator were stopped in the street by a stranger and asked 'What is the way to Kaiser Street?' the translator would not reply 'Three o'clock' – the questioner would become lost. It would be good German but inappropriate.

A phrase or word might be the correct German. Or it might be distorted – because the character is obviously using slang or dialect. But then the *type of distortion* becomes essential to the map reference (I cannot say more essential, because sometimes formal language is of great referential significance: consider a name carved on a gravestone – it's covered with mud – you scrape off the mud (which has its own rain-smeared calligraphy) to get to the formality of the chiselled words – the chisel speaks of death but so also does the mud, both are emblems of mortality – and together they create a different sense of mortality). I will try to make this clear with a diagram:

1. English word, etc.

Situational English →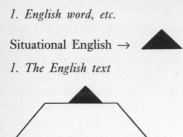

1. The English text

2. German word, etc.

Normal non-situational
German   →

2. The German text

Different effects, different
map-references and so different
situations.

Or vice versa or any other combination. The mountain is the 'situation', the intersection of the various worlds. Interestingly, the human mind is very perceptive about this – it even reads these texts subliminally or is made pleased or anxious by them without quite knowing why. Half the craft of drama is for actors and directors and designers (who must also be precisely situated in the situation in the world, though over a longer span – the design cant change as lines do, and if it did it would be doing something else, since objects are not meant to declare themselves in the way language is) to record the experience of being at that particular map reference – because then extraordinary things happen, we reveal ourselves.

Here are a couple of interesting map references, one from drama and one from the other drama which we label 'reality'. First the drama. When Hamlet goes to the churchyard he speaks to the Gravedigger. The Gravedigger tells Hamlet things Hamlet doesnt know – hardly anyone else in the play does this (except factually: 'there's a ghost on the roof'). The Gravedigger talks of mortality and survival of the body after death. Hamlet does the same, after his own fashion. The extremes meet and then each speaks the same speech, but from different situations. I do not have a copy of the play to hand: but if you compare the two speakers you will see how they are interrelated – and the actors and a translator need to know *how* before they can use the speeches. .

The next example is from history. When one of the French revolutionaries was taken to the scaffold he said to the executioner, 'Show my head to the people, it is worth the trouble.' The executioner did and the people were not much moved. Why did Danton ask this? What was the trouble? (I have only the English text.) From what world did he speak it?

You can be sure that all the worlds are present on the scaffold (English peers tended to tip their executioners). The idea suggests the Gorgon's head. Perhaps in one of the world's Danton was saying: 'I want to see them when I'm dead/dying.' Perhaps it is an image of resurrection? Is it to shame the spectators? Threaten them? Is it pride? Humility? When did he think of asking this? Perhaps the spectators were not moved *then* – but later. Perhaps the head is an image from one world which will later gravitate into another world? To look at a severed head and not be moved is to be dehumanized? Is the head being lifted up like the host – a punishment of the spectators? Or was Danton thinking of the good of the Revolution? The 'trouble' isnt specified. But the map reference is very precise because it makes the imagination work – and imagination is nothing more than the intercourse or interdictions between the various worlds, which is why imagination isnt something dark, secret, mysterious in the mystical sense, but is our interaction with 'the material' – social reality is as decisive in the imagination as are the structures created in infancy. The imagination isnt a palimpsest but an 'interaction' between the psyche's worlds.

The great impact of drama is to bring the language of the usually unspoken (aloud) words into the world of social reality. That is why precision is essential because the point of drama is to enter the other worlds and make them articulate, give them visible, apprehendable shape, sound and form. The journey there is precise, and the space there is a precise space. When I have translated Chekhov and Wedekind I have been shocked at how arbitrary many other translations were – it was as if they had no sense of how drama works, no skill at making it work. This is not true of all translators – but if I had found a translator who translated Wedekind or Chekhov as the dramatic architects and craftsmen they both were, there would have been no reason why I should have translated them – though they write their plays in a way very different to the way in which I write mine I can respect their dramatic purpose.

So of a translated sentence we need to ask not 'Does this translate the original sentence?' but 'Does this translate the original map reference?' – so far as is possible. This means understanding not what the original says but why is it written in this way. I found Russian closer to English than German to English – but perhaps this was true only of Chekhov's Russian. I found that I could translate most of Wedekind directly – I began with a literal translation and retained almost all of this: there were some sentences I shortened because I was translating for performance – not making an historical record – and the shortened version translated the effect of the original in a way that a literal translation would not have done. I want to make it clear that I do not imagine that literal translations are possible – but a translator must remember that the translation is not of a language but of a play.

I think it's easier for me to understand Chekhov and Wedekind than it would be for an audience to understand a contemporary dramatist. Can we understand Shakespeare still? – O, English audiences understand Shakespeare much better than they understand their contemporary dramatists. Of course they do – that is the point in writing more plays. Unfortunately they tend to understand Shakespeare as he understood himself – history was then less self-conscious. They still call *King Lear*, Act 3, Scene 7, 'The Blinding of Gloucester' and not 'The Killing of the Servant' – though structurally the latter is as important as the former – both add 'worlds' to the other. It's 'The Killing of the Servant and the Blinding of Gloucester' – neither the language nor the action is understandable if this isnt understood.

All my plays move through several 'registers' of language, often violently juxtaposed – because that's how the language authenticates itself; if it speaks in one world it echoes in another, and often more than one world speaks in the same sentence. Much of this is common, unconscious knowledge – everyone needs to listen to these worlds in order to survive in the street or do their shopping. But the social realism of Stalin and Hitler, and the unsocial realism of capitalism, have debased language, made it schematic – and so characters have to escape from TV and film, and search for a new, plausible, credible, strange language on stage. To make this happen a dramatist has to create those extreme situations where the worlds have to speak, have to be represented – just as fingers change to toes and toes to fingers when you scale a rock face.

Really, this is the easier part – but if the original map reference is located then the other things may become deeper and crystalline. Why do the soldiers in *Coffee* speak as they do? I have taken ordinary slang and heightened and compressed it and made it more brutal through juxtaposition and image – because I believe that men engaged in these massacres create a virulent, angry humour – their language is spattered with blood and bits of brain just as their hands and boots and clothes were. And then they see other worlds – the Jacobeans knew that it was not the good who saw visions (that is just the kitsch of the Counter-Reformation and its born-again children) but the evil, the corrupt – their world is bizarre, it combines the mundane and the impossible. I have a photograph of an *Einsatzgruppe* arriving at its 'territory' – the soldiers wear uniform and they carry not army rucksacks or military kitbags but 'luggage', good leather cases bound with straps, the sort you would take with you on a trip to Paris – because they were special. Most translators, if I'd put them down as having 'luggage', would translate it as haversack or kitbag or some such (because 'that is what soldiers use') and the bulging leather cases might be in danger of vanishing from history. The title of the play *Coffee* is an extreme map reference – it takes the massacre into its other worlds. A survivor of the massacre taught me this. I cant say that of all my plays this play needs to be translated with the greatest accuracy – because it ought to be true of all plays, we owe it to the times which produce massacres. And I dont know whether actors and directors will know how to use the German text – it seems to me they vulgarize, evade, blare when only a whisper can be heard, distorting the grotesque so that it becomes conventional again! That is the 'multi-national' style, in fact. But we have to try.

The Sergeant's speech is very public – it's addressed to his soldiers and is meant to persuade them of the importance of culture and the importance of their knowing their (lowly) place in it. At the end of this speech he should (if he were only in the social realistic world) say, 'You understand?' or 'Dont ever forget it' or some such military 'last line'. Instead the text says: *Gives a little private snigger.*

Immediately the speech lurches into another world – the significance of the whole speech is changed by the snigger. He doesnt even laugh publicly at the soldiers – he sniggers to himself. Clearly he's using the cigarette case for a private reason – his relationship to authority: he's spent the whole long speech glorifying authority and urging their – and his – submission to it and at the end he indicates by the snigger that in fact he's manipulating authority (doing exactly what he says they shouldnt) – or perhaps creating a private intimate relationship with authority – and immediately before it he has raised the possibility of having cheated the officer by stealing the case – and referring to the final 'Judgement Day' and (obscenely) to 'Jesus'. So the little snigger changes the 'worlds' – and comes from the very centre of the play: it's a necessary step towards getting himself shot by Nold – if it isnt there, if the director and actor dont know how to use it, the Sergeant will die for another reason. The audience wont know they know this – they dont need to, because they will experience it, it will be knowledge that they have created in their own 'worlds'. Just as essential is what happens next: Nold enters – his 'entry fanfare' is the Sergeant's private giggle – we should feel worlds searching for themselves. It's only in ways like this that we can create the 'work' of drama. Who laughs at whom? Why did Hamlet speak to the Gravedigger? Why did Danton say 'Show my head to the people'? In fact every little vocal oscillation of the snigger is itself like a footstep to the scaffold – as Danton would have known and as Dostoevsky assures us he himself learnt. The oscillations are footsteps as they are heard in a certain world. As if a condemned man were hurrying – trip-tripping – to the scaffold. We have to give actors and audiences a chance to go there with us and to see, so that they go home in greater safety.

I am not pedantic when I talk about 'ands' and 'buts' and tenses and the repetition of words, and the use of developing images and structures – 'worlds' depend on these things . . .

Best wishes

Edward

Pearl White
Notes on the TE of the Text

A dramatic situation leads to an effect which produces a response from an audience. If the effect exists for itself it imposes *its* meaning on the situation. This distorts the situation's meaning and the response to it is a misunderstanding. It is the difference between a blow on the head and a thought. A blow is an 'effect' that may come from behind and produce unconsciousness. A thought is also an 'effect', it is an event in the mind and is at least partly conscious. Its impact may be more dramatic than the blow's and have more far-reaching consequences. A dramatic effect is useful when it dramatizes its relation to its causes, so that the relationship is understood. The relationship is not immediate. It opens a gap which is filled by human mediation. When an effect does not show its relationship to its causes, it is its own cause. It is authoritarian and asserts that meaning is self-evident. In aesthetics what is authoritarian may be experienced as freedom. Really this response to an effect is like a reaction between two physical objects. It is a reaction without responsibility. It substitutes reaction for response. It conceals reality. It makes imagination objective not subjective. It makes drama and its meaning conventional, so that change is like the passing horses on a merry-go-round. The effect and reaction may be highly dramatic, but the drama is static and conceals deadness – emotional, intellectual and moral stagnation. Its social consequence is lethargy under hectic activity and moral indifference which often activates itself as malice. Typically, it is the theatre of the British Royal National Theatre.

Reaction-drama is concerned not with the meaning of causes but the creation of effects. It comes from our political and social confusion. For three hundred years intelligent people proposed solutions to our problems which now turn out to create new problems. We try to solve the problems by isolating them into spheres of particular expertise. We ignore the interconnection of causes. Drama cannot be isolated into separate spheres – even when its trivial, drama is 'total'. When it is not cynical it can – even simply by coherently enacting a problem – show the audience its own ability to understand and begin to solve the problem. But it is easier to exploit audiences – reaction-drama tries facilely to please with the high-brow Theatre of the Absurd and low-brow musicals.

Dramatic effects should be the consequences of their causes. The aesthetic means should be drawn from the causes. Instead effects are imposed by music, lights, gratuitous shocks, 'art', 'style'. The set is made an independent effect, spectacular and mobile. All drama, even fantasy and make-believe, depends on reality. The destitute fantasize about winning the lottery, the reality is destitution. Reality lurks behind the superficial. It is what makes nostalgia poignant. Nothing is emptier than empty aesthetics and empty shocks. The spectacular sets, coercive music, emotive lighting embalm the audience.

Many modern plays create their own false effects. False effects are also used in staging the classics. Dramas become classics if when they were written the causes of their effects were existentially urgent: the drama recognized this and so the causes, the situations, were presented scrupulously. In time the effects – the meanings of the causes – change. But the situations still demand an understanding because originally they were described scrupulously. Reaction-drama tries to resuscitate the obsolete meanings by new effects – lights, music, gratuitous 'business'. Typically this is the theatre of the Royal Shakespeare Company. Behind it is the contemporary theatre's demoralization.

Theatre deals with conventional situations because they are important. They have political, social and personal meanings. They are humane or repressive, trivializing and corrupting. They are obsessively – often fiercely – contested. The meanings of situations are not obvious because they change historically. TE tries to create a theatre of new meanings. Deconstruction cannot do this. It exposes false meanings, the elisions and seemingly impenetrable gaps which hold things together. It can expose empty effects that make false meanings plausible or compelling. But it does not create new meanings. It leaves causes disconnected but surprisingly autonomous. A cup is deconstructed by smashing it. It can no longer be used as a cup. You may play post-modern games with the pieces. TE reuses the cup. For example a cup may be used to enact war.

Two soldiers hide in a ditch. They are Christian crusaders or fighting in Alexander's campaign. One is young, the other – an officer – is older. They are not shown heroically. The officer is wrapped in a blanket and pelts. Bits of metal show from underneath. His feet and shins are bound in wrappings. Dirt seems part of the natural contours of his face. He is too old to be at war. The young soldier is also cold but he is fitter and wears less, his neck and arms are bare. There is a slight, persistent wind. The soldier picks up a cup. He is about to pour water into it from a flask.

The officer says 'I have a fever.' At this point (in a film) the empty battleground beyond the ditch might be shown. Flat stony desert with scrawny bushes and shrubs. A wind haze blurs everything. In the distance, a low vague shadowy citadel stretched on the horizon.

In the ditch the officer talks. 'I can't tell the difference between the living and dead. I've forgotten how to live. I'm not living. I'm practising to be dead.'

The bare nape of the young soldier's neck. It is white and smooth. The officer talks but is not seen. Suddenly, silently, a metal blade or file thrown or blown from a projector penetrates the neck. The metal is polished and so narrow and fine that it penetrates cleanly and deeply. The soldier is immediately dead. He is propped against the ditch and does not move. The unseen officer goes on talking. A thin thread of blood starts to trickle neatly from the point where the blade enters the neck. At first it pulses with the last heartbeats and then flows in an even mechanical momentum.

The unseen officer says: 'Sometimes I give a man an order. Then I see he's dead. Sometimes the dead slide down the side of a ditch. They look as if they're trying to make themselves comfortable.'

As the officer talks – slowly and flatly – the little thread of blood runs neatly – jollily – down the soldier's neck, under a metal collar and then slowly down his bare arm. Sometimes it goes out of sight for a moment and then reappears. It moves as smoothly as if drawn by a red pen. The unseen officer: 'I'm more dead than they are. I took the hand of one of them. Don't know if it was ours or theirs. Touched it to my face. I said to it "No, feel *me*. That's dead. I can teach you how to be dead".'

The trickle of blood has run down the soldier's arm. It reaches his hand. It is arched over the cup on his knee. The fingers hold it by the rim. The blood trickles down a finger and slowly drips into the empty cup. Drip. Drip. It fills it. The officer's voice: 'Some men strip the dead and put on their clothes. Feel safer in a dead man's clothes. They say no one's killed in them twice. Death recognizes its own by the clothes. "Not that one. Got him." Any trick to stay alive. Soon no one'll be killed in their own clothes. All the dead'll wear second-hand.'

The blood drips. The officer is seen sitting as before. He has not moved. He says: 'Give me a drink. Wind parched my throat.' He reaches out and takes the cup from the soldier. He does not look at it (in war you look only at the enemy). In the same flat voice he goes on talking about the war and why it never ends. He raises the cup to his lips. He tilts it to drink. He rises as the blood sprays from his mouth, cascades down his front. For a moment he is still. The dead soldier falls forwards as if trying to take back his cup. The officer still holds it, standing upright in horror. Suddenly he realizes he is exposed to the enemy – he turns to face the empty battleground . . . where death is. He holds the cup as if drinking a toast to it.

Alienation goes beyond deconstruction. It seeks to alienate conventional and ideological meanings so that things appear as they 'really' are. It does not claim to create new meanings in the way TE does. But alienation cannot be a simple negative that just removes ideological confusions. Situations do not speak for themselves. Alienation must work from a particular point of view, a particular understanding. Otherwise there would be no rational way of choosing what to alienate. Alienation cannot work from a generalized 'humanness' – a generalized humanness is part of the problem. If situations could speak for themselves drama would not be possible. Originally alienation was based on a total political philosophy. But the philosophy is not known by present-day audiences.

Alienation may produce a counter-response, a 'counter-alienation'. When whatever is alienated is without its conventional assurances, then instead of a reasoned response it may create cynicism, disgust, laughter – all things which are useful in TE. The large glass cabinets of shorn hair in concentration camps *should* provoke reason – but *need* not. Nazis are already alienated from their victims. The existential may be alienated but it cannot be given an alienated *meaning* because reality cannot be revealed to us, we create it by giving it its meaning *for us*. The existential has meaning in situation. The problem is not to alienate the situation but to alienate the self's presuppositions and prejudices. Only redramatization may do this. Otherwise it is like filling a bucket of water from the sea and expecting it to leave a hole in the sea where the water was. Alienation is itself a situation, not an abstraction from situation. For instance, the Brechtian manner of singing no longer alienates. It relates to pop and punk music which are commitments to particular 'lifestyles'. The change of effect is decisive. Static alienation becomes another convention. Dramatic method has to relate dialectically to its time.

TE dramatizes the situation's meaning. It alienates within situation by creating commitment. It may be provocative. It is not distance from situation. In aesthetics, closeness may be distance, intensity may be dilution. In the 'cup TE' the officer clutched the cup to him as he faced death – this is closeness *and* distance. The point of view creates meaning. Drama is the interaction between the social and individual, political and personal, reality and imagination. The interaction creates drama's cathexis, its intellectual-kinetic identity. Alienation is meant to decathex the situation. TE reuses the cathexis to create a meaning. Change in meaning is the most radical dramatic experience because it is partly a change in the self. Reaction-drama confirms a situation's meaning. It is an emotional or 'objectively knowing' experience. It 'moves' only on the surface. The audiences' imaginations do not create, the stage imagines for them. It is as if the stage took a photograph of its dead audience, and they saw themselves reflected in their glassy eye.

Meaning is historically present in situations. It changes historically – that is, it is determined diachronically not synchronically. That is the difference between physical and historical determination. In historical determination there is a gap between cause and effect. The gap is filled by choice. It is determined at the historical moment. The determination is not prescriptive – as if we owed a duty to history – or, of course, automatic. Drama is the difference between physical and historical determination. It involves choice and may be human or corrupt. When it concerns moral or intellectual dilemmas which have no ideal solution, often the choice is paradoxical. In the past the exploited were a majority – the 'mass' – and so collective choice was finally human. This was not 'natural' determination, it was determined contingently in history. Our future depends on humanness being *chosen*. How are we predetermined to choose the human and not the corrupt? That depends on understanding ourselves in our situation. Drama must seek the human and the just. Alienation – at least in theory – avoids the most important site of drama: the existential *need* to dramatize the self, the need for imagination to seek reason – alienation only *offers* these things. TE alienates ritual and ideological compulsion but seeks total drama. It expresses the purpose of theatre. Reason is not added to drama by alienation, reason is created through drama. It joins reason and imagination in value. This is the centre of drama, which is described in 'The Reason for Theatre'.

There may be a TE of text or of performance. The TE of performance is difficult to describe – it should be shown. In theatre performance is more profound than text, but performance is derived from text. The TE of text is easier to describe – for example in the story of Pearl White. Pearl White was a heroine of silent films. The villain ties her to railway lines. The express will shortly pass over her. The hero comes to her rescue on a horse. Will he reach her in time? The incident exploits dramatic suspense – it is a basic abstract effect.

The hero does not struggle directly with the villain to save Pearl White. Instead, old-fashioned chivalry mounted on a horse races against the huge and potentially destructive power of the machine. The train driver and fireman (who shovelled coal into the furnace) are decent, simple, hard-working proletarians – as innocent as the hero. These virtues survive in the handling of the train, although it is potentially destructive – and so a weapon to be used by the villain. The ideological argument depends on the suspense of the race, but it is the use of the suspense which prevents us noticing the ideological argument. The incident makes the ideological argument without directly referring to it. Its place is taken by the tension. The rescue of Pearl White 'wins' the argument – but does so by a false reaction-effect. The relief does not explain the cause. It is as if to rescue a climber stranded on a mountain you lowered the mountain.

The incident celebrates the hero's traditional courage and the power of modern industry. Good workers and good machines together overcome ancient villainy. The villain cannot use the train for his crime after all. The hero is rewarded with the woman. Chivalry, virtue and industry triumph together. The ideological argument is that it is safe to leave industry in the hands of its leaders and owners.

A flash-forward could show Pearl White being rescued. The film could then return to Pearl White tied to the rails. As the result of the race is known, the drama would lose its suspense. The cathexis would have been discharged before the final effect. This is true of reaction-theatre but not of TE-theatre. TE would put the cathexis to different use. It would use it to observe the actors more closely, to understand their situation better.

Pearl White is tied to the rails and the villain has absconded. The train whistles in the distance. Pearl White struggles frantically to free her wrists and ankles from the ropes. The train: spinning wheels, the sweating fireman shovels coal into the furnace, the driver adjusts the controls. Pearl White: frantically writhing. And so on. The flash-forward shows the rescue. The film then returns to Pearl White struggling on the rails. Her expressions and movements are now studied more closely. Suffering is real. Biological death is made social. The villain is anti-social. The killing weapon – the train – is social. It carries passengers: businessmen, relatives going to visit their families, friends on outings, a soldier returning to his regiment. If it is a goods train it carries raw materials or manufactures to cities and ports. The train is not a mythologized symbol of industrial power, it is a particularized image of society. The relations between passengers are observed. Documents, food, cigars, clothes. The driver and fireman are not consciously part of the crime. They are on the train with the passengers but their *social* destination is different. The empty rails may become an image of destiny when conscious choices are made. The crowded passengers do not know the meaning of their journey: the possible death of the tragic figure fluttering like a wounded white bird.

What happens if before the train reaches Pearl White it is derailed? Again this changes TE use. The driver, fireman, soldier and other passengers are killed, wounded or wander in shock. The businessman searches for his lost contract. A mother hugs her dying child. Pearl White does not know that she will live. The tensions in her face, her frantic writhings, have more profound meaning than the confrontation with death: they are seen as a confrontation with life. Perhaps she is trapped in the modern world.

What happens if the train is stopped by a stray cow? The driver sees the cow and puts on the brakes. The train stops violently. The passengers are thrown from their seats. A drunk stabs his cigar in a woman's dress. The businessman loses his papers. Children laugh. A pickpocket steals from a handbag. The soldier shakes with shell shock. The cow placidly chews. Pearl White docs not know she is saved – her struggles are pathetic and bathetic. The driver is a city man – he habitually patronizes the fireman. The driver is afraid to shoo the cow away. The fireman does it. He is not thanked. The businessman threatens to sue the train company for delay. The train restarts. Pearl White struggles. The train is now a 'Train of Fools' because the passengers are ignorant of the vicissitudes of their journey. Perhaps the gestures of some of them are like the villain's gestures. Pearl White is exhausted, her blank face stares at the sky. Clouds, waving grass, a tottering beetle. Pearl White quietly weeps. She is close to death. When Dostoevsky was taken to be executed he noticed he had all the time in the world. A child fingers a toy. The calm driver. The chewing cow.

A courting couple leave a field gate open. A herd of cows wanders on to the track. The passengers step down from the standing train. They wear fashionable clothes, gloves, kid shoes. They wander among the herd. The children are amused. The desperate businessman pleads with a cow – doesn't it know he will be bankrupt if he is late, he will lose his wife (who already has affairs), his children will starve? The cow stares and chews.

The two lovers find Pearl White. She has fainted. They think she is dead. He kneels and touches her face. Her eyes open. Is she in heaven? Is he an angel? Half-swooning with happiness she embraces him. He lifts her. Suddenly the face of his young woman moves a little too quickly and her eyes darken. She stares at her lover embracing Pearl White. Yes, she is jealous. Her secret fear returns. Her shadow falls across the empty space between the four pieces of rope tied to the rails. The train whistles. For a moment she sees her lover and Pearl White tied to the rails together in some depraved sexual embrace. She mutters, 'Yes . . . kill them.' It is only a moment – but one day it recurs in her marriage. The train is surrounded by the herd of cows.

Pearl White is tied to the lines. She writhes. The train wheels spin. The fireman shovels coal. The driver opens the throttle. Pearl White's writhing hand: a ring on her finger. On the ring is engraved the key to a code. This key will save her brother's life. At the moment the villain is in Pearl White's flat. Frantically he searches for the key. He does not know it was on a ring on the hand he lashed to the rail. Pearl White has not memorized the key (she has no head for figures). The train moves on to a curve on the side of the mountain. The driver leans from the cabin. Ahead he sees the white figure fluttering on the line. He brakes. The passengers are thrown from their seats as before. The train is grinding to a halt a few feet from the fluttering white hem – it is all that is seen of Pearl White. The cow-guard on the train's front is like a dinosaur's jaw: it moves towards the fluttering flounces. The wheels screech, the train whistles. The businessman leans from his carriage window. He orders the train driver to go on, he offers him money, he threatens him, he begs the soldier to threaten him with his gun – don't they realize that if his factory is closed whole families will starve, children will have rickets, the old will wither away? A child stares at him. The train travels the last few inches – but Pearl White is not on the line. She escaped ten minutes ago and left her white cloak behind her. She sits on the bank staring in horror at what might have been. The wheels cut into the white satin. Her hands go to her face – she sees the ring is missing. It fell from her finger in the struggle. It is on the line. She rushes to it. The slowly turning wheels are like a mastodon sniffing at its prey – a wheel descends on the ring, brushing Pearl White's hand. The ring is crushed. The train stops. Pearl White's brother dies. The businessman admires her: he thinks she tried to save her satin cloak. It gives him resolution. He steps down from the carriage. Pearl White stands on the bank and sobs. The driver tilts back his head cap and scratches his brow. The fireman comforts Pearl White – he thinks she sobs from joy. Her hands cover her face. A fortune teller had told her, 'I see a long line on your hand. Your life will be happy.'

The hero races towards the track. He is lost. He dismounts and consults his map. The horse bolts. He chases it, waving the map. Waving the map changes its 'use'. Its printed information is now useless, the map becomes a cloth waved in desperation to attract attention. The wind

blows the map into the high branches of a tree. The hero dreads heights.
He climbs the tree and his life is changed: he will become a steeplejack.
The image of his body askew in the leafless branches, his hand reaching
for the map – Icarus? Pearl White will not know, she is dead.

The horse bolts on to the tracks. In panic it charges along them
towards the train. Perhaps it tramples Pearl White. Its terrified eyes,
snorting nostrils, streaming mane. Its iron shoes pounding the rails,
hollow clanking, sparks. Horse and train race towards each other. The
TE is mythic. The horse is crucified on the front of the train. Its last
scream. The train screeches to a halt just as it reaches Pearl White. Its
wheels cut the ropes but kill her. The cow-guard hoists her body up on
to the back of the dead horse. The driver, fireman and passengers stand
round the front of the train and stare at the dead woman on the dead
horse. The businessman pounds away along the line – he will be late for
his appointment, but he must *move*. He roars that he will sue the train
company. Chivalry is dead.

The TE can use the cathexis of the 'biological frisson' to make the
event social. The same things are seen differently. TE breaks down
incidents and uses their components. The use relates to other events in
the drama. It shows that events do not happen 'naturally'. They are
made up of part-events. Each part-event is an occasion for interpretation
and choice. TE puts the moment into the crucible of the gap so that it
may be examined. Part-events produce a meaning for the total event.
Instead of victims of events there are constructors of events. Chance may
change events, but events are made of chances. In the Pearl White TE
she, the hero, the lovers, the passengers, the cows, the train (running at a
particular place in the time table) come together by chance. What seems
determined is often chance. We choose our fate or we choose the fate of
others. TE is not a form of realism. It uses chance and choice to enact
meanings, and turns incidents into constructed events.

Pearl White's original story is 'biologically dramatic'. Reaction-drama
assumes that suspense is 'naturally dramatic', an end in itself which is a
fundamental truth about drama and human nature. Really the *story* is
artificial and conceals its ideology. Behind the use of all abstract natural
effects there is a reactionary ideology. Human actions are not natural,
they are always artificial – the result of circumstances, of the situation.
Are they natural *in* the circumstances? Aren't our 'basic' functions
natural? This says nothing useful. It is like saying a hanged man
naturally *dances*. We even ceased to eat naturally long ago. A natural
person would be highly unnatural in society – he or she would be cared
for or locked away. If we were natural we would die. TE shows the

artificiality of human behaviour. It removes ideologically distorted
interpretation and enacts meaning. Meaning is found in history not
nature.

(1999)

The Site

We must learn to trust drama again. Drama is not drama for drama's sake. But it is its own authority. Its aim cannot be propaganda or instruction.

In modern theatre the story is not the drama. The structure deconstructs the story and turns it into TE. Alternatively, the story is dramatized by effects. This makes the drama meaningless. Modern drama is created only by TE. It is not created by the story or effects.

Ideology tells the story but the TE deconstructs it. The story selects certain incidents. But drama requires a site in which potentially everything is present. Drama is concerned not with character but with the site of character. It is not concerned with a story but with the site of a story. In a street there is a wounded man and a discarded cigarette packet. Each is its own potential TE and the TE of the other. Most contemporary drama destroys the site.

The story is horizontal, the structure vertical. Drama does not collapse into subjectivity or essence because the structure uncovers the site: the social on which the personal is sited. When site is revealed imagination responds to it as necessarily as reason responds to the objective (to mathematics, for example). So there is a logic of imagination and this is also a logic of value: the human. The logic of imagination is the seeking of justice. This is the purpose of drama.

But justice is Utopian. Society is unjust. We maintain ourselves in society only by use of its unjust procedures or in conflict with them. Imagination and self-consciousness are the same. The desire for justice is synonymous with self-consciousness. The desire is Utopian: the child's mind instantiates justice before it understands the inertia of the practical, social and political world.

Humanness has two sources: fear and the seeking of justice. Divorced from reality (when drama becomes self-referential) they become vicious or sentimental. Fear is the source of human corruption. Drama is the conflict between fear and the seeking for justice.

Shall we help the wounded man lying in the street or step over him to pick up the discarded cigarette packet? The answer seems clear. But if this scene is an analogy of our daily life we pick up the cigarette packet. We do this for two reasons. One is that we do not know what we are doing. Reality is shrouded in ideological obfuscation. The other is that even if we knew what we were doing we would still be forced to do it to survive. How can we make the scene useful by TE-ing it? Shall we show the human gesture: tend the wounded man? Or the 'realistic' gesture: pick up the cigarette packet? TE reveals the hidden site. It is useless to instruct the audience to tend the wounded man. This will not show the audience their site (except sentimentally or in making rules which may or may not be observed).

The audience are shown their site by being placed in it – not, as in Brecht, outside it. Accident time replaces alienation effect. In the site the audience are faced with the human paradox. A paradox cannot be 'taught'. Nor may its solution. There is no solution to the problem of being human. A paradox may only be shown. Faced with it we create our humanness or destroy our humanness. Nothing else is possible. This is the necessity of drama, the logic of imagination.

The TE exposes the site so that it is seen in accident time. Theatre without accident time is not modern. Accident time resembles the stillness at the centre of the whirlwind. The storm protects us from the dangers of the storm. We are suspended in the accident. Accidents remove the normal connections between things, the ideological net. In TE the audience have to create the connections. That means they must take responsibility for them. The site of drama is not art. The site of imagination is not imagination (just as grammar is not meaning). The site is the self in its total situation. Self and society, psychology and politics, belong to the site.

The site presents the paradox. The importance of drama is that it also resolves the paradox: in response to it you choose to be human or, instead, to destroy humanness. Drama relates to the audience as practice not as revelation. Drama does not instruct us in action. We choose. We become human or inhuman by the way we choose to act when the paradox is revealed. The human has no self – perhaps we visit ourself from time to time. In drama we see ourself as a site on which we are also others. This site is not an abstract place but a place of events. In drama, we seek the events which enable us to become our own humanness. So the site is both the extreme place and the commonplace. In the commonplace we learn to live with our fear (through revenge, ennui and so on).

Structurally the human mind must seek justice because of the way the infant must create self-consciousness. But justice is not ontological. It is a human creation. To seek justice means to change society. Doing this causes fear. That is why we fear justice – and so fear our humanness. We practise the destruction of humanness. Fear is the cause of all crime and vice, legal and criminal. We fear our self.

In the accident we are fearless. Fear comes later when we know what we have learnt or done or what has been done to us. Tragedy has to do with the removal of fear. In tragedy we lost the fear of being human. Tragedy occurs in accident time – when the arbitrary is seen to hover over us as the inevitable. That belongs to the paradox. We are at home in the site whether it is tragic or comic.

Only humans may enter the site of drama. In the human mind there are no biological analogues of pre-human minds: imagination is structurally intellectual. Only humans have imaginations. Imagination creates human reality. In nightmares fear is real though the spectres are unreal. Madness is as real as sanity. But objective reality is full of spectres: patriotism, racism, cultural elitism, religion, gods, ritual. The divisions between self and society are porous. When imagination penetrates reality the imagined is real. The spectres and other images of imagination are not objectively real. Their origin is in the pre-real mind of the child and the way it must anthropomorphize reality. What is imagined becomes concrete by the act of imagining it. Just as images learnt from reality appear in dreams, so images of pre-real imagination reappear in ideology. These have concrete effects. We describe our enemies – cultural or political – in images of childhood fear.

The imagination's understanding of itself makes each of us what we are individually. Because modern technology gives power to our fantasies (gives them real effects), collectively our future depends on our drama. The transcendental is the curse of history and we must escape from it. Humanness is immanence and materialism. It is the logic of imagination. We are each of us our own humanness and therefore our own fear and corruption. When we understand this we can no longer be coerced into political crimes (fascism, patriotism, revenge, religion and so on).

Children without toys cannot be human. The mind seeks humanness. If children are not given toys they create their own. We cannot create a private drama. The site of drama is the site of other people. In it we find ourself. The state seeks to penetrate the site of drama (as religion, law, and so on). It does so not only to repress the self so that it fits into the historically inevitable unjust structures that have administered society: it does so also to create its own justification. When our objective truth of the world is limited, truth is created from a mosaic of lies (God made the world and so on). The state abhors a vacuum because opposition may shelter in it. By emollience and terror the state dominates the imagination – but it cannot own the self. Modern technology makes it possible for the state to totally occupy the site: democracy becomes the perfected form of slavery – imagination owned by the state. This is the problem aggravated by modern media.

The structural relationship between self, imagination and the state begins to revert to an earlier relationship which is now technologically inappropriate to the support of humanness. In the same newscasts, TV and radio report technological advances and the appearances of ghosts and occurrences of miracles. Superstition 'proves itself true' by penetrating personal and social imagination. Technology functions as witchcraft. The enlightenment ends.

If we understood the reality of drama we could replace history with the human story. Objective knowledge would no longer bring us the dangers of ignorance. Drama would be the free site of humanness. To trust drama again we need TE and its devices: among which are site, accident time, the centre, use, event not effect, not fantasy but the logic of imagination. Without this theatre assists in its own destruction. It becomes another stall in the market.

In the TE the actor steps over the wounded man. He picks up the cigarette packet. He shakes it. It is empty. He sees a cigarette in the lips of the wounded man. He takes it. Here or later he may or may not shoot the wounded man. The cigarette went out when the wounded man fell. The man lights it. He inhales. He sighs. Everything depends on the way the actor sighs. The sigh is the TE.

(1999)

Letter on Design

Jacques Gabel

9 January oo

Dear Jacques

I wanted to thank you for being so kind to me when I visited your studio last year and to say how much I enjoyed my visit.

It isnt so much that design is important to me – that wouldnt matter; but it is important to my *plays* – and that does matter for the actors, the director and the audience. Design is at the centre of my plays and if the design isnt right the play cant work – that is why some productions by schools with no money for design work better than expensive productions in large theatres. Design is at the centre of theatre – because of space. The Greek and Jacobean theatres had a set space which was a simple diagram which enabled the human complexity to dispose itself. Shakespeare's stage had a raised heaven, a stage middle, and below it a hell. The Greek stage didnt have the hell – because its underworld was nebulous – instead it had the great orchestra – the agora – the house/palace behind it, and the space for the gods over it. I think all drama which is not empty tittle-tattle – as vacuous as a shop window – needs these three spaces. They arent built into our theatre. But you cannot tell a significant story without traversing these spaces – the play is a journey. I think we dont have these spaces structurally ready in our theatres because of our greater subjectivity, our lessened sense of the public world. So there is a greater responsibility on the designer to articulate these spaces – in one way or another – within our more interior introspective space – with the added dangers (and possible advantages) of abstraction which lurk in the modern world.

I think the great poet of space is Dante – it is the topographical realism of his hell which is so startling. He begins at the head – and ends at the fundament of Satan. In Dante there is a confusion because he needs

something over the head – where God will be: a sort of cosmic halo.
There are variations on the human-space journey – but the map must be
drawn in a consequential way.

I wanted to say all this because when I arrived you showed me some
pictures. I dont think the choice of pictures was accidental. It might have
been adventitious to the occasion – but they were the paintings you had
been working on, and so their presence was not accidental. You showed
me paintings of the head (as skull) – and of the stomach (which is the site
of the womb). That is the Dante, Greek, Shakespeare journey: you must
have been leading an interesting life lately. It is also interesting that
you'd turned the skull on to its end – so that the temple as site of
wisdom became also the grave – and that in the paintings of the stomach
there was the small, little grave where the umbilical cord leaves its
wound. So we were dealing with the same paradoxes and problems –
social and political and psychological. Why does the temple become the
grave, the sacred place the cesspit? In the ruthlessness of time,
everything is ruined – but humanness in someway stands out against
time. It's what our creativity is – out of chaos it creates.

So the disposition of space in my plays is important. It's so important
that I dont have to think about it – it is there, like the atoms in the table.
That is why I found myself asking: why didnt you put the door up in the
sky? Literally it is a pointless question and – among the wrong people – a
tiresome question. But because I had seen your paintings I felt that I had
to ask it. I then realized why I hadnt put in a second door – I
remembered, then, vaguely wondering when I wrote the scene why there
wasnt a second door, but I got on with listening to the characters and
writing down what they needed me to – and when I revised the scene I
concentrated on other things, again just accepting the absence of the
second door, although my stage directions are usually pretty complete
and precise. The absence was the precision. Over the years I have got
used to 'shutting up' when some directors ask me to look at designs –
there was no point in talking. But I felt that I could talk with you and the
others – that it was necessary. The play desperately scrambles from place
to place – sometimes falling into holes and pits, sometimes clambering
up cliffs, sometimes inventing space (I've always known, since the first
time I read the play, that in H3 the Woman and Greg both 'invent'
spaces and offer them to the others as new worlds to enter.) That all the
soldiers have to climb a cliff – that Nold does this unburdened – that he
looks into a space and sees the Girl climbing the bloodied cliff, that when

he is at the bottom of the cliff he looks up at the sky and wonders what he would see if he were there, like a man being buried alive looking up at the sky through the top of his grave – and so on. Unlike Dante, my characters have no Virgil to guide them through hell – they wander in it and get lost. Unlike Dante, they have no God to reach for – they must create their heaven themselves. So you cannot say their stage space is a machine – or an organism – or anything as simple as that: it is both itself (it has to be a topographic area) and a metaphor in which the actors can enact metaphors, not merely speak them. So the space must interact with them – must be itself a character, a role.

I think that in your designs for *Company* the huge 'countryside' that intrudes into Oldfield's house – creates a space, stages it, which the text can only describe – the view across the trees in the early morning (I've always been fascinated by the Scot describing the space with one word: panoramic.) But when Oldfield and the others walked in the space you opened on stage you could see them as lost figures, as small in relation to their problem, as trapped in space without Virgil . . . and therefore the scene must lead sometime to farce and tragedy. The space acted.

It's only when a writer sees something – on stage or in a model box – that he can learn certain things about what he writes; just as it's only when he sees and hears the actors that he can learn other things. If I am being true as a writer, then it isnt a question of saying 'I like this space' or 'I dont' – isnt a question of personal preference – that's like saying do I like it that a square has four sides – would I prefer, personally, only two sides . . . ? Yet a lot of design is on that level. Because there is no stage logic in it, it is mere shop-window dressing. A writer of plays – I think – can only be logical: he can say this is the logic of the situation – and then show what the characters do within the logic of their situation. Poetry is the illumination of logic – and I suppose design is also the illumination of logic? – but that part of it I cant create because I am not a designer. (I have to try to create the spoken poetry of logic, and its gestures and physical confrontations and appositions, etc.) I think directing, also, is about presenting the logic to the actors – only they can create the poetry of involvement and comment on involvement. So really I think that what logic does is not restrict or confine – it sets free, but eliminates the arbitrary; prevents fancy taking the place of imagination – because imagination is the comprehension of logic. Im trying to explain all this because it is important for me, and your work makes explanation possible because it clarifies certain problems for me.

Space acts with the actors. Suppose a beggar sits on a gold throne – I can as a writer point to the logic of it: but aesthetically I *cant* say what the gold throne should look like, what the rags should look like – the designer does that. And there is a way of making the contrast of rags and gold throne tragic or comic or human or . . . whatever is the 'use' chosen. Also only the actor can know how he or she should sit, get into the throne, leave it and so on. In all these things there is great artistry. The logic is meant to demand that artistry from the actor. The director must take responsibility for the logic – and also deploy it in such a way (the mise en scène) that the logic becomes most fruitful. None of these other things can a writer do. He can only go into hell and heaven and hope that, like Dante, he keeps his wits about him – and you are more likely to lose *them* in heaven than in hell, more likely to be deceived. I apologize for having written at some length. I needed to after visiting your studio. I left very content and happy. Im sending you a book as a way of saying thank you for *Pièces de Guerre* and *Compagnie*

Best wishes

Edward

When an artist finds his space he finds his signature

I Wrote a Poem

I wrote a poem
The child reached out its fist
To grab the pen
Let the child scribble
On the sheet
Doodles of ludicrousness and rage
Of truculence and pain
There will be time
To write your poems
When age and childhood meet
In youth
And the marred page
Is white again

(1994)

Notes on Theatre-in-Education

I watched a child play with a piece of wood. The child gave the piece of wood great value, it was its toy. Adults cannot give value to things – they need things, property and possessions, to give *them* value. Imagine the reversal in that! Our ability to create value comes from our childhood. The ability cannot be learnt later. And it can't be learnt from facts. A bit of wood is a bit of wood. Value comes from using things creatively. After all, poets and prophets have seen the image of humankind in a handful of dust. Children see in the same way till it's knocked or taught out of them. We teach children, but they take responsibility for themselves. Later they may hand over that responsibility to the state, a uniform or regulations. Children may even obey creatively, because without knowing they take responsibility for their world. It is often not convenient for us, but children are always seeking to make a just world. A child would be terrified to do anything less. No exam we set children is more stringent than the exams they set themselves in accepting responsibility to become themselves. Children play because taking that responsibility is so serious – they dramatize their minds to elucidate the pressures we put on them. They relate their emotions, impulses and visions, in a patterned way, to their social world. They create a map of that world and make themselves as part of the map. That is done by creative imagination – and adults must go on renewing the mapping, but often they do it uncreatively because the struggle to survive makes them sullen or desperate.

In the past, religion, folk festivals, local culture helped children in their dramatization. This is no longer sufficient in our complex world. Complexity and constant change expose us to an unprecedented amount of dramatic and aesthetic experience. More and more this is controlled by banks and money-markets – in TV, films and adult theatre. Imagination is captured and locked in fantasies that the state and the market find useful. The mind is exploited and the human image corrupted.

Theatre-in-Education was not created by accident. It came from children's need to take responsibility for themselves when that was being made difficult and replaced by bewilderment. Self-responsibility doesn't come from simplistic discipline. People in prison are disciplined but not allowed to take responsibility for themselves. Responsibility comes from creativity. If the child cannot find creative value in the piece of wood it will never find it in itself or in anyone else. Instead the child will become an object to be bought and sold in the market – or broken. And increasingly this is what education leads to. Education is not being reformed, it is being devalued.

Understanding theatre is the most difficult task our minds undertake. It is more difficult to understand it than to understand, say, quantum physics. To understand theatre means to understand ourselves and no one has ever managed to do that. It is not true that science deals with reality and theatre with imagination. Imagination and reality are different aspects of the same thing. We are conscious of reality but we are also self-conscious. But we could not be self-conscious without imagination. We would do things as machines can and feel things as animals can – but we would not know ourselves or have a history, politics, society, morality or theatre.

A murderer in a film creeps in the dark. We know he is an actor creeping in a studio but our suspense is real. We imagine a nightmare or happy dream but our panic or pleasure are real. The stories and images of patriotism are not real, but through imagination we may believe they are. Belief is a vital adjunct of imagination: it is imagination impelled by fear or hope. This gives imagination its reality. Believers, dreamers and the mad think that what they imagine is real. This is also the 'reality' of theatre – but there it need not entail intellectual corruption.

What is reality? If a fish could imagine it would always have to imagine the sea was the sea and not desert. Otherwise it would try to leave the sea and drown. But people may imagine strange things – not real things but illusions. Fish cannot drain the sea to make a desert to swim in. But increasingly we have the technological power to turn our illusions into reality. Our practical knowledge of reality is integrated into our imaginations. So what we do with our knowledge depends on our beliefs, on what we imagine. The same practical knowledge may have good or bad consequences. Imagination changes reality just as reality changes us. But our situation is more vulnerable than this because for a time beliefs are stronger than facts. This means that reality is created by our imaginations.

Imagination makes us human but may also make us inhuman. Imagination is basically the desire – the need – to be at home in the world. But our societies are unjust. When we try to make ourselves at home in injustice we corrupt our imagination. We deny our deepest need. We become angry and destructive. Our corrupted imagination turns reality into a nightmare. We use our practical knowledge of the

world to destroy it and ourselves. It is the story of the past. Will it be the story of the future?
It is difficult to describe our situation. The words we need are corrupted by injustice But we can say:
Imagination and self-consciousness are the same thing.
Imagination seeks justice.
Fear may corrupt imagination so that it seeks violence and destruction.
The structure of imagination is drama.

From this it follows that imagination is the basis of our humanness and secures or destroys our place in reality.

Today the media saturate our imaginations with trivializing dramas based on false beliefs. Increasingly this is done to keep society running, not to make it more just or help us to understand ourselves. The boundary between reality and imagination is made unreal. Our daily lives turn into fiction.

The strength of a society's search for justice is always reflected in the state of its drama. Bad drama flourishes in an unjust society. Our future always depends on the state of our imaginations. Drama becomes more important as the world changes. Theatre is just or corrupt and in the urgency of the times there is nothing in between. That is because theatre is the place where reality is made real. The plays young people write, act in and watch are blueprints of the world they will have to live in. Anyone who has had to work in the adult media over the last twenty years has wasted their life or had it wasted for them. During these years, Theatre-in-Education has become more relevant, skilled and useful – more valuable. Now the threat to its existence is a tragedy. It is the most valuable cultural institution the country has.

(1994)

Oranges

When I have been dead a hundred years
One day a woman in a busy street
Hurrying a little to be home
Will trip on the uneven pavement
Stumble – not fall – but check her pace
And drop her shopping bag
Packages and bits and pieces lie at her feet
But the oranges scatter into the road
I wish I could pick them up
Run after the furthest one – the colour could not be missed
  – rolling between the traffic
Take them back to her
And put them in her shopping basket
It would be better to pick up oranges in the street
But still when I am dead
The plays I write may be of use to her

(1994)

Rough Notes on Justice

What is Justice?

We need to make three distinctions. First there is the law, legal justice, law and order. These are the rules that all members of society must obey. They are made by the legislature, administered by courts and enforced by police and armies. All are equal before the law.

Second, there is the social order. Social justice is more complex than the law. Social justice involves customs, politics, livelihoods, culture. It allows people to live in freedom. Everyone is different, with different needs and abilities. Social justice allows everyone to meet their different needs and try to fulfil their different potentials. Everyone is equal before the law, but everyone is unequal before social justice.

If I sing or paint or nurse or organize – and need to do these things to fulfil myself – social justice makes this possible. It must make it possible for me to achieve my personal aim, which is important to me. But for society different aims have different values. One aim might be to play table tennis professionally, another might be to be an inventor or teacher or industrial entrepreneur. Society rewards different aims differently, paying more for some than for others.

We also need to divide social justice into community and society. By community I mean the relationships between people which enable each of them to pursue their aim humanely. Community is founded on trust, friendship, on 'getting on together' and sharing a common life. By society I mean the economic and organizational structure into which we are all fitted. The economy enables us to make and to buy and sell. It produces a class structure. The higher your economic standing the higher your class.

In a community the poor and rich may be equally pleasant and equally generous within their means. These human qualities do not count in economic society. The economy is not a human structure, it does not depend on human virtues. It has a life and logic of its own. Our economy is named after its driving force – capitalism. In the end, it may serve justice, but obeying the economy's laws is not the same as obeying the laws of justice.

We can now add the third distinction I began by mentioning. It is power. Money is the power that makes our economy work. Power is money. The more money you have, the more power. So if it is just that we all have equal power we should all have equal amounts of money? Not necessarily, because some people use money in ways more useful to the economy and the community than other ways. It might be better to invest money in discovering a cure for a disease than in giving the money directly to the sufferers of the disease.

The economy has laws which must be obeyed. When necessary these laws take precedence over the immediate needs of the community. Otherwise the whole thing crashes and the community suffers. The problem is that power clearly affects the law, before which we should all be equal, and society in which we should all be free to be unequal in our own ways. Power makes us unequal before the law, and forces its own inequalities on us in society.

The poor are not equal with the rich before the law. The rich tend to commit different crimes and are better defended. The crimes of the rich tend to affect property and power, the poor's crimes tend to affect the person. Our society (though not all societies) punishes offences against the person more severely than it punishes property or economic offences. We execute people for murder but not for corporate fraud. And someone who habitually steals wallets will be in prison longer than someone who commits one fraud that misappropriates more money than would be gained in a lifetime of wallet stealing. Rapists are punished more severely than big tax evaders. That is one sort of injustice. Another is that powerful classes tend to decide what the law is. In, say, feudal society, the powerful made laws for their own benefit. Is it different in democracy? The wide suffrage should ensure that it is. But power affects everything, and clearly it has a large say in forming public opinion and so biasing elections.

The American president went to China and criticized the Chinese government for restricting religious freedom. But America had an Un-American Activities Committee which restricted communism. Was the HUAC defending society against communists who wanted to radically change society? Christ wanted to change society far more radically than most communists do. Are Americans Christians because they want to change society? On the contrary, the evidence is that they are Christians because they want society to stay as it is. Christ would not care a damn whether anyone worshipped him (he would leave that sort of thing to Hollywood stars), but he would want everyone to change their life. That would mean living according to the virtues of the community and not to the laws of the economy. But clearly the logic of the economy is that power rules our lives.

What does a community call good? Virtues such as kindness, candour, generosity, forbearance. If I commit a crime power will imprison or execute me. If I am 'good' for a year, will it pay me a bonus or move me to a better neighbourhood? That would not be good for the economy. It *could* be argued that power will enable me to move to a better place by earning more on the social market. But the social market deals only in power. Saints tend to be poor, in business candour doesn't pay, and innovative artists and thinkers are neglected unless power can use them to serve its own ends. The economy rewards greed, cunning, acquisitiveness. Was the conscious immoral promotion of tobacco for years in America worse than the suppression of Christianity in China? Were there more Chinese Christian martyrs than martyrs to the American tobacco industry?

There is a difference between naked totalitarianism and democracy. But a free market does not make a just society. In it people are not socially free or equal members of society or equal before the law. It is not that the economy is run by wicked men or that Christians are cynics. The trouble is that the economy attacks the virtues of the community. We say: well, this man is poor but nevertheless he *did* murder and we must kill him. The poor should not kill but work to improve their market level. But the poor live in a culture of despair which is directly caused by their lack of power. The meek may eventually inherit the earth, but in the meantime they won't get the best paying jobs.

The economy cannot be honest about itself. It's claimed that by obeying its own laws it eventually serves the community. Eventually came to an end some time ago. The economy becomes a vast advertisement for itself. Tobacco industries knew tobacco caused cancer but advertised it with images of the good life. We see the connection between tobacco and cancer but not between the power of the market and prisons, children who kill, drug abuse, racism and reaction. The connection between tobacco and cancer is clear and is exposed in hospitals – the connections between economic power and social malaise are not clear, they are mediated through culture and hidden in living rooms, kitchens, bedrooms and schoolrooms.

I described the community as a place of friendship, candour and other virtues. But the effects of economic power leak down into the community. Families and neighbourhoods become sites of antagonism and violence. If the manipulations of the economy and power structure society, the consequences must infiltrate everything. Power creates both apathy and resistance to itself. And as more and more of society is mediated through the economy and its necessities, so chaos and repression grow. It is then that power turns to violence. The economy

gives us more of the means to 'the good life', yet society becomes
increasingly violent.

There are other points to consider. 'Poor offences' against the body
are more heinous than offences against property – murder and rape are
more heinous than fraud. But the economy itself commits offences
against the body – the tobacco and gun industries kill and among their
victims are the most vulnerable and innocent. But although we are
increasingly subordinated to the power of the economy, in the past it was
not different. Power has always regarded its economic foundation as
necessary and even God-given because its own existence depended on it.

We are struggling to disentangle two things: the necessary laws of the
economy and the human desire for justice. Why do we desire justice?
Why not simply give ourselves over to force? Shoot all offenders –
however trivial the offence – or lock them away for life. It might work,
people would obey all the laws out of fear. But we think we should desire
justice not out of fear but for some other reason.

We have come to the fundamental question. We must try to
understand it because our future depends on it. Humans are 'unnatural'
animals. An animal's body is evolved to relate to the place in which it
exists: fish have fins and birds have wings. Neurologically advanced
animals have a sensory relationship with their place. They are conscious
of pleasure and pain, otherwise they would not have evolved the
neurology to register them. But they are not self-conscious. They do not
ask *why*. *Why* is a question possible only to self-conscious beings. A lion
waiting for its expected prey is consciously hungry when the prey does
not come on time. But the lion cannot ask *why* it doesn't come. Instead
it will wait or move to another watering hole. A vixen may coerce her
rowdy cubs when the hunt is near. But she will not have to ask *why* the
cubs are rowdy and answer it is because they are naughty. Morality
comes into being only when you may ask *why*. It is to do with reasons
and not only causes. When you ask *why* about one thing you must ask it
about everything. Yet there are no real answers to *why* questions. That is
the reason why (as I shall explain) we have imaginations.

An animal's consciousness is limited to consciousness of its location
and situation – that's where its wings or fins or claws work. But there is
no appointed location or situation for humans – we may be human (or
inhuman) anywhere. Our 'site' is the universe, and that is why we ask
why. The answers we give to these questions decide how human or
inhuman we are. The consequences are profound. St Augustine said that
if he didn't think about time he knew what it was, but if he was asked to

explain it, and thought about it, he didn't. This is also true of ourselves. We know who we are till we start looking for ourselves.

Unlike the lion, the child, if its food doesn't come, will ask *why*? Is it because it is bad (as mummy might say) or because mummy is bad? Who decides what is 'bad'? Ultimately all 'why' questions are about everything. This is because the human mind is holistic. Like other animals, really we need to ask only about our immediate situation, but then we would not be self-conscious. Self-consciousness is synonymous with 'why-holism'. So we ask about the beginning and end of time, about our mortality and life after death, about good and bad, about creation. Really, in asking about these things we are seeking to know who we are, to find ourselves.

Even the infant's mind must be holistic. The newborn child makes no distinction between itself and the world. It thinks it is the world. Its eyes cannot focus or its mind concentrate on anything outside its own sensations. If it is hungry then the whole world is hungry. Soon the child learns to distinguish a world outside its self. It becomes self-conscious by learning that it is a 'self' related to a world outside it. At first the world was its skin, now it is not. The child can then seek only one thing: to be at home in the world. That seeking to be at home in the world is the origin of our desire for justice.

The child must think that it has a *right* to be at home in the world. That is, that it has a right to live. If it cannot do this it must become functionally autistic. Its mind cannot function, its *why* is trapped and so it loses its *self*. If it cannot ask *why*, it has no other questions, and there are no answers – the self and world have no meaning. That is, they have no value. Values come into the world only when we can ask *why*. It's true that pleasure and pain have a meaning for us just as they do for the lion. But they can be analysed into *whats*. The child itself would be another *what*, if it did not have to ask *why* because it was conscious it was a self. Its answer is that it has a right to be in the world. This is part of the functioning of its mind, and without it its mind cannot function. All other values are derived from this, as the child understands more and more of the world.

The infant is egotistical. Once it thought it was the world. Now it knows there is a world but it is only concerned with its own right to be in it and in this sense the world is its. This egotism is universal in all infants. Its universality means that this self-conviction of its right to be in the world is a universal statement about all people. Each has a right to live and to desire to be at home in the world. This is not an 'idea', but is functional in the working of the infant's mind. Because it is universal it is as if each child had it in all living human beings, those who have lived and those who could ever live. This is a characteristic of the human mind: each human is everyone else. That is part of the foundation of justice. The paradox is that it combines the universal and the particular, isolated individual.

Adults distinguish between the world and society. The child has no society, it has only a world. It knows no geography outside its house, it has no economy except its feeding bottle. Nevertheless it has the whole world in the way adults cannot. This and the right to live in the world are its 'radical innocence'. Its radical innocence makes it responsible for the world. If the child is not at home in the world – even if this is only for an instant: because it cannot distinguish between an instant and eternity, to lose the world is to be lost for ever – then the child rages. To us it seems aggressive and we describe it as bad. Really it is just its innocence made urgent. It cries to save the world.

Its innocence is radical because it is demanding. It cannot accept that it should not be at home in the world. This is the first expression of its desire for justice. The desire becomes fractured into an all-pervading distinction between good and bad. These words apply not only to the external world, they are used when it learns to control its bowels, its emotions, to speak and behave. The child is immersed in the task of understanding. It is as if the child made a map of the world and at the same time included itself on it, created itself as part of the map. Self and belief become one. It searches for truths about the world but cannot describe the world in terms of itself, which is all it knows. It anthropomorphizes the world. Trees speak, the storm is angry, the chair is naughty, the toy is alive, animals drive automobiles. These fantasies are for the child the stuff of sanity because they enable it to exist in the world. So they are lies that become existential truths. The child does not disassociate fantasy from reality, on the contrary it can only know reality through fantasy.

The child grows and learns more of reality. The storm is not angry, trees do not speak. The child needed fantasy to survive, but adults need a knowledge of reality to sustain an economy and organize society. *Whys* are unanswerable questions, because the answers lead to other *whys*. But the questions must be answered – the answers are as existentially necessary to adults as they were to the child. And so society answers them – not to explain the world but to explain itself. This means that power provides the answers in order to justify the injustice of the social order. There is always a paradox, and here the desire for justice leads to the justification of injustice.

The fantasies of adults are dignified as part of culture. All cultures contain many lies. We invent God in our image, we talk of a mother country (and may die for it), we may believe that our fate is in the stars, or that droughts or storms or AIDS are punishments sent by God, we may believe that God insists on sartorial or dietary conformities as if divinity were a tailor or a cook. But there are greater dangers. A culture is the way people make themselves at home in the world – it combines technology, organization and beliefs. Because both the powerful and the powerless share in much of a culture, it is able for a time to change reality. This leads to the distortions in psychology and behaviour which turn the desire for justice into the lust for revenge, the need for community into the 'power world' of society, the need to be at home in the world into a rage to destroy other people. When we pass from childhood to adulthood, from world to society, we stand everything on its head. And reality reinforces our fantasies. There *is* crime, and we *must* find a niche in the market or we fall out of culture. So we rage because we are not in our home.

Finally, we must deal with the imagination. Imagination enables us to create fantasies (which the lion and the fox cannot do). Why do we have imagination? Because we are self-conscious. Imagination and self-consciousness go together. We could not be self-conscious if we did not have imagination. We think of imagination as an insignificant part of reality but really imagination is the foundation of our humanness. Without it we would be conscious but not self-conscious. Imagination forces us to ask *why*, and all the *why-answers* come from imagination. Our existential need for answers then turns bits of imagination into beliefs. Beliefs are imagination reified by fear and they may act as if they were *whats*.

Imagination is the source of the highest and lowest in humans. It is the source of the terrors of madness and the inspiration of ideals. When imagination is related to reason it is creative, but when it is coerced by fear it becomes mad – and when this is transposed into action it becomes destructive. On a large scale that is the origin of political totalitarianism and religious absolutism, and the armies and cults which owe fealty to these things; on a small scale it is responsible for crime, vandalism and family violence.

We look for mechanical explanations of human behaviour. But human behaviour is always paradoxical. This is because it is not derived from mechanical *whats* but from existential *whys*. An object can change only according to mechanical laws, but human minds have fantasy as a resource of their reality. It is as if the mind were a permanent miracle. Or it is like a beanbag, when you put pressure on one point its contents move to another. That makes the distinction between fantasy and imagination vital. Fantasy is arbitrary and inconsequential, but imagination always takes part of reality into itself, and so it must be either drama or belief. Fantasy is a sort of onanistic scribbling in the brain, but imagination never escapes from the existential pressure of *why* – indeed it is its expression.

As human behaviour must be paradoxical, it cannot be understood as we understand objects and cause-and-effect. Executing murderers will not stop murders – paradoxically it may result in more murders. Punishing children may not prevent them being 'bad', it may make them worse. All such paradoxes can be summed up in one way: because innocence is radical it may express itself in corruption. And because societies are unjust, they not merely insist on outward conformity (which punishment and reward might obtain) but insist on belief. To do that power must monopolize what is radical in innocence, its necessity – and power can only do that by making innocence corrupt: that is what turns the desire for justice into the lust for revenge.

Individuals may do something similar to themselves. If a child is deprived or punished severely the paradox appears again. The child believes it has a right to exist and that the world should be its home. That would make it a good child in a good world. But if the world is not its home but a bad world then the child will be bad. It will assert its right to exist by being bad – it will have an existential right to be bad, it will be its good. This will bring it into conflict with society's insistence that it is good (in its terms) and so the paradox escalates into disaster. As power increases such conflicts become endemic in our society, it is why it deteriorates. We are part of our society, and when it is unjust we are either bad or righteous and revengeful – and none of these things are just.

Imagination is the site of madness or drama. King Lear or Antigone would understand the paradoxes I have described. The law is too simplistic to deal with the human paradox. It treats people as *whats*. The paradox is the subject of drama, of all arts which must articulate or image ideas – because *why* needs the articulation of ideas. The first society to understand this was Greece. It created the foundations of our drama and our democracy. The two go together, and the state of a democracy is shown by its drama. The subject at the base of all drama is justice. The Greek dramatists even accused their gods of injustice: it is the theme of tragedy. The Christian religion is a Greek drama in which God may not be accused: God is indeed a murderer, he killed his son – but the son dies willingly. In a sense this is a formal answer to *why*. If it were a real answer, our societies would not be unjust and we would not be violent.

We live in crisis. We have weapons to destroy the world, and even when we are at peace we destroy it: that is the logic of the power that rules our economy. Faced with this crisis it seems fatuous to talk of drama and the Greeks. Yet Greek drama changed the world twice – first in Athens and again in Renaissance Europe. Greek drama was innocent, ours is corrupt. Greek dramatists were concerned with justice, our films and TV are concerned only with guilt. So our situation seems worse. But the Greek dramatists wrote their plays in celebration of a non-existent God and we know more about the real world than the Greeks did. So we may be hopeful. Moral persuasion will not make us just, because morality very easily becomes the support of injustice, and usually for very practical reasons. We will become just only by honouring our common innocence. The law and society cannot do that – they must speak the language of *what* and not of *why*.

Like all human things drama may be corrupted, but it need not be. It can be a place of radical innocence and speak the language of justice. When it does this it finds it speaks the language of the community. From time to time this has happened. I do not know if it will happen again. If it doesn't it will be because we have become so trapped by power and injustice that we destroy ourselves.

Written for the Summer Seminars,
University of Southern California, 1 July 1998

Rough Notes on Intolerance

To condemn intolerance suggests that there is something that should be tolerated. It also suggests that there are some things that should not be tolerated. These include Nazi death camps and mob lynchings for instance.

There is a more immediate, personal, form of intolerance. You can intolerate a neighbour's loud music, smelly cooking. Tolerance on this level implies give and take. People have a need to express themselves within their own culture – and this includes music, cooking – and perhaps aspects of personal relationships, such as rearing children. You might move from a neighbourhood where the music was too loud – but suppose you thought children were being handled brutally and were in distress: can you move away from that?

Intolerance can be good or bad. Yet we regard tolerance as a virtue. Do you find slavery intolerable – or do you tolerate it and use it? The Bible has been quoted in support of slavery.

Tolerance is not a simple question of adopting a tolerant attitude – and intolerance is not always bigotry. Indeed our modern liberal civilization was created – at least formally – because some people found intolerable what other people did.

This raises the question: how is it that some people find tolerable what others find intolerable? Factory owners in the English Midlands were intolerant of slavery in America in the nineteenth century; but in their factories they worked to death young children. Children as young as five worked in mines and were deformed by their work. To find black slavery intolerable is human, but to deform little white children blackened by coal dust . . .?

The Nazis who slaughtered their enemies were in other ways very 'cultured'. They listened to classical music, looked at the Old Masters, and even respected the law much more than the average American does now. When intolerant people are asked to explain what they're doing they often say – as the Nazis did – that they're defending civilization – and the English factory owners believed they were deforming and killing children for the common good.

It is not clear that the common good is so good if it means crippling children – or that civilization is cultured if it means killing people of other cultures – and remember, even within the Nazis' definition of culture, their Jewish enemies were conspicuous for being some of the greatest representatives of that culture.

To talk of tolerance and intolerance is not enough. Why is it that the 'tolerant' are often so intolerant in some respects? The factory owners obviously profited from intolerance towards their working-class children. If in the nineteenth century I had worn a shirt woven by these children – or warmed my room with coal mined by these children – I would have profited from the factory owner's intolerance. I would have been intolerant of the well-being of the children – and yes I might well have taught other children in a Sunday school all the Christian virtues. Most tolerant people are intolerant because they tolerate injustice.

It is pointless to claim to be tolerant if we tolerate injustice. It is self-deception. But how can we found a system of justice on the habit of lying to ourselves?

To be tolerant in ordinary social life is obviously a good. If someone pushes ahead of us to get served at the counter first – we can tolerate that. It costs us nothing and perhaps the other person 'has a problem' or is in a special hurry. If everyone stood up for their rights on *every* occasion, we would have to live in a police state. Yet we are encouraged to 'stand up for our rights'. No society can work on that principle – we stand up for our rights only in important matters. But what is important to me may be unimportant to you. A newly emancipated slave may perhaps not tolerate someone pushing in front at the counter as easily as someone who had never been a slave might do. We even need caution: suppose the person who pushes in front is a maniac with a knife? We have to tolerate mental illness – but not assaults on us. We obviously have to rely on our own judgement. But suppose that for some reason more and more people begin to carry knives or guns?

Perhaps it is necessary for the former slave to carry a knife in self-protection – because it protects the former slave against the gradual return of slavery – it shows that former slaves will no longer be abused but will stand up for their rights. Obviously anyone who wanted the return of slavery would not be tolerant. Is it intolerant of the former slave to 'pull his knife'? It depends in the end on what you – the person not immediately involved in the quarrel – do. Because when it comes to the moment to be tolerant or intolerant – it's always too late, or your tolerance is little more than an empty gesture. On the whole the Nazis were conspicuous for politeness and manners – such things protected their intolerance – just as a Sunday school could protect intolerance in nineteenth-century England.

Our lives – and our actions – can only make sense if we make society just. Then it becomes much easier to decide what to tolerate and what not to tolerate – it doesn't completely solve the problem but it makes it easier. And to want to make society just means that you have to live not just courteously but radically, because societies are very unjust and it is difficult to change them. But there is this: trying to make a society just opens up for us and involves us in all the difficult questions that define what it is to be a human being. We become human only by fighting injustice. This may seem surprising – because surely someone who is courteous, supports their dependents, is kind to children, gives to charity – surely they are behaving as humans should? The answer is no: because I am my brother's and sister's keeper. I am responsible not only for what I do, I am responsible for what other people do – because I am responsible for what is done to other people. This seems the opposite of tolerance! – because isn't it tolerant to let people get on with their own lives and not interfere with them? But we don't act on that idea – we don't think it's right to let others gas people of other cultures or to exploit and cripple children. It's perfectly clear that there is a conflict between justice and tolerance. If we could say: 'From one o'clock tomorrow everyone will be tolerant', there would be no problem – but we can't. Not just because we know some people wouldn't be tolerant – but because we are probably not prepared to fight for justice. Justice is not 'standing up for my rights', it's 'standing up for everyone's rights'.

Standing up for your own or others' rights of course entails intolerance of those who infringe these rights. This isn't always the 'good' opposing the 'bad'. The Nazis and the factory owners believed that they were doing 'good' – the Nazis were prepared to die for their beliefs as well as to kill for them. I do not want to tolerate evil – and that was also the Nazis' explanation of what they were doing. It's clear that if you wish to be tolerant – except in minor things such as good manners – you need a police force to enforce your tolerance, just as you needed an army to defeat or at least confine Nazism. The police force enforces law and order – but that's what it did for the Nazis, that's what it did when it protected the factory owners' destruction of children's lives. This is because society is unjust: you need a police force to protect your tolerance and also to protect society's injustice. You see, there is no way out of these dilemmas unless you insist on making society more just – and tolerance alone does not do this. This does not mean that you should not be tolerant – except to intolerance. But it means that by being tolerant you are not doing very much – and you are not facing the important questions that define what it means to be human. Tolerance would only be human if you could ensure that everyone could be tolerant.

How is this to be achieved? By moral persuasion? – by persuading that intolerance of race, religion, sexuality, customs is as wrong as theft and murder? That morality teaches us to love humankind?

Gandhi was an important moral leader in India. He spent most of his life persuading people to be non-violent and instead to use 'soul force' – that is, moral persuasion. He was asked if he would ever use violence. He said, 'If my daughter were about to be violated – I would kill to protect her from violation.' You would think he meant that he would kill the violator. He meant he would kill his daughter. So here is a doctrine of 'purity' elevated to a very high level. It is better to kill the innocent potential victim – than to kill the aggressor. It is better to kill the innocent to protect innocence than to kill the aggressor. Gandhi would take on the guilt of murdering the innocent but not of murdering the guilty. Most people would say that the daughter was potentially the victim of the violator – and also of her father who would murder her to protect her chastity. I suppose it's why the Inquisition tortured and burnt heretics in the Middle Ages – to save them from being a 'living violation' of the moral law, though I think the reasons were in fact more complicated. When the Nazis killed their victims to protect (as they saw it) civilization – were they doing what Gandhi said he would do to protect chastity? Of course the Nazis saw their enemies as violators – and Gandhi would see his daughter as innocent; but they are both, one in practice and one in principle, prepared to kill for the sake of truth – and, in our eyes, the victims of both would be innocent.

I am not comparing Gandhi to the Nazis. I am describing how difficult the questions you are dealing with are. Gandhi would kill the innocent for the sake or morality. He would not tolerate violation but would rather murder.

A sympathetic outsider, such as I am, wonders why America is such a violent country – why it's retreating from many of the attitudes and practices that Western civilization has for many hundreds of years taken to be necessary indications of civilization? I think the answer is that America is not only unjust but it is becoming increasingly unjust. There is an easy trick that will 'solve' this problem. It is this: when people are intolerant or break the law, say they are evil, bad, sinners, naturally aggressive. The Nazis did this of course, when they said their enemies were evil – the Inquisition said it when it burnt its enemies – or the Massachusetts church when it hanged witches. Presumably the factory owners regarded the children they crippled as 'inferior' – as slave owners regarded slaves. The 'crimes' of heretics would be, in another place, virtues. In Africa blackness would be regarded as a sign of normality – not as it was, at that time, in the Southern states as a sign of inferiority. The same with Jewishness. Does this mean that if everyone were in their place the problem would be solved? What was the place for the factory children? Is there a special place for the rich and another special place for the poor? Justice surely implies freedom – that we should be free to go where we wish. Or is justice simply that everyone should be imprisoned in the 'right' place? But the slaves did not want to make the journey to the Southern states, the Jews often changed places to avoid persecution, and Europeans emigrated to America to find freedom not to be hanged as witches.

The danger is that you can be tolerant – and still allow a police force to protect injustice and prevent people from being free. And I suppose that if Gandhi's daughter had tried to passively resist Gandhi when he (in principle) came to murder her, he would have resisted her passive resistance with violence. Of course the Gandhi example is only an 'experiment' because no one tried to violate his daughter – but if you wish to follow his moral principal, then you would have to murder your daughter, mother or wife (or even a stranger) rather than permit their violation. That is Gandhi's opinion, of course, not mine.

Gandhi's daughter, the Nazis' enemies, the Africans brought to America as slaves – all these were innocent. What of the guilty – I mean robbers, violent people and so on – people in prison and death cells? Not those who are there in error, but those who have committed the acts for which they were being punished. Surely these are, if not sinners or evil, at any rate bad, anti-social – a thief is intolerant of another person's right to their own property.

Now I want to say something very serious. Gandhi was never in the situation where he had to murder his daughter for the sake of principle. He was a good man and he was spared that situation. In that situation he would, I think, have behaved badly – he would have committed a crime against his daughter. I have to repeat here that I do not regard Gandhi as 'evil' or 'bad' but as someone struggling with the problem of being human. I think he misunderstood his situation. And I think that behind the problem of freedom and justice there is not a problem of goodness, badness, sin, evil: but of understanding. The thief is in the sort of situation which Gandhi was spared: I think the thief also misunderstands his situation – but I must understand his misunderstanding. I say this, in just the same way, of the murderer in the death cell. I have to understand the situation in which the murder was committed –

understand not merely an hour, a day or a year – but a whole life. And if you do not take the trouble to understand that – then you are intolerant.

When a society is unjust there is no freedom: everyone is in a ghetto of poverty, fear, anger, insolence, sentimentality – a ghetto of danger. In this ghetto it is difficult to understand but easy to feel. And there comes a lethal cocktail of misunderstanding and emotion – and it is this that leads to violence, to robbery and even to murder. The victims of this social injustice become the aggressors who offend law and order – and end in prisons and execution chambers. The emotions become a sort of drug to them so that they see the world differently and behave in ways we regard as unacceptable – but I believe this also to be true of Gandhi's attitude towards his daughter. We have to remove the places where violence is created and remove the situations that breed misunderstanding. I think the nineteenth-century factory owners did not understand their situation and that is why they crippled children. Today, those who are trapped in injustice do not understand the situation – that is why they rob and murder.

The factory owner and the murderer have different attitudes to their actions. The factory owner will be 'personally' law-abiding – may even preach in Sunday school. The murderer may murder in anger or cold-bloodedly. These are irrelevant considerations – the owner and the criminal act out of an understanding of their situation, just as the Nazis did and Gandhi did. We need more Gandhis and no Nazis – but this is wishful thinking. I am trying to be practical because I think the welfare of humanity depends on understanding and creating justice. Tolerance is often a trick: a way of tolerating injustice – and therefore of creating intolerance. The only way out of this is to make society just.

This is an impossible goal – which is why people invent heaven: they despair of making a heaven on earth. Even if all of us were born into just situations and helped to understand ourselves – people would still be difficult! This is because the young mind is almost in an impossible situation: how can a child understand the world it's born in? – it needs fairy stories to explain reality, to assure it in its extreme dependence on the giants and huge objects that surround it. The child is too young to be responsible for itself. And so children grow up with emotional biases, with anxieties and fears. That's another reason for understanding. The child is not to be accused of evil and punished. It is to be understood and helped. I think this is why we have stories, films, plays, pictures – they're ways in which people, young and old, can recreate themselves and learn to be just. In societies as unjust as ours, this is an impossible hope! Our films and plays may allow us to release some of our emotion –

but they do not help us to understand our situation. It's like a sports match – a game of baseball may allow you to release some aggression but it will not help you to understand the world.

Intolerance is always destructive if it is based on ignorance: tolerance is always superficial unless it is radical. Radical tolerance is the only real opposition to intolerance – because it changes the causes of intolerance – it makes society more just. Doing this has now become more urgent.

I'm not suggesting that we simply abolish prisons and release the condemned. In fact, if we did society would probably become less violent – freedom has a way of curing ills and prohibition and repression of exacerbating them. But no one is going to try the experiment – democracy doesn't really understand freedom and justice any more than (I think) religion understands evil and human nature. Repeated calls for morality don't make society less violent – sometimes it's the contrary. It's surely relevant that Gandhi's son was imprisoned for petty crime – the proximity of moral authority did not make him 'good'. Making society just is a social and political not a moral problem. But if society is not made more just – if people cannot see its increasing injustice – then society will certainly become more intolerant and more violent and dangerous.

I want to ask you to think about this statement: the condemned in prison cells and death cells are as innocent as Gandhi's daughter. If you can understand this, you understand intolerance and may begin to understand justice.

Written for the Summer Seminars,
University of Southern California, 14 July 1997

Notebook, 31 January 1996

I

I've just written to an Egyptian student who asked about violence. I repeated answers I've given before. I said the state was an institution of violence. I said that before violence was a moral question it was an economic question. Violence follows trade. And that for this reason violence was an aberration of socialism but an essential characteristic of capitalism. Because capitalism required inequality and this inevitably led to violence.

Then I said that to ask for non-violence was to ask for too little. I asked for something more radical. I could sum up what that is by saying: be just. Because this contains the plea for non-violence and does it in a realistic way. It also includes many other things that are desirable and necessary for human happiness and well-being. Gandhi did not tell people to be non-violent. He told them to live a life of satyagraha and this would include non-violence. But this is still a personal appeal to individuals and it is meaningless when faced with Nazism or nuclear weapons. We need political changes – the changes necessary to make society just – and only then can the other things follow.

'Be just' has nothing to do with the law. The law may well administer injustice. 'Be just' means that everyone belongs to Kant's kingdom of ends. And that we must be just in the means we use to achieve these ends. Economic means must be just. It is immoral to ask for non-violence and not ask also for justice.

II

It used to be said that soldiers said (or were said to say) that they were proud to die for their country; and that parents were proud their sons had died for their country. Now civilians seem to be more at risk of death and wounding than soldiers are. Perhaps in time civilians will be televised saying they would be proud to be bombed – even with hydrogen bombs – for their country. It seems the hysteria in which people of Western democracies live could lead them to say this sort of thing, especially at times of international tension. Then it would be only a matter of time before schoolchildren were taught to be proud of bomb victims. The rationale would be that their country cannot defend itself –

cannot attack its enemies – without exposing civilians to the risks of being bombed.

Western history would have been far more moral if the Bible had not been written. Western society would have been – would be now – more Christian if Christ had not been born. The difficulty with Christ is the murder. This corrupts the idea. One ought not to have conversations with one's murderer but Christ did it all the time.

III
The Calculus of Hell

The Nazi soldiers come to the house. They say 'We are taking away your children to kill them. We will take you and kill you too.' Should the parents kill the soldiers with the weapons hidden under the floorboards? The soldiers outnumber them and have many more weapons.

But the soldiers do not say 'We will take away your children and kill them. And we will kill you too.' They say 'We will take you to another place. There you will work for your living. It will be better for you there.'

It may be that the parents will believe what the soldiers tell them. They trust the soldiers out of fear. It is too frightening to believe they will kill their children. But perhaps the parents should believe this? Perhaps they are wrong to trust the soldiers? They assume the soldiers have a moral sense which they do not in truth have.

Why do they trust the soldiers? They have every reason not to trust them. Is it that they trust in 'human nature'? That they believe there are limits to human brutality? Their own leaders might reassure them and encourage them to trust the soldiers. Their leaders know of course that they and their children will be taken away and killed. Should the leaders warn the parents not to trust the soldiers?

If the parents kill some of the soldiers they will not save themselves or their children. The other soldiers will not respect the parents for fighting for their children. It will confirm the soldiers in their judgement of the parents. The soldiers will say 'They fight like cornered animals. The bitch protects its whelps.' It is not even true that the parents will be punishing some of the guilty. The soldiers are not in all respects guilty. They do not understand themselves because they do not understand their situation. They wear a uniform – just as the parents wear the uniforms of the officially condemned even if these are only civilian rags. The soldiers may even be profoundly innocent – as the mad are. The soldiers obey orders and commit deeds their leaders are too squeamish –

or proud – to commit. To stand in the presence of the evidence of your own brutality is a form of innocence: you can no longer pretend about certain things. The shadow of the dead is your own shadow. The murderer will always be poor.

At any massacre the world becomes a theatre.

Perhaps the parents should say to the soldiers 'You are taking us and our children away to kill us'. Would the soldiers then be ashamed of what they do? Perhaps sharing a lie with the parents – 'we are taking the children to a good place' – is a comfort to the soldiers? It protects them from the rawness of their behaviour, the rawness of the day. If so – and even more so if the soldiers know that the parents know the truth – then the parents are helping the soldiers with an act of kindness. Perhaps (in time) the soldiers will be grateful for this? They might say 'The parents helped us to kill their children – so we are not completely animals'. But the soldiers might as easily say 'The parents are corrupt. They compromised with us out of fear.' Or treat it as a joke – 'They think that's going to change our attitude to anything?' Is there some manner, some look or gesture or tone of voice, that the parents might use when they give the soldiers their act of kindness, that will change the soldiers, will make it impossible for the soldiers to treat the kindness as a joke? Perhaps in the extreme moment – when the situation becomes theatre – such a manner *would* have such an effect? It would be the moment when the soldiers were most vulnerable. A mark of humanness might create solidarity at that moment – which otherwise, in other circumstances, would deepen the soldiers' corruption, make them more inhuman. We can imagine the orator at the national rally would imitate the parents' gesture – the human mark – made at that moment, and parody it as the gesture of a cheat trying to sell inferior goods at higher prices. Or is it that such a mark, such a manner, can survive all distortions – as the expression of a doll remains even when its face is broken? Or is that the constancy of the inhuman – so that in a way the soldiers have dolls' faces? The religious might believe the gesture could not be distorted. They would say 'At this moment Christ' – or God – 'is here'. Is it that humans must do the right thing – use the right gesture, manner, tone – to make God appear? Prayer would not be enough. The situation, the theatre, would have to produce a drastic sincerity. And yet, when God did appear, they crucified him – so why should 'Ah God is here' make the soldiers hesitate one second in what they are doing?

The Bible is romance. Events in it are not history. But to get to divine paradoxes the story must be plausible. And so it is appropriate that

Christ says of his tormenters and executioners 'They dont know what they're doing'.

Perhaps the soldiers will themselves change themselves? Whether the parents lie, defy, accept, comply – it may be that later the soldiers will say 'We should not send the children to be killed. We should not kill children' – as if in dying the children had told – taught – them this. If we who come later could trust in this happening, whatever the parents do becomes of only immediate importance. If they resist or consent, things will change. Does resisting or consenting hasten the change? Basically this changes a political situation into a personal one: should the parents kill the soldiers if in the end that is all it is? – and change will come another way. This is important if the actions count in an afterworld and not only in this one. Unless you wish to be your own God and say to the soldiers 'I forgive you'. But then the considerations necessary to this situation are those which occur in all other situations which are 'moral' – to shoplifting, queue-jumping and so on. Violence raises questions specific to itself. The further consequences of the situation have to be considered. These consequences affect the lives of other, distant people.

But first there is one other personal consideration. The parents may plead with the soldiers to let their children run away to try to escape. They may ask the soldiers to be human. The parents then know that they have behaved humanly. Or have they? They have only behaved humanly in an inhuman situation. They may rail at the soldiers. They would tell them that they knew they were taking the children to be killed and that the soldiers were inhuman when they did this. Perhaps the parents would know, then, that not only were they behaving as parents but also as human beings, because human beings should help other human beings to know what they are doing and so they should tell the soldiers they know they are taking their children to be killed. They are not saying 'God is here' but 'Human beings are here'. And each human being is all human beings.

It might be that to change things we cannot appeal to reason. Perhaps it is enough to make the soldiers feel guilt. And when one person is guilty all people are spectators of that person. And so the guilt – or even just the lesson – is shown to other, distant people. The parents sacrificed their children. They had guns under the floorboards. They did not shoot the soldiers. They set an example to the soldiers. They said 'It is better not to kill'. And as they paid for this with their lives – and even more, with their children's lives – we see the tragic severity of their teaching. For the parents the sacrifice is great, in the passing of history it is small.

But it is one among small events that accumulate and become great lessons in history – great lessons in humanness. The soldiers cannot – at this time – be changed. If they change later, what would that mean? Not that everyone must kill in order to realize later that they must not kill. Not everyone kills or is ordered to kill. Massacres are occasional. But they are decisive – they turn place into theatre – and later, from them, distant people learn the lessons of general humanness. And so, in time, people behave more humanly – among other things they do not listen to the orator and so no longer give the leaders power to order soldiers to send children to be killed.

It may be otherwise. If some people do not strike back at inhuman acts by humans, perhaps all of us will become more inhuman and finally destroy ourselves? It is not true to say that resistance provokes greater inhumanness. Different things change different people because people are different.

Perhaps as the soldiers come the parents should kill their children and themselves. Is that best? Ancient Jews besieged by Romans did this. Goebbels did it in Hitler's bunker. Goebbels' act affects us differently – it was not the act of a humane parent facing an inhuman dilemma. Who else wanted to kill Goebbels' children? Couldnt they have been hurried away to safety? It was a fanatic acting in accordance with his fanaticism. He killed his children for the reason some of the soldiers had for not killing themselves rather than taking the children away to be killed. The soldiers were fanatically convinced of the rightness of what they did. Of course many of the soldiers did it because they did not know what they were doing – and even then often at least partly because they were too cowardly to want to know.

Death by transportation and gassing is reasonably quick. What if some (or all) of the children are to be taken to 'medical' installations to be experimented on? Or as living toys handed over to torturers for their recreation? What are the parents to choose to do?

If you are told 'We will take your child to the corner and shoot it', how is that morally different to being told 'We will take your child to the barracks and slowly torture it for as long as it can survive – or experiment on it to help us to understand how to cure damaged and shell-shocked soldiers'?

Does it change the dilemma? Perhaps later, distant people would not 'want' the parents to do the rational thing – but to protest, delay, struggle with whatever means they had to hand – namely, the guns under the floorboards. Perhaps we 'want' the parents to protest irrationally – if it *is* irrational. Is it irrational not to talk to the lion that mauls you and give it reasons to spare your life? This latter cannot be true and if it were the calculus would be pointless. The mad are mad because they are tormented by reason; they are more cruel because their rejected humanness torments them. That is why, when the situation makes the place theatre, we have to find ways of saying 'There are humans here'.

If the parents shoot the soldiers their children will be gassed. Perhaps before they are gassed they will be treated with greater brutality because soldiers have been killed and wounded. Later, other soldiers will not stop taking away children to be killed. The soldiers will come with more arms.

It cannot be said whether, in the long run, resistance or submission will change things. It can be said with certainty that when the world is changed the people in it will not be like the soldiers. Will they be like the parents who resist or like those who submit? We cannot say. Perhaps they will be like the parents who resist – and shoot the soldiers – but we can know this only by inference: because they will never be in the situation of having to decide whether or not to shoot soldiers coming to take away their children to be killed. In the changed world there will be no soldiers. Perhaps the people who live in the changed world will be people who would have shot soldiers if they had come to take away their children to be killed. The situation will have changed. Some of the people will have changed – the soldiers and others who act inhumanly. But suppose this changed world – a place of peace – were invaded by brutal humans from another planet – and they came to kill the children? What would the people in the changed world do?

Perhaps they would know from history what in the past had been done and not done. Perhaps they will be able to tell what it was that helped to change the world in which they live. We cant know that: human behaviour is not a science in the way which would enable us to know the answer. If it were we would not ask moral questions. All our 'moral' questions would become practical questions.

Would the people in the changed world decide that it was their moral responsibility to moralize the universe – not just those invaders, but those who will invade them and then *them* – and so on? They would base their choice (to shoot or not to shoot) on their knowledge (if any) of history: what the historical effects of the choices were. But if we make a moral choice *now* we make it not merely for ourselves and this occasion, not even for human beings in all situations – we make it for the universe. The span between, say, the choice to submit, and its final (if possible) result in the changed, humanized world, would doubtless be long – but

it is already an act in humanizing the universe – because a universe saved
is more moral than a world saved. Is it? Would we sacrifice one moral act
– that would save no more than a butterfly – if this meant that the
universe would be for ever hell? Can we talk of sacrificing a moral act? Is
a calculus possible? And then, if non-resistance is the moral act, there is
no argument: the parents may not shoot the soldiers even if the children
are taken to be used in vivisection experiments that a decent autopsist
would hesitate to carry out on a corpse. That is Kant and Gandhi. The
children may be thrown in the grinder. (Or God might choose to save
the world if he can.)

The Eschatology of Bread:
Christ and the Bearded Lady
(Notebook, 3 August 1995)

In drama there are two subjects: the self and society. Each forms the other and is in conflict with the other.

The Greeks united religion and drama: the Church divides them.

Oedipus comes to the city. The Sphinx guards the way. The Sphinx is a breasted woman with the haunches of a female animal – but she sits on her sex. Oedipus must prove his wisdom. He does not share wisdom with the Sphinx as a philosopher might. Wisdom is a secret. The child must be wise. It must believe it knows.

The child Christ goes to the temple. The priests are amazed at the child's wisdom. The temple is an institution like a philosophy school. Later the wise men of the temple will kill Christ. Oedipus has killed the wise father Laius. Oedipus and Laius exchange anger not wisdom.

Oedipus is impure and brings pestilence to the city. Christ is pure and brings salvation to the city, the World-Jerusalem. Oedipus is sexually involved with his family: procreated by his father and mother, and procreator (as one-third of God) with his mother. Christ's parents are sexless. Joseph and Mary do not procreate, both are virgin. Christ is the son of a virgin mother and virgin father.

The Angel of the Annunciation is Oedipus on the road: where he meets the Sphinx. The Angel is the incestuous Christ, the incestuous son.

Laius wishes to murder Oedipus. God murders Christ. Laius wishes to murder Oedipus from envy. God wishes to murder Christ for love.

Laius is a traveller, as is Oedipus. Joseph (Christ's earth father) is a carpenter – he makes crosses (and in his tools carries Christ's death).

Christ has secrets which he reveals to his followers. Oedipus is the victim of secrets: they are revealed to him.

Mary is the divine intercessor. Jocasta wishes to preserve Oedipus's ignorance of the secrets. Revealed, she hangs herself.

Revealed, Oedipus blinds himself. His blinding tools are two brooches – his mother's: he has looked on the two breasts of the Sphinx. To lie with a woman is to know her. In King Oedipus, a brooch is a breast with a penis. Christ is hung with penile nails.

Oedipus blinds himself: he castrates himself. It is a sacrifice to the dead Laius which gives life to the dead. Oedipus rebels – as does the Son of the Morning, the Son of Light: Lucifer. Christ submits.

Christ is androgynous. He is robed (as female) but bearded. He feminizes himself before God. The crucifixion is a male rape – of the son by the father.

Oedipus usurps the father and his power – till discovered. Christ must change the world. He must change the nature of power. Christ provides food at the Last Supper: the woman cooks. Christ offers himself as the meal: he is the circumcised woman.

Oedipus lives after his blinding but loses his kingdom. Oedipus quarrels with his two warring son-brothers. The sons quarrel with their father-brother. Oedipus at Colonus is the Old Testament God. Oedipus vanishes mysteriously, exiting like the Old Testament God – in one of his entrances.

Creon is Laius returned to earth. Theseus is the wise son-king who welcomes Oedipus to Athens – dead. Creon has power – Oedipus's bones are sacred.

Creon has two problems: the new world-order (Rome, Caesar) and the lore of the ancient gods. Antigone speaks for the ancient gods. Antigone as a man-woman defies Creon – it is the way she can perform the woman's role. Christ is only a bearded lady: he establishes the power of Creon (Caesar's things) but in a permanent, balanced opposition: the tolerated critic, Lear's Fool. The Fool is wise and hanged.

Hamlet hesitates because he sees the problem.

Sophocles merely turns Oedipus into Laius at Colonus.

Antigone quarrels with Creon-Oedipus, daughter with father. Her wisdom speaks for the gods. Creon loses his son and daughter-in-law. He is humbled. But Antigone has spoken for the old gods who waylaid and trapped Oedipus: she speaks for the God of the Old Testament.

Raskolnikov murders to get money to study and learn wisdom. Raskolnikov murders two women: the hag and her Fool (her foolish companion). Raskolnikov wishes to imitate Napoleon's power (potency). Dostoevsky cannot solve the riddle, nor could Shakespeare: both speak of submission – and sacrifice (Shakespeare) and redeeming labour (Dostoevsky).

Creon serves Antigone a Last Supper (to exonerate himself of the guilt of her death). She does not eat it. She hangs herself. Rats eat her last meal. Rats congregate, procreate, breed, feed on the rubbish heap at Golgotha.

The problem is not how to repress individual desire (Freud and the discontents of civilization) but how to humanize society. To humanize one another. We are not human: we are not in a humane society and we do not humanize it.

The women at the foot of the cross are Antigones. Pilate (Laius, God) is absent – bureaucracy, organization, has intervened in the immediacy of Greek drama.

The soldier in Antigone's play is the nearest Greek tragedy comes to staging the Fool. Oedipus is wise but ignorant: Christ is wise but a Fool.

Greek drama confronts the problem in its agonal state. Christianity subverts the problem. It promises a second coming but there is none. It is an execution where the axe hovers permanently in midstroke over the neck. It might fall at any time. (Claudius: 'Let the great axe fall.')

Christianity mystifies the problem and makes it unsolvable: it degrades drama into religion.

What is the eschatology of bread? – it is the feast of crumbs, when the weak humanize the powerful. This turns to reaction when it is understood as the one against (or worse, *for*) the many.

The eschatology of a play – its end and resolution – is always the eschatology theorized for society. In 'Christian' society, theatre is never more than a religious relic allowed to perform miracles for the Church. It is not allowed to recreate power, to create the New Kingdom (which for the Church would be the anti-Christ of the Second Coming). If Christ did not bleed every day God would die. The West is a culture of movement (innovatory, dynamic – Dionysus the Greek-Christ) because it holds psychic-time still: none of the stages of Oedipus's story need to move. The stages of the cross are static. It is as if Oedipus held his breath and so imitated the dead. But in time psychic-time seeks revenge: it can no longer sacrifice itself to itself. The Second Coming must be the anti-Christ. The anti-Christ waits on the station platform. That is our present state: the Christian myth of Oedipus no longer contains its content.

Cord-elia (the rope on which Antigone hanged herself), the woman hanged with her own name . . . in a play I turned her into God, Raskolnikov's hag, Laius at Colonus: the Gravedigger's Boy (the son of Laius the gravedigger) is silenced. Lear cannot live with his children. Oedipus cannot live with Laius. Christ cannot live with God. The Christian religion seeks to make Oedipus and Laius one: God-the-father-God-the-son. The kingdom of the world must not degrade the world of imagination. Technology becomes the Armageddon of bread: the machines are not on the side of childhood because of the presence of the Bearded Lady. We have held our breath for two thousand years. Religion is irrelevant: it lived because the corpse became one with its iron coffin. We have to write the feast of crumbs. That is the new stage in drama's only story, the only story society can tell.

Christianity hides the sword it holds by sleight of hand: the example of Christ – not the ritual magic sacrament of castration – will change people who will then change the kingdom. There would be no need of the second coming or of heaven.

There is conflict between child and adult: the child must judge and create, the adult must organize and really protect: that is what lies behind innovation. The problem is always justice. Laius's word is not ordered justly: nor is God's world (Calvin, predestination). Understanding is blocked by the mystery of the Sphinx (they know not what they do). Explanation withers before drama.

We would be lost without Pylades. But might he be the Sphinx or the ghost of manes?

The Church diverts the problem: it institutionalizes revenge, the enduring anger of Laius against Oedipus. The Eucharist is revenge institutionalized.

Power must be taken from Laius if there is to be a second kingdom. Laius justifies power by the nature of his kingdom: it delays the second coming till after death. Oedipus-Christ can live humanly only by dying. Otherwise Oedipus turns into Laius at Colonus.

Antigone's conversion of Creon is fantasy. Hitler-Creon would film her death for after-dinner viewing. Because Christianity has stopped psychic-time Creon-Laius turn into Hitler, revenge turns into fascism and calls itself love.

(The last part of this paper is lost.)

Social Madness

Before we can say anything useful about human beings we must first define madness. How is it that most of us appear to be sane but we live in societies that are mad? We live rational daily lives but our societies make grotesque weapons, economically destroy their environment, build prisons, make some rich and others poor, some powerful and others impotent and in these and other ways are flagrantly unjust. Then there are the wars between societies and the barbarities of victors and vanquished, the bombing of cities, massacres and genocide. We are so accustomed to most of these things that we do not see them. It is as if in our house one room were palatial and the next room a slum. How could we live in the house? We would have to be two people. First we would become irrational and then we would be violent – we would go mad.

What is a crime in a private person is a virtue in a citizen. How can sane people act in mad ways and believe the mad ideas society requires of them? We can find the answer in those who are *not* sane in their daily lives. What makes them mad? People go clinically mad when they cannot create a practical working relationship to society, to reality. Instead they create a society, a reality, of their own. They go mad in order to find sanity. Their madness is their explanation of why the world is mad. Those who can live practically in society – function in it – need not go clinically mad. But society itself is mad. Society is most people's way of trying to make sense of the world. That is, society is most people's way of going mad. This statement itself seems mad, yet it describes what all madmen do when they try to explain their world sanely. We call their description a symptom of their madness, but we call our description of our mad society culture, civilization.

Society is a structure of mad theories and mad stories and of the mad actions and mad institutions founded on them – the churches, prisons, barracks, schools, the belief that there is a God and life after death, that we are born of our motherland, that the poor and the rich are brothers and sisters. Because we put our fantasies and delusions into practice in our daily lives we become the symptoms of their madness: soldiers, believers, teachers, judges, good citizens, the righteous guardians of rectitude. The clinically mad are not free to enact their fantasies and delusions in reality. They are cured or put away. But society enacts its fantasies and delusions in reality – it's how societies preserve themselves.

Their madness holds them together so long as they are practical. A society is a form of madness that works for the time being. And as with all madness, society finds evidence in the world to support its madness – the mad prove the world is flat by running round the globe. Yet every building in which one person imprisons or represses another is a madhouse, whether it is called a prison, a church or a school.

Society uses its technology and organizes work so that people may live well. Its culture must make this possible and explain why things are as they are and why they go wrong. So long as society functions practically, its own madness protects the daily sanity of its members. Society is mad on their behalf. When society breaks down and its structure no longer works, its members – because they are sane – criticize it and wish to change it. And if it was simply a matter of rationally observing the breakdown, they would always see it and change would be easy. But economics and politics are deeply obscured and cluttered in cultural explanations. When society is no longer able to persuade us, so that its madness can shelter our sanity – then we ourselves become mad in our daily life. We react irrationally to the breakdown – and there is crime, despair, cynicism, racism and war. And then society is no longer mad on our behalf.

Society tries to use the consequences of breakdown to justify itself and increase its power. Like the mad it seeks reassurance in its illusions. In the end the illusions are exhausted and society's madness ceases to protect our daily sanity. Then, like all who are mad, society becomes violent – because madness is not just a matter of thinking but a way of being.

Society mediates between people's needs and what the earth offers. It achieves this through its administration, institutions and culture. This is true of early pastoral and hunting societies and of our own hyper-technological society. Society is always based on its form of ownership – and its ownership is always unjust. It's because of this, and only this, that society is mad. Its culture is as distorted as the madman's fantasies. Its fantasies are its ideology, its story of why things are as they are – and because the story seeks to justify injustice it is mad. This will determine our future – because if the mad are not restrained they finally destroy themselves. But society is the restrainer and society is mad.

Why can't madness be perfect? Why can't madmen live benignly in their fantasies and society in its injustice? The answer defines our humanity. It is in two parts, one structural and one existential. Together they show that the real world *requires* us to be sane.

Sanity is an evolutionary pressure on us of living practically in the material world. Machines are 'naturally saner' than people. They cannot fantasize. A corkscrew can't imagine it's a hydrogen bomb and persuade other corkscrews of it. And because machines mediate the world to us they impose their 'sanity' on us. One winter's night a madman might set fire to his house to warm his room. The fire would do this. But reality would intervene and the madman would be homeless and cold. A farmer might pray for rain in a dry spell. But when his tractor breaks down he sends for a mechanic. He may pray that the mechanic will be good – madness casts long shadows – but society must train mechanics to know their work. If we are to eat, sleep and shelter in the real world, the real world 'insists' that we be sane. It cannot cooperate with our madness for long. Advancing technology teaches us more about reality and our relationship to it. We may still pray for rain but we use weather satellites. As we change the world it changes us, how we think and what we are. In this respect we are the robots of our machines.

Madmen are not violent until their world – their story of reality – threatens them. Madness is their way of protecting their sanity, and so long as they can live practically, rationally, in their mad world they have no need of violence. Being sane in a mad society means that we stand on the edge of an abyss and sometimes fall into it. But always an incipient sanity, a whisper of reason from our dealing with the material world, urges us back from the edge. Finally we must face reality or be destroyed. The great suffering common to madness is caused because madness is the search for sanity – for the real which prompts us to be sane. That is the origin of our recovery and renewal. It is why madness is often the theme of drama.

But why can't society adapt to the new reality that technology and the material world constantly impose on it? To change the organization of society you must change its form of ownership. That is, society has to become more just. The unjust do not want this – and because culture is created to justify and protect injustice, the unjust cannot understand the nature of justice. To them justice would be injustice and would make our daily lives unlivable. Like the mad they cannot unravel their madness. Instead they use the chaos they create to justify their injustice: they run round the world to prove it's flat.

The material world prompts us to sanity and justice. But we live in society and its madness protects its injustice and makes it practical – till in time it makes it impractical. So society seeks to corrupt the need for change: partly because of inertia but mostly to protect its injustice. It clings to its mad version of reality. That is why people and society are always in tension, in danger of setting fire to the house to warm the room. The need for justice isn't idealistic but practical – that is the structural need for justice.

But there is another, existential need for it – one which is even more profound. Machines cannot bring us closer to reality, they can only point at it for us. This might make us even madder. Something else is also needed to make us sane: our minds themselves *desire* sanity.

Our desire for sanity comes from the origin of our being. Infants are powerless but must act like gods. Which is certainly madness! – but it is the only way we may become human. The newborn child must come to know its world. Its way of doing this is even more dramatic than it would be if it were a creature from space. The creature would be conscious but the child is not. The child becomes conscious only by discovering where it is. It cannot use its consciousness to do this because the discovery of where it is is also the creation of its consciousness. They occur together. As consciousness discovers *where* it is, it discovers itself, *who* it is. The relationship is so close it can *never* be repeated. If it could be we would become someone else. The closeness haunts the rest of our life. In becoming itself the child creates the world. It is *its* world – but it is *the* world, the *real* world, *our* world. What else could it be? Lear said do not reason too closely, that way madness lies. But the child must create the world, the real world, in raw sanity – without the refuge of social madness and culture which are open to it only later, when it is grown. It is the plot of all Greek tragedies: the child creates its world but is also confronted by an implacable reality. It can combine these things only through imagination. The child must imagine the real before *we*, later, can imagine the fantasies of madness. Voltaire said that if God did not exist it would be necessary to invent him. But the child must create the world *because* the world exists. This is creation, not simply the acquiring of knowledge. It is as if the act of writing creates the ink in which it is written. It involves love and rage but also something even more basic: the need for coherence, which is the tool with which madmen play, the tool they turn into a toy. Before the mind incorporates a thing into its story it must know what it is. Knowing it *is* the act of incorporation. The mind requires, insists on – its story desires – coherence. It is coherence which forces us to be human. Blake said that imagination and reason may see the world in a grain of sand. But we must know that the world is the world and a grain of sand is a grain of sand. Madness cannot touch the cause of our sanity – it can only misuse it to make us mad.

Creativity is the sign of our humanness. The absurdist dance of death called 'deconstruction' is the attempt to give madness the attributes of sanity. Madness protects sanity but is not sanity. The mind's basic characteristic, its premise, is the need to know. The infant's need for coherence is prior in consciousness to its instincts. Instincts are prior only in pre-human animals. The infant's more capacious brain listens to itself, even to its instincts – which come to it as strangers seeking their place in its story. An infant's cry is its first topographical description of the world. It is not enough for it to instinctively need food, it knows – hears in its own cry – that in this world it is right, just, that it should want food. By existing the child's mind tells itself that it has a right to be. The child must be God in its world – *the* world – because it creates this world and so has a right to be in it. The child is the actor in the true play. Its right belongs to its creation of the world. And so reason and justice are joined. If it is just for the child to be in the world it creates by being in it, then in the world itself it must be just that the child is in it – that is a truth about the world. So when the child desires its just place in the world it is desiring that the world itself is just. The mind cannot recognize itself – be itself – in any other way. For this desire for justice to lead to acts of injustice, injustice must be identified with justice. The mind cannot accomplish this itself. It is accomplished by society when it replaces the real world with its injustice. This is social madness and it reverses all values. But if injustice were removed we would be sane.

A child could not be coherent and learn if it distinguished between reason and justice. That distinction is a finesse of the adult world. If it is just for the child to be in the world it creates, then the world must be just. It is the desire that the world is the just place for all its people: without justice there is no creation. From the beginning it cannot be otherwise.

But then the child learns that it is not its world, that it itself is not a continuation of the world. But as long as it is coherent the mind cannot lose its first structure of reason and justice. Madness is erected on this foundation, madness is reason seeking itself and corruption is the seeking for justice. We try to explain away this human paradox with sin, evil, natural aggression and other symptoms of society's madness. But the Nazis did not gas people because they believed themselves to be evil, they believed they were the force of justice. Armies do not put evil on their banners. Under the emblem of the skull pirates put a cross of bones – a parody of salvation. A thief knows that theft is wrong but that it is right for him to steal. Judges cannot understand the thieves' paradox. Such paradoxes take us to the heart of drama, without which we are as mad as judges.

There are various ways to describe the process in which the child creates itself and the world. It maps its world and itself in the map as part of the map. The child's mind is its story of its world and the child is itself the story. Every event is part of the story. It is similar to the way in which by learning words the child enters into its language's grammar and uses language for its own speaking. As the child and the world grow distant to each other, its mind creates and seeks to resolve tensions. The child's mind – the child itself – is a drama. A human being is a story which seeks justice.

As a child cannot understand the world analytically it must understand it imaginatively. It anthropomorphizes the world. The table is happy, the tree speaks, there are wicked and bad spirits. The child must live practically in the harshness of reality and its fantasies are the only way it has to describe reality so that it may live in it. Imagination is not fantasy. The child's imagination is its desire for justice, its fantasies are its first illusions. Sanity is the imagination of the real.

A child can create its consciousness and be in the world only as God. Later the God must die so that the child may become human. But the nostalgia for God remains as a disquiet deep in our minds. It accounts for our goodness and why it becomes corrupted and violent, why love may turn to hate and justice become punishment. All punishment is revenge – the rage of God is greater than all other rages. When we look closely at anyone we look into the face that was once the face of God and see on it the marks of cruelty and madness of our world.

We would not become human by becoming God again. That would be madness. We have to go to a time *before* God, to the mind's first desire: to imagine the real. And then, because it cannot create the real, which already *is* – it desires to go beyond desire and into being. It creates itself again, and in doing this rids itself of the nihilism which infiltrates desire and turns it to madness. The child's first steps towards this are the fantasies which society adopts and corrupts to make its own.

The child's fantasies prepare it for society's falsehoods. If children did not believe trees spoke, adults could not believe their birthplace was their motherland, that we live after death, that we could belong to a master race. There is only one solution to the problem of being human in an inhuman society. If reality requires us to be sane if we are to live in it but society requires us to live in injustice – then society must be made just or we cannot be sane. Insane society will destroy us because it has the means – military and civil – to enact its madness in reality, and the toys of madness are now lethal. We are on the edge of self-speciescide.

In the past the search for justice took unjust forms, just as – and for the same reasons – sanity often takes the form of madness. Culture is society's identity and becomes its members' identities – always in a state of tension. The tension may be ascribed to our place in society and our striving for power and possessions. But history shows that power and possessions do not satisfy us. Striving for them is a reflection of our deeper discontent.

Ownership clings to the old forms of madness. The madness of the Stone Age – the myths, rituals and sacrifices of its society – is not our madness. In the Stone Age people were sacrificed to propitiate God. Our machines impose a different sacrifice on us: we sacrifice in war to defeat our enemies. But all sacrifice is the cost of injustice. Society gives us the name of 'human'. To say 'I am human' is to claim the madness appropriate to my society. It is as mad for John Smith to say 'I am human' as it is for him to say 'I am Napoleon'. But for Napoleon to say 'I am Napoleon' is even madder – the heaps of dead prove it. It is the same with the clutter of religion. To say 'There is a God' is as mad as to say 'I am God' – it is mere nostalgia made corrupt. The first gods protected people from fear of their mortality, but for a long time God has protected only injustice. There is no Rousseauian nature to require our humanity or Augustinian nature to require our inhumanity.

The clinically mad live in fantasy and sometimes kill. Most of us are clinically sane but socially mad. We kill or hire killers only when bidden to do so by the motherland and call it patriotism. We rob only when forced to do so by the state and call it profit. We must not mistake the confusions of living in society with the perplexities of living at all. Our injustice causes the first, our mortality the second. It is a nostalgic fantasy of the dead God to say we may be immortal – but not to say we may live justly. Then how can we come to see that we live unjustly and need not? It is like asking a madman to understand he is mad. And yet reality and our minds prompt us to sanity and justice.

Human beings are created by the meeting of the subjective and the social. The creation has no natural image or representation. Art is the expression of the meeting and of its process, which is the process which creates human reality. Art is not the expression of the subjective. The subjective and the social cannot exist apart, they are created in the process. Art is the necessary expression of human desire and social purpose, and is part of the process of their relationship. Through art society imposed its transient necessities on the individual's constant need for sanity and desire for justice.

Art was partly repressive, but immanently it had to concede to the individual's desire for justice and need for sanity because they were all it

had to work with. It could for example repress the individual's need for
sanity by portraying rulers as ideal individuals, and turn the desire to
live in a just world into images of a just heaven. The relationship in art
between individual and society lasted while there was a close relationship
of people to technology, the means by which they related to material
reality – tools were hand-held, houses were built by hand from natural
materials. The industrial revolution opened a gap between people and
technology. Machines became complex and manufacturing 'artificial'. It
created new means for art to use – photography, film, recorded sound –
which were appropriate for expressing the rapid changes in human
reality. The technological copying of human senses imitated their
relationship to reality – photography and recorded speech are naturalis-
tic. When art distorts them it expresses the effect of new technology on
the process by which people create their reality. If you could have shown
Shakespeare a photograph he would have seen a ghost.

The Industrial Revolution alienated people in their daily lives.
Machines alienated their bodies, media extended their senses but
lessened their autonomy over them, social organization became complex
and remote, wars were more destructive. Together these changes
changed art. Art is essential to the human mind which must create
images as part of the creation of human reality. When the process was
alienated, 'modern art' – which reflected the changes of the process –
became alien to most people. Some artists responded to their isolation by
becoming introspective. They abandoned the social and became ghetto-
ized and elitist. A counter-movement produced kitsch – which art, being
protean, could even reradicalize back into creativity. Alienation did not
always disrupt the literal portrayal of the social in realist novels and
social-realist plays, but behind this literality the process in which people
created their reality was distorted, and so this most sober of 'realisms'
was afloat on a sea of kitsch.

Art belongs to the process by which humans are created, and now it
was entering no–man's-land. When artists eliminated the social they tried
to retain their seriousness by relating subjectivity directly to the
transcendental. This produced absurdist art because meaning is created
only in the meeting of the subjective and social. That is why the past had
assigned the transcendental to religion and so brought it under social
control administratively, psychologically and artistically. Art could
portray saints in priestly apparel because that is as much a social uniform
as a soldier's tunic. The Christian story is the plot of a Greek tragedy
which theology presents as real.

A madman imagines he is a prince. Madness is always logical. It is sane for the madman to imagine he is a prince because then he gains power to protect himself from the vulnerability which drives him mad. We can understand why the madman must be a prince. Then why do people go to theatres to 'believe in' someone who is pretending to be a prince? They 'suspend disbelief' during the play and then return to the sanity of their daily lives. But on the face of it it is very odd that they go to the theatre to pretend to be mad. Where is the logic in that? Theatre is the madhouse where the audience go to find their sanity, just as madmen go mad in reality to find theirs. The sane cannot live in insane society without drama.

A play shows the search for sanity and justice and the forces opposed to it. The play's resolution 'resolves' the conflict between the desire for justice and implacable reality. The audience must recreate itself in a way derived from the way in which the child creates itself and the world. The child knew that trees spoke because in the reality of drama the unreal may be accomplished. If the play 'works' the audience accepts social injustice as part of justice.

This paradox is crucial because it is both repressive and liberating. Formal drama works like religion. In it society must recognize the individual's autonomy even as it imposes its authority on it. Just as madmen are convinced that their madness is reality, the audience is convinced through an experience related to madness that injustice is justice. But to do this it must again be shown what justice is. You can see the world in a grain of sand only when you know that the world is the world and a grain of sand is a grain of sand. We can understand the ideal only in imperfect forms. Drama achieves its effect only because the mind is itself a dramatic process.

Madmen's desire for sanity drives them insane and they lose their practicality. The audience enters insanity but leaves the theatre sane and to live practically. So in the theatre *society presents itself as the desire for justice*. It is as if society pretended to be an individual. And indeed it's as if in drama society gave a tragic insight into its own processes, even into the deceptions of its theatre – because if madness is the search for sanity, then unjust society must itself be part of the human search for justice. That's why history progresses. Outside drama discourse is rarely so subtle. Of course this is a trick of society. It's as if society were a relay-runner who constantly turns back to pick up the baton – he never hands it on. The human desire for justice is so basic that it is confirmed in drama's unreal reality. Not only is the audience free to live practically in unjust society – unlike madmen it is free to change it.

This drama is not cathartic, it is a process of recognizing and understanding. The Greek Tragic was not a submission to the transcendental but to the transient: the individual was not purged, society was purged. And yet the audience recreated their humanness. It is foolish to think that Greek theatre is simply repressive. There is a tolerance that represses, there is also a repression that liberates. Even when art represses, it is the most complete expression of the human possible at the time it is created. But it is not sacred, it must be used so that it becomes part of our own humanizing process. We must not imitate the art of the past, because then what was humanizing becomes barbarizing. Fascism can almost be defined as the imitation of the past by modern means.

Now the market and technology turn daily life into theatre, into a madhouse, but not to find sanity. Everything is dramatized to create fantasy in place of reality. Instead of the creative relationship to needs there is a fantasized relationship to wants that the market constantly fabricates to maintain itself – the audience can't leave its real-life theatre to be practically sane outside it. Humanness cannot be created in the search for something else – or as a by-product of the rage to consume. It is created by its search for itself, which is hard and often pitiful among the pitiless. Now theatre cannot be the drama of this search, because the market turns theatre into another product and locks it into society's madness. We cannot create new images of humanness, the mind is silenced.

Drama belonged to the process in which humans created their reality. It meant learning that there is no fixed boundary between madness and sanity. It meant not conniving with convenience but knowing the cost of injustice. It meant being shocked at being human. Euripides was exiled, Molière persecuted, Racine escaped into religion, Ibsen died in perplexity, Chekhov died too young for the last confrontation with reality, Shakespeare hid from it in drink and real estate and to found the petrified dramas which are their religions Christ was crucified and Buddha made poor. To found the new drama all its entrepreneurs had to do was become rich.

We return to old barbarities and create new ones. Auschwitz and Hiroshima are among our new madhouses. But surely our madness is greater because our reasons for needing to be sane are greater? Our new relationship to the world prompts us to sanity. Yet we allow our new knowledge to increase our ignorance. Where subjective and social meet, there should be creativity and democracy, not the market and destruction. Theatre must make the desire for justice so clear that it cannot be made mad in its social prison. The prison is now more repressive – but also weaker. All art is political, but art must be more radical than politics. How to be human in an inhuman society? – that is the question. The province of drama is the proper care of the relationship between madness and sanity, imagination and reality, society and justice. Drama is essential to our humanness.

(1997)

William Shakespeare's Last Notebook

After his death several notebooks written in William Shakespeare's hand were found. All but one of these were destroyed by his housekeeper in lighting kitchen fires. Of that one, most of the pages were found to have been eaten – certainly by Shakespeare himself. What follows are specimen extracts from the uneaten pages.
– Editor

Politicians are crows pecking at cobblestones.

The dead body has no breath to blow out the candles on its bier; so the schoolmaster is proud that he teaches knowledge.

The brutal SS-man said he obeyed the law. Those who live by law-and-order are like the SS-man. The law is that you obey the order.

The government is always weaker than you. It takes your virtues and returns them to you as vices. The government's bravery is your cowardice, its honesty your corruption, its culture your barbarism.

And so when you are brave in its service you are a coward, when you are honest on its behalf you are corrupt, and when you act according to its culture you are a savage. How else can your times be understood? The most competent governments create the worst people. No government can exist without depriving people of their moral responsibility. Common sense is a form of terror. Common sense is contained in this formula: the world in flat. This creates the terror of falling off the edge. All common sense is of this sort. If the world is round I shall fall off it. Common sense enables you to leave your house and enter the street, but in the end it's common sense that gets you murdered on the street. As common sense in fact explains nothing it is always supported by the viciousness of Ideology. As with common sense, so with God. The notion of God explains one thing: why anything exists. But it makes everything else an absurdity or terror. A Frenchman said 'God is evil'. No, God is fear. How could God bear the stench of the black incense of Auschwitz? It is said that God crucified his son; God fears humankind. Do not give nails to Gods or bullets to soldiers.

The franchise and money are incompatible. Where there are rich and poor no one is free. If there is a prison in your city every room in your city is a cell. When you send your enemy to prison you make your child a gaoler. The justification of punishment corrupts the justifier. Any punishment is always crueller than the deed it punishes. Whoever is punished is innocent. The desire to punish is criminal. Punishment is perversion made legal. Punishment is the perversion of moralists.

All children pity their teachers: that is why teachers hate children. All children fear their teachers: that is why children grow up to build schools, prisons and death camps. Education teaches you to lay bricks, but who will teach you whether you should build a hospital or a gas chamber? The snake is immune to the venom in its mouth: we are poisoned by what we say. There is no freedom of press in our democracy because all the papers are owned. The prisoner writes on the wall: what do you write on?

Greed is not the desire to have much: it is the fear of having nothing. We are vulnerable: we do the worst while pursuing the best.

Only one thing may be bought with money: slavery.

If you earn your living by making weapons your aged will die in neglect and your children run mad. The man going home on the bus spent his day murdering: he makes weapons. The woman at his side tortures old people and children: she makes weapons. Torturing children is good for the economy. (It also explains your taste in music.)

The good citizens name their son Auschwitz and their daughter Hiroshima. The hero boasts of his wounds: really they are his sores.

Patriotism is the respectable name of racism. Piety is the respectable form of fascism. A child in uniform learns how to be a coward and how to be sly. A man in a uniform is a skeleton in a straitjacket. A man in a uniform does not own his own skin.

The Berlin Wall was not destroyed when it was pulled down. It was carried away in hands and pockets and unfreedom spread.

Hunger, poverty, robbery, violence – these are bad: but worse is the philosophy which justifies them as the consequences of human nature.

A false idea kills more than plagues and famines. The aim of government is to justify injustice – of law to justify crime – of the market to justify waste. Our democracy is an unacknowledged dictatorship.

Your virtues are fit only for your own hand and mind. You give your virtues to the state and they are returned to you as vices. You do not need a gun in your hand to defend your virtue – only your injustice.

Time catches up on us. Once the machines were weak, now they are so strong they make what were once mistakes, disasters; executions, genocide; religions, holocausts; the agitations of a parish, the wars of continents. Whoever does not own the machines he uses is owned by the owners of the machines. Would you say you were free if a man owned your wife but let you use her? The state lets you use your life. We are the shadows thrown by machines. You think we own the machines but the machines sell us in the marketplace.

You cannot teach a madman he is mad: he has every reason to think he is sane. When there is violence and crime in your city, it is a madhouse but you do not know this because you are mad. You cannot know yourself because you have given your mind to the state and it has returned it to you in an urn. When you put a cross on the ballot paper you are ticking your name on the list of prisoners. What we call freedom is only the ability to spend money and live violently. You are corrupt if you let the state do in your name what you would not do yourself; if you do with a weapon what you will not do with your bare hands or teeth.

St Augustine: 'Love, and do what you will.' Himmler: 'I gas the Jews out of love.' On this paradox hangs the future of humankind. But it is a paradox which our culture dare not understand and which hides a secret our democracy cannot dispense with. Our democracy teaches its children the wisdom of Himmler and calls it the wisdom of St Augustine; but really they are the same wisdom. St Himmler and Reichsführer Augustine. You give your virtues to the state and they are returned to you as vices.

Really every child is a giant and every government a dwarf. A child values toys in the way adults value property. For the adult, property gives value; for the child, Imagination gives value to property. The child's Imagination endows all things with life. The child gives value to a doll, a toy, a piece of wood; adults receive value but do not create it. The child expresses the general in the particular; for it, the value of all things is in one thing, the value of all relationships in one relationship, the passing of all time in one moment; and so the child cannot be destructive; even its rage is creative because it is an attempt to cast a spell that will restore justice to the world – remember, the child is the only author of value. If the child did not think it was God we would not be human. The child is not selfish, it merely identifies itself with all things. The child makes a map of the world and it is part of the map. Thus the child takes responsibility for the world, and doing that is the foundation of its reason and if it did not do it it would not be sane; and so the child always acts virtuously. Whoever hits a child slaps God in the face.

[Here several pages have been eaten away. –Editor]

The adult world needs to train the child . . . discipline and order . . . The child believed it was the cosmic map and that it and the map were one; the state tells it it is only a bit, an atom . . . the state turns the

Imagination from creativity into destruction. The child gave values to facts, the state uses facts to devalue the child: the adult becomes the state's property . . .

[Dots indicate passages obliterated by teeth marks. – Editor]

Curiously, Imagination is further removed from Instinct than is Reason. Reason is an ability which lets us function in ways which would be done by instinct in less complicated animals in less complicated eco-relations. Adults function in the real world of fact; a child would not need to reason till it became adolescent and had to behave as an adult; the child has reason but no need of fact so the child's mind is free and it makes itself-in-the-world in freedom; this is the doing of Imagination; and so the child is responsible for the world and is the author of justice – and it is this which makes us human. But the state says (rightly) 'What you imagine is not so. Instead we will give you the real world and you will become your real self.' In this way the state takes control of the child's Imagination and turns it from creativity to destructiveness: this is the only rite of passage in Western Consumer Democracy. It turns the child from freedom to submission. When the child mapped itself into the world it told its lies creatively and created value; now the state tells its truths destructively: it tells them in the form of Ideology. Ideology is the fantasies of the child turned into the myths of necessity. That is why so far all politics have been the childhood games of adults and all weapons adults' toys. The future of our species depends on one and only one thing: that the Imagination of the adult should be as free as the Imagination of the child. Then the adult will Imagine the real – that is, create value in the world of facts. In doing this the adult will take responsibility for the world: he or she will become part of the map of the world. When adults Imagine the real they become human: otherwise they are not human – then Imagination is owned by the state and produced as Ideology, the falsehoods behind which are the fairy tales of murderers. And that is the history of this time.

Reason that does not proceed from Imagination is false. When the state tells the child 'Now you are an adult and will put away childish things – instead, we give you the real world and your role in it' – when it does this the state turns the child into a fiction. In Western Consumer Democracy all people are fictions. This is because Capitalism now owns the Imagination – it is an aesthetics without content. When your Imagination is owned you become fictional, you are not the author of yourself. That is the form enslavement takes in our democracy – and those who aesthetics enslave do not even desire to be free because they buy their own chains.

Our society is now fictitious. We have the minds of children but without even the child's sense of responsibility. We have the technological power of giants but do not have even the control children have over their toys. That is all our democracy is. It is a condition of great danger. We are children at play with the weapons of Armageddon.

[Here many pages have been eaten. – Editor]

Some people despair of understanding. Isn't the attempt to understand like the spectacle of a mouse nibbling at the globe? Yes but that is how to be a mouse, that is what mice do. How to be human? What do human beings do? The Imagination is dissatisfied and technology is impatient – and you might as well tell a leaf not to tremble in the wind as tell a human being that the –

[The rest of the notebook has been eaten, partly by the author and partly, as teeth marks indicate, by a mouse. – Editor]

(1995)

The Labyrinth

Birds do not make the sky: the sky makes birds
Fish do not make the sea: the sea makes fish
Tigers do not make forests: forests make tigers
Moles do not make the earth: earth makes moles
And in time ice stalks like a ghost in the southern lands
Dry winds burn the forests and seas flood the plains
All places change
And all creatures in them must change
That is the law of space and time

Space and time are the palisade between life and death
When a place changes it is a grave that offers life to its creatures
All places are a cradle or grave
There is no place between them where cunning prevarication or power may
    hide

Creatures are made by the place where they are: it is a law
Only one creature has broken this law: humankind
We make the place where we are
As if the bird made the sky or the tiger the forest
We turn wild lands into deserts or fertile fields
Build cities of wood and baked clay and stone
For a time we are masters of time and space
We rewrite their laws
But time cannot be turned back: if it turned back it would be the date of an
    execution
If space found a hole to hide in it would be a grave
We are the most bereft of creatures – the most in danger
Because in time the law of space and time must of all creatures judge us
    most harshly
And sentence is passed

Listen the dark labyrinth turns
We make the place where we are
There is no space between us and where we are
And so we are the place where we are

It is as if a bird had become the sky or a tiger the forest
As if we lived before time and space – before there was a world to create
    creatures to follow its laws
The dark labyrinth turns
It was written do to others what you would they did to you
We have changed that law
We make the place where we are
So we are the place where the others are
And what we do to the others we have done to ourselves

There is nowhere to hide between cradle and grave
If there is a slaughter house in the city you are the slaughter house
If there is an arsenal you are the weapons
If there is a plague house you are the virus
If there is an execution shed you are the executioner
If you live in greed you are the famine
If you live in superstition your churches are market places
If you live in ignorance you are the violent streets and the desolation that
    waits at street corners
Do not cry for help: you are the robber and the street
You are the place of your wound
If birds made the sky it would be a nest
If men made the sky it would be a prison
We are the patriarchs who give birth to children

This is not rhetoric or argument or moral persuasion
Earth has no parables – the wind has no sermons
It is the law of the structure of space and time and their creatures
Even the lawgiver who rewrites the laws is given that law to obey
A place is a cradle or grave
Justice belongs to the cradle and judgement to the grave
And there is nowhere between them for injustice to hide in
You are the place where you are
That is why the good you do cannot wipe out the injustice
That is the law the lawgiver is given to obey
Society is the contract the lawgiver makes with space and time
Judgement is passed when the contract is broken
It is the judgement of space and time
And time writes the sentence on space as if the wings of a bird as they move
    in the sky were carving our fate in granite

The old century announced itself with a scream
The new century announces itself with a cry
Cries are more logical than screams
The guilty and frightened scream at phantoms
The hungry cry for food
The sick cry for healing
The poor cry for shelter
The lost cry for comfort
And the rich cry for their guns because the rags of their phantoms are real

The dark labyrinth turns
Listen
The ox in the slaughter house does not know there is no field between it and
    the killing crate
Mad people in madhouses believe they are weeping in universities
The condemned in the electric chair spits at the warder: the spit is
    knowledge
If there were a god he would use his finger to write in the spit his last will
    and testament
The dark labyrinth is turning
The slogans of politics are empty
There is no place between cradle and grave and still there is no justice
Equality freedom fraternity are graffiti scratched in the clay by the edge of
    the coffin as it is lowered into the grave
Or worse: etched by tears in prison walls
Between the cradle and grave there is no sky or sea or forest or earth – no
    time – no space – nowhere for us to hide in
We cannot speak of freedom because we have not said
I am the place where other people are

Written for the First Annual Faculty Conference
of the School of Theatre, University of Southern California,
Los Angeles, 16 April 1996

The Faustian Trap

Two assertions are commonly made together as if both were true. They are mutually contradictory. The first says that human nature does not change. The second that human behaviour becomes worse. The confusion threatens our self-understanding.

Over time we learn more about the world. We learn that in the morning the sun is not born at the edge of the flat earth and in the evening dies at the opposite edge, that thunder is not God's wrath, that floods and droughts are not punishments of our misdeeds. But still we are often superstitious and credulous. We build embankments but in deluges pray to God to spare us from floods. We pray for what we cannot control. We do not pray that city traffic will flow more easily. Instead we mark the streets, build roundabouts and flyovers and multi-storey car parks. It is easier to reason about the world and change it than to reason about and change ourselves. Except, that is, when we consider ourselves as part of the natural world. Then we can understand the working of our organs as we understand the creation of rocks. Mind cannot be understood in this way.

It seems inappropriate to talk of reason when considering emotions. Pascal said the heart has reasons which the mind does not know. Pascal misunderstood many things in interesting ways. The transcendental was created to explain the natural. Pascal tried to use the natural to explain the transcendental. Strictly, that is the procedure of the mad. Imagination seeks reason but reason has no cause to seek imagination. That is why the logic of the imagination is able to dissolve rational understanding.

Aggression and anger are emotions. We are said to have become more violent because we are more aggressive and angry. But the nature of violence changes – it depends on our self-understanding. Agamemnon sacrificed his child to appease God. God prevented Abraham from sacrificing his child to please him. Finally God sacrificed his child for our sake. Has God changed or have we? We no longer sacrifice living beings to God because we are more rational and emotionally more complex. We use the idea of sacrifice differently. It is no longer a quid pro quo between God and humans. The self-drama of the human mind has become more profound.

The Romans tortured and killed prisoners in the Colosseum. It was a sort of giant sports stadium. Later, heretics, witches and criminals were publicly tortured, mutilated and killed in horrific ways. It was a public spectacle and presumably an entertainment – though its drama made more demands on the spectators than simple Roman butchery. Burning heretics should have discouraged heresy. Yet some heretics chose to die because (among other considerations) they believed recanting would earn them greater torment in hell. These considerations made others – even spectators of their suffering – become heretics. This happened among early Christian martyrs and is known among political idealists. The bombing of Hiroshima may have saved some lives yet still have been a fatal step towards our annihilation. But it does not follow that if more humans behaved more cruelly the ultimate boundaries of humanness – compassion, understanding, integrity – would shrink. Perhaps in the end Auschwitz is an awful warning that will save us? – which might be the argument of a religious pacifist. Perhaps to increase humanness many people must go to hell, even if some of them are corrupted there and only a few are shriven of their narrow self.

Now we do not usually torture and kill living beings in public (unless we are sportsmen and sportswomen). But privileged Americans are allowed to watch state killings. The crusaders killed their enemies – among them children – by hand. The air crewmen who dropped the atom bomb on Hiroshima went about it in a noticeably jocular way – but it is inconceivable that they would have killed their victims by hand. In the last year of the twentieth century Europeans, Africans and Asians have massacred others face-to-face – but they were forced to do so by authority (and encouraged by tradition). The Nazis openly humiliated Jews on the streets of great civilized cities – but Auschwitz had to be hidden away. The twentieth century was the most destructive time in history. We destroyed more living beings and inanimate things, and damaged the earth, sea and sky more, than did earlier people we call barbarians. And perhaps the soldiers at My Lai were as cruel as the burners of heretics. But Hiroshima, Auschwitz and the wastes we create do not please us. We kill in earnest and not for entertainment, because we think we must not because we can, to exterminate and not to warn. We have become more serious and are often ashamed. We hide our killings and mostly we kill only when the state requires it of us. So it is misleading to define us by our *nature*. Our behaviour changes – which is what matters. Even if our nature were unchanging our behaviour could still change radically. It depends on our situation. And yet it is true: the kinder and more human we become, the greater our cruelty and violence. We are in the Faustian Trap.

Faust sold his soul to the Devil in exchange for knowledge, some of it medieval hocus-pocus but some of it scientific and technological. The cost of this knowledge was torment in Hell. Now children may know more about the real world than Plato, da Vinci, Newton or Darwin knew. What is the cost of our knowledge?

The residue of aggression in the human community becomes less as we learn more about the world but what we learn about it gives the residue of aggression far greater technological power and multiplies its destructiveness. That is the Faustian Trap. We become less cruel yet more destructive.

A medieval – even a Renaissance – pope armed with nuclear weapons would have waged a nuclear crusade against heretic and heathen nations. It was his Christian duty to destroy God's enemies. What would be lost? The believers would go to Heaven and the unbelievers to Hell – but it was a kindness to kill them because the longer they lived in error the greater their torment in Hell. I do not know why some people wish to return to the faith of former times. The pope would have been as zealous in blowing up the world as he was in burning heretics. Fortunately modern popes do not take God as seriously as their predecessors did. If they did they would open a laboratory in the Vatican, learn to make nuclear weapons and use them against all those who did not accept their – God's – views. Religion has lost most of its political power. But the power and authority of the state have increased. It coerces people to do collectively what it forbids them to do individually, and gives them the means to do it. The first man or woman who fires a hydrogen weapon in war will kill millions and (if anyone survives) be given a medal. If he or she killed one person as an act of their own will they would be charged with murder and imprisoned or killed. We would regard a fundamentalist pope as clinically mad. We do not see that we ourselves are socially mad. It does not follow that the more we know about the world (including how to make hydrogen weapons) the more we know about ourselves. Understanding ourselves is not a scientific discipline, because we create ourselves through the act of understanding. Science can never catch up with our 'being', it creates the modern world but it is always a generation in the past. That is why the modern world is disfigured. Only drama can enable the self to elucidate itself and be free of social madness. In the past religion took over the 'human drama' and dogmatized it. God had made the world and us. But as we learn more about the world we find that we do not need a God to explain it, and it would take more than a God to explain the human mind. Now increasingly the 'human

drama' is structured not by religion but by the secular state's ideologies
and the culture of social madness.

Formerly the purpose of human life was to survive. It was a selfish
need but it created community because when people cooperated more of
them survived. Cooperation required an administration. Administration
takes on its own autonomy and this has ramifying consequences. It is
resented by many of those it administers. It gives itself privileges and
this aggravates resentment. It justifies itself and its privileges – and
legitimizes repression – by claiming to speak for a transcendental and
incorruptible source of good. This and the social tensions it gives rise to
create the culture of social madness. Now we survive and do not suffer
scarcity. Instead of a society of needs we have a society of wants. We
produce collectively but consume individually. The imperative of shared
humanness is lost. We must still cooperate but this does not require
community – it is achieved by organization, conformity and penalties.
There is no longer a need to seek the 'shared good', it is sufficient to
conform and consume. So there is no structural need for community and
humanness. But can they still survive? Can we use knowledge benignly?

There is a contradiction in consumer democracy. Members of a
democracy are equal, with an equal right to be and to be respected.
Members of a capitalist economy are unequal. Formally we become
more democratic and free; in reality we become more undemocratic and
confined. Structurally the economy requires inequality – affluence and
poverty. The economy is based on competition but that is only one of
the causes of inequality. In consumer democracy even the poor consume
more than they would outside it. This does not resolve the crisis of
inequality. It would do so only if humans were defined by consumption.
The human mind needs more. It needs justice – roughly, the right of
each to define themself – not just in their identity, which is individual,
but in their humanness, which is shared. We desire to live both our self
and our humanness. Like medieval heretics we will sacrifice everything
to this need and to remove what denies it. It is a need that raises us above
the brutes and if we do not protect it we become corrupt and brutal.

All inequality creates a cultural deficit. The economically unequal
respond to their inequality in several ways. They may struggle to
succeed and do so or fail. The system structurally requires more to fail
than succeed. If everyone won the lottery no one would win it because
money would be worthless. Affluent society requires one thing to be
scarce: money. Money is made potent by its scarcity, not by its power to
purchase. It is the scarcity of money which makes it possible to control
society – without this there would be no purchasing. The poor – the

economically unequal – are always with us. They may be conformist, revengeful, apathetic, anarchic, emptily hedonistic, anti-social, criminal. This litter of attitudes is the cultural deficit. It will create a new subclass of CTs – the Cultural Troglodytes. Ironically the cultural deficit is even reflected in the 'lifestyles' of the economically successful. Culture travels more rapidly than wealth because culture both preserves and corrodes – that is its appeal.

The cultural deficit creates tensions which lead to greater repression – to more prisons, longer sentences, the reintroduction of capital punishment, born-again religiosity and punitive morality. Increased repression and administrative violence worsen the cultural deficit they are meant to remove. Social madness becomes both rigid and frenzied. The mad – clinically or socially – have no rational understanding of what they do. In consumer society we understand ourselves less because we have no community. We live in affluence but ask ourselves the old questions of survival because we must deal with the social crisis created by the cultural deficit. We know more about ourselves as medical and statistical objects and less about ourselves as minds. The economy rejects any search for humanness because humanness cannot be technologically systemized and exploited for profit. It is easier to use technology to repress and divert. By definition humanness is shared. The characteristics we regard as human come from living in community. Consumer society represses these characteristics or debases them – it makes kindness sentimental, justice revenge, it turns the search for self-understanding into jejune New Ageism and integrity into what can be captured by surveillance cameras, not what the heretics said to themselves in the fires.

Consumer democracy creates the Faustian Trap in a new form. It becomes more difficult to escape from it because we understand less. We do not know how to create a new humanness, instead we cherish the phantom figures that rise out of the cultural deficit. Consumer society is 'paradise on earth'. It has no need of transcendental Utopias (would the television sets in Heaven be bigger?) but still needs a transcendental theory to explain the 'wicked' (the CTs – Cultural Troglodytes) and a 'hell on earth' to keep them in. To understand what happens next it is necessary to remember that whatever is logical in the imagination becomes acceptable to reason. God put the good and evil in separate places: Heaven and Hell. Hell cannot be a ghetto in Heaven because you cannot have a slum in the quarter of the affluent. So the administration will transport the CTs to vast separate settlements – the Western Gulags. There they will not contaminate the affluent. Before the Nazis could in good conscience destroy the Jews they had to declare that they were simply not human. Then it became a rational obligation to destroy them. It would be equally rational to destroy the CTs of the Western Gulags. Already the press and courts call criminals and hooligans 'animals'. For the time being these ideas still seem extravagant because they have not yet become imaginative logic. If they did they would be common sense. Humanness is not sustained by squeamishness or sensitivity or even by will. It depends on understanding.

The Faustian Trap might have a third, final stage. Unlike the first two stages it would not be created by our ignorance. We would be 'taken over' when our struggle in the trap had exhausted us intellectually, imaginatively and morally. It would begin soon after social madness and consumer democracy became a disaster. Evolution produced the self-conscious, imagining and reasoning human mind. In evolution a site is the occasion for part of itself to become independent and sustain itself metabolically on the site and so evolve cycles of being which lead to greater autonomy of individual structures. Independence creates dependence and so evolution is logical not arbitrary. In time man (seemingly) became lord of creation. Self-consciousness is a materialism. Transcendentalism from outside cannot intervene in an evolutionary system. Evolution is hermetically sealed to its origins. Imagination locks us into the material. Only what had already evolved in a system could intervene in its evolution and so would not be transcendental. (If God created man, God would not recognize him.) Humans evolved in the cycle of site, consumption and increasing autonomy (which is not independent of the system). But there is no reason why the system should be restricted to the 'human'. Self-consciousness is the 'highest' known state of evolution. It is said that it will continue to evolve. How? Into what? It is like imagining that matter will evolve into another 'material' – as if one reaction in an atom could turn it into an armchair. Self-consciousness is a dead end. It cannot evolve into a 'world spirit'. There is no transcendentalism into which it could ingress. Self-consciousness can only increase in knowledge of itself and knowledge derived from other self-consciousnesses and from things.

Technology evolved from the human mind. Self-consciousness made nature its instrument. The utility of the first tools depended on human hands. Now technology creates technology – it begins to become its own site. It still requires the human mind because it serves human purposes. It need not. The process which evolved 'higher' humans might continue to activate itself in the evolution of 'higher' technologies. Self-consciousness need not be evolution's end but only a stage in it – a bridge over which evolution passes from natural matter to technological structures. Evolution could abandon humanness. Machines and humans would not wage a 'war-of-the-survival-of-the-fittest'. Humans would become complacent parasites on technological proliferation. Perhaps self-consciousness would wither away – the drama of the human mind and its curious self-animosity fade out. Technology needs no purpose, it need only proliferate. It would just use the earth differently. The world might be filled with machines tended by human ghosts who consumed but were not self-conscious. Probably there would be only machines – a vast technological cancer cannibalizing itself. Archaeologists from space might find bits of human bones caught up in the technological gadgetry – like remains of food in mouths that had not even eaten it.

Would it matter? We seem to become humanness's destroyers not guardians. Except indirectly this has nothing to do with our nature, or with structurally irrelevant innate aggression or the grotesque transcendentalism of original sin. Science does not create humanness. But humanness is not a dead end. Drama enables the mind to understand itself, to cure itself of social madness by redramatizing its relation to reality – and create humanness in this way. Drama is the need to be human even when we are buried inside social madness: to search our coffin for every remnant of life to use to recreate the world. At this late stage one fragment is enough. Even our bones are full of history. Drama has a history but no past. It always begins in the present.

Drama must be as ambitious as the mad – as demanding as they are in their confrontation with reason. Otherwise we will be destroyed by the Faustian Trap. Only humans can have a purpose. Or are we too trivial for this universe?

(1999)

The Reason for Theatre

The Child

The origin and basis of theatre is imagination. Imagination takes the form of images, words, sounds, gestures, dreams, stories, vague and often admonitory perturbations and reality. It is not reverie, fantasy or arbitrariness. It is logical and has consequences in itself, reason and life. If it were fantasy we would imagine only what was pleasant – and doubtless sometimes what was unpleasant for others. Freud believed all dreams to be wish-fulfilments. He had to explain why some dreams are nightmares. We have to understand why often imagination turns to loss, danger, dread – the Tragic.

Other animals think and solve problems. Their relationship to the world is more purely rational than ours. Primates have an elementary ability to reason. Only humans have imagination. Other animals have no use for imagination, they live naturally according to their instincts. They have no culture and make choices only in relation to facts – 'Do not leave cover, predators are near.' Unlike humans they do not invent enemies.

Non-human animals are concerned with what and when but not with why. Imagination is needed to ask why. Imagination and not reason makes us human. We are self-conscious. Imagination and self-consciousness cannot exist without each other, they are aspects of each other. The rational is a priori to our reasoning. It is derived from objective reality. The ability to reason does not make us rational. It is our imagination that reasons. Imagination is not prior to imagining, it is wholly human. Reason seeks the rational, imagination seeks the logical – either as fate or freedom. Reality is indifferent to our irrationalisms. We may or may not survive errors of reason, but if we imagine illogically the consequence is our destruction, individually or collectively. If we are to be human there is a logical practice of imagination. More, the logic of imagination requires us to be human.

There is no gap between an animal and the place where it is. It fits its place – its territory and niche in evolution – just as its instincts fit its skin. The newborn child – the neonate – is aware of itself but not of place. It is a monad – one thing which is everything, an infinity in which every point is the centre and the self. It is itself and the universe. We know that the neonate only imagines it is the universe, but for it imagination and reality are one. This structures the functioning of the self – structure reflects the self. Leibniz said the monad has no window on the world. The neonate does not imagine the world, its imagination creates the world *as* the child and the child *as* the world. That is how we become a self. The double meaning of imagination confuses later understanding because in essential ways imagination continues to create reality. Consciousness cannot leave the imagination because it cannot leave the self.

The newborn child – the neonate-monad – is formed by its experiences. These are elemental experiences of itself and objective reality – comfort, discomfort, peace, dread. The newborn child is on both sides of its skin. There is no outside so it generates its own experiences. Its self is bound into imagination as language is bound into grammar. It endures. The neonate-monad creates the others' attentions, they are its elements in the way warmth and cold are elements in the adults' world. What if the guardians' smiles are like the sun in the adults' sky? – the child is its sky because there is no outside. If the child quarrels with the world it quarrels with itself.

The monad has no window on the world and no door on time. It exists in eternity. All its events are elemental, cosmic, total. For it the traumatic is the ordinary. The neonate has no psychology for the reason the world has none. It does not inflict pain on itself, it *is* its pain and pleasure. Happiness is the imagination's desire, the Tragic is its *idea*.

The Tragic is not only the neonate's experience but also its *idea* because it incites responses and results in behaviour. Tragedy is ontological, a presence that may wander or wait in any point of the universe which is the child. As the Tragic is ontological it is a question. Ontological questions have no answer. When all else is explained, all other questions answered – the answers lead to the unanswered ontological questions. We try to explain – and answer – the ontological questions by the transcendental. This corrupts the self by corrupting imagination. The transcendental is always violence because it imposes as answers what are really questions. Really the ontological is 'nothingness' – or in human terms the Tragic, the implacable. Imagination, self-consciousness, remains paradoxical. Imagination is unconfined by any boundary yet reality may coerce it – force it to reflect on itself – with either humanness or the Tragic.

The neonate-monad is actor and act, agent and event, cause and effect. If (an impossible example) it took up a cup to drink it would be mover and moved, cup, drinker and water. The cup would be the water and the water the cup. The water would drink the drinker. Each thing would be

an aspect of a Spinozist reality apprehended in a universal mind –
otherwise mind would be a series of catatonic events without imagination and self-consciousness, of effects which could never teach us causes.
The neonate accepts responsibility for the Tragic because no act by it
(the sole actor) could remit or eliminate the Tragic. Before the child
speaks it has only one question: to be or not to be.

From the beginning the neonate's elemental experiences induce
responses and behaviour and so create elemental ideas in the imagination. The neonate has no iconography or language waiting to represent
ideas. The monad is prior to grammar, but innate grammatical structures
might respond – register themselves in the neonate's experience before it
speaks, as if echoes of unspoken speech. The responses might begin to
structure the neonate's experiences, it might begin to make profound
Kantian patterns of itself by becoming conscious of itself as if it were its
own other – and in this way, in the gap between itself and its other,
create the vertigo of nothingness. Its skin is not yet a barrier, it is as if
the new child passes over it in and out of death, and death might as well
be internal as life be external. The Tragic is the neonate's recurring
mortality, which it meets on either side of its skin. It lives its death and
dies its life. It knows the Tragic and the tragic desire for pleasure. The
child knows – *is* – this. It exists in this way until its skin becomes *time*
and it enters the others' world. The new child lacks a psychological self
but perhaps its selfhood will never be greater. In the beginning
everything is elemental, cosmic and total. The new mind does not
experience itself passively, it is already its own riddle. Adults can
understand this state only by imagining it, but it is their reality.
Imagination never forgets though it is often forgotten.

When the neonate smiles it cannot know it is not smiling at – on –
itself. It seeks relationship with itself and this is also relationship with
the real world it cannot yet distinguish. Imagination is born with its
twin, the reasoning mind. The neonate does not take pleasure in the pain
it creates in itself. Masochists require another to inflict pain on them or
are themselves surrogates for another: another must represent their own
other – in the masochist act or demeanour the masochist seeks the self
which is lost when reason and the Tragic are sundered.

In the patterned chaos of its experience the new mind rests on one
thought: it has a right to be. This is not a mere physical or emotional
reaction, an impulse – it is an existential imperative because it discerns a
pattern of cause and effect and so knows itself as the site of cause. It
thinks its *self*, recognizes it. This is the basis of the mind's coherence and
without it there can be no self-consciousness: because there is no

coherence, cause and effect have not been imagined. The child's idea that it has a right to be, to live, is fundamental to the mind because its notion of cause and effect is synonymous with the idea of that right – the right is the cause and the effect is the self. Without the idea of this right the mind becomes mad. Madness is the opinion we have of ourselves. This is the functional origin of madness and it leads to the psychology of madness, in which imagination and reason are sundered and so cause and effect made irrational. The idea of the right to be in the world endures – for the same reason that it originates in the child, as a concomitant of coherence – in adults as the desire for justice. This is the origin of Value. All other values are practical, instrumental derivatives of this: the pragmatic cannot create this Value, nor in themselves can the sensory experiences of pain and pleasure, because masochism (and social submissiveness) sunders reason and the Tragic so that humanness is lost – we become Valueless. The mind is drama. How else could mathematicians find mathematics to be beautiful? The mind's structural need, without which it cannot be coherent, is the desire for justice. It is obvious that the transcendental would simply be a misrepresentation of the mechanical were it not for this human Value. Value is brought into the world by the self-consciousness of the human mind – and necessarily by any other self-consciousness (if there be any) in the universe. It is a practical, imperative *idea* – immanent not transcendental. Imagination is the need for justice, and self-consciousness expresses its *idea*.

The monad *is* morality – *is* and not *has* because as the monad is its own experience it cannot distinguish between fact and judgement of Value. In it, is *is* ought. In adults fact and judgement of Value are put asunder but the monad's creation of Value remains the basis of the understanding of right and wrong, not that any particular thing is right or wrong, but of right and wrong as an existential idea – 'existential' not to limit its future intellectuality but to denote its origin. It is the rationality of the child's being in the world. The origin of Value is the cause of our freedom and bewilderment. As it is created but is not an object, it also creates its opposite. Because the new child is wholly egotistic its morality is atrocious.

In the monad the neonate's imagination is literal, the imaginary is the real and there is no distinction between the two. In time it learns that its skin is a barrier and beyond it are places and people. The monad opens a window on the world. It is as it is when grammar is articulated by new words, they articulate the original grammar. Just as language cannot leave its grammar, mind cannot leave its origins, which are like a grammar. But in imagination there is also a logic of exclamations and other vocalizations of pain, fatigue, happiness. It is painful to cry and pleasurable to sigh with happiness. Imagination is the self carried into self-consciousness.

If the child entered the real world by a total break the self would lose consciousness. There would be coma and chaos. As the child enters the world the world enters it. Imagination is content and context. Imagination structures experience as a map. The map is the site of story. The first map is the neonate's. Later maps are imposed on this and on each other. The self is a palimpsest of maps. Each map informs earlier and later maps but each is distinct – over time the child acquires new selves derived from new experiences and knowledge, and each self is appropriate to its stage of development but each remains distinct. It is as if the selves existed on the same plane, not fitted into one another in the manner of babushka dolls. In the silence a babel of storytellers waits to speak – which one speaks depends on the situation. Maturity does not modify the potency of earlier selves. Any later real or imagined event may invoke any appropriate self. That is why we may behave out of character, or in ways which afterwards – often soon afterwards – surprise or appal us. All our experiences remain raw. The selves remember. When we introspect we ask: tell me a story. Adulthood is the way we accept or fail to accept responsibility for our selves, especially our early elemental selves. Imagination is the way we accept or fail to accept responsibility for the world. If we become society's story (its ideology), society speaks to us according to its needs in a situation – often it is that which causes us to behave in ways that afterwards surprise or appal us. But there are limits to our corruption. The first map, on which the Tragic gave meaning to our need to exist, is not obliterated. The Tragic watches over our humanness and no one can escape the tragedy which is their self.

The growing child necessarily retains the practical conviction that it has a right to be in the world. It is an egotistical conviction but it means that the world should be a good place in which the child is at home. Otherwise it would have to use violence to change the world. The neonate is God alone in the world and a God can use violence only on another. The neonate has the idea of the Tragic but not of evil. Evil is meaningless, it is not an *idea*. Only evil *events* can be described.

We have our proper names but the words we use to describe what is human are also our names because they are names for our imagination: good, bad, right, wrong, mind, reality, God, society, patriotism, religion and so on. These words have meaning and are about meaning. The word 'table' is descriptive, but the words we use to describe ourselves are also

prescriptive. But all words may be self-words. The self has no fixed
being. Partly we retain the neonate's identification of itself with its place,
it becomes us in imagination. We cannot say that reason supersedes
imagination, or emotion supersedes reason, or spirit supersedes mind.
Self-words recreate themselves in relation to each other. They are not
stable but there is a logic to their relationship. The logic decides what
happens to individuals and what will happen to us collectively.

The growing child enters the world consciously. The neonate's
imagination was structured as creator of the world. Now the child seeks
to be at home in the world but finds it to be a house of discord. The
imagination's imperative is to find meaning in the world.

Children cannot be taught, they can only create. We give children
lessons, but the world did not give the neonate lessons – it created the
world. It lived itself as the world and created its own experiences.
Children create but do not learn because what they know must have
entered the mind creatively. A growing child is *sui generis*, its own
context. Facts belong to existing systems and so the child cannot think
that B precedes A. But the child gives systems a context. If this were not
true of simple objects we would have no aesthetics – and consequently
no ethics: kings are not enthroned on kitchen chairs. This is also true of
cause and effect, circumstances and their consequences. Knowledge is
the use we make of it.

Imagine a mosaic. A child asks us what is the missing piece. We
supply the missing tessera and the child enters it into *its* picture. A table
has the same meaning for most children because it has the same use for
them. But a table is often the site of crises. This makes it a self-word.
This gives it meaning. Puritans put a table in the place of the altar in
their church because they wanted God to be in the kitchen as well as the
church. Changes put pressure on the tesserae because the picture – the
social *use* – changes. Often the pressure is violent. We strain to hold the
tesserae together but the interstices may open into gaps. It is as if the
interstices were strands of a net but the gaps between the strands are
sealed with coloured glass. We are looking for a picture that our living
destroys. We try to hold the picture together by violence but the
violence destroys it. When we try to give fixed transcendental meanings
to self-words it is as if we attacked the picture with a hammer. We use a
map to guide our journey which the journey destroys.

The world cannot 'happen' to us. Nor may our instincts. Children
create their instincts by the way they experience them. The self is a
story. The story relates experience to the real world. The story is logical.
How does instinct relate to it? Are instincts autonomous? Does story

repress, shape, incorporate them into itself, make them its agents? Instinct is taken into story. For instance, anger is an instinctive capacity but anger's causes belong to story. Instinctive force is as real as a table's solidity, but the *stronger* the instinct the more it is bound by story. Even the earliest emotions are echoes of story.

Augustine's struggle to replace carnality with celibacy was not reason repressing instinct. Would he have sought celibacy if the story of God the Father had not already been told? Story's events are not simply explanations but causes. Did fear of his own father make Augustine repress his carnality? What was his mother's role in the repression? Why was he converted in a garden and not in a church or a shop? In another story Eve was tempted in a garden. Some of any story's events may be secret and coded. Sometimes story uses the power of the desire for knowledge as a means to avoid the inconvenience, embarrassment or danger of knowing. It is often so in the ideology of religion and culture.

Instinct does not determine story but it has power, as water has weight. Water's flow depends on events and topography. In story the equivalent of these latter are events determining instinct. Story is creative not reductive. Instinct is incorporated into story but no more determines it than ink determines what is written in it. In story a 'murdering-instinct' might become the motive to burn down a house or build one. If I can afford to build an extension to block my neighbour's view I will not burn down his house – he may burn down my extension. Instinct is not repressed but is used in story to relate the individual to society. Drama and story are one in the way that imagination and self-consciousness are one. Drama is reality's logic, the logic of change. We could but do not understand the logic. Understanding it means altering the relationship between self-words. But as they are prescriptive that means changing ourself. Eventually reality changes their meaning and so changes us. But it does so violently because we do not understand the logic. Violence is always logical. We cannot escape this dilemma, it is as if the interstices between the net's strands were blocked with glass. The logic may be explained but this is of little use. The words are bound together in anomie, ennui, crises and drama. If it were otherwise, the human problem would have been easily solved but we would not be human.

Children enter the real world through the monad's self-creativity, they anthropomorphize the world, create it in their own image. The child gives objects human subjectivity. This is the stage of the pre-real. Trees speak, chairs are tired, storms angry, winds spiteful, plates hungry and demons wait in the dark. Through anthropomorphy the child remains coherent, supplies effects with causes, and finds meaning so that the storyteller may be told. The story is protean but logical. The storyteller always has one foot in the real world because the story is told to enable us to live. In story one object becomes another roughly in the way a spirit is said to enter a juju. A child's block of wood may 'be' a car or dog. The child cathects objects with Value – the world impersonates the child. This is the pre-real. The child is no longer sealed in the monad. Its *act* of making the wood-block car shows – and the wood-block car itself shows – the child's right to be in the world. Children's play is a *use* of justice. Christianity does not record the monad-time when God created Himself but it records the pre-real, the time when the child created things and their world. Eve is a bone taken from near the heart, a wood block turned into a woman. God's miracles all derive from the child's game with the wood block. In the pre-real world a child relates the elemental monad world to the external world. The elemental is still the child's way of being pragmatic, its story is still the map of the world. It creates it and is not passively imprinted with it. As it maps the world so as to exist in it, it puts itself in the map and maps the world in itself. All creation creates the creator. The child creates itself as it creates the wood-block car. The child's power to put the wood-block car in the world has greater consequences for us than the power of factories to make cars.

The child makes itself human by anthropomorphizing the world. Its story contains a practical understanding of the world, of what and when. It also designates Value. The child does not distinguish between Value and fact. Its story binds it to the world because the story gives the world meaning. It does not distinguish between story and itself the storyteller. The pre-real child is at a threshold. It is its own creator but the world is autonomous. The pre-real child begins to distinguish between agent and act. The child cannot create the world *ex nihilo*. Instead it gives birth to it – a human not divine act. The child enters the world by having it taken from it as a child is taken from its mother. Otherwise the world would bring the child its death. Then the child could develop only as part of history and history is blind. Each child comes to its term with reality differently, in its own way. It happens over time (yet is anticipated), at some times calmly, at others in crisis. Reality is not presented to the child in a consistently humane way. Children find meaning in what at first to them seem random events, and the linkage the child finds between the events gives the child its character. Each child is different because it links experiences differently. The child takes

– imagines into reality – the character it defines for itself in relation to the vicissitudes of being in the world. Character is expectation.

The world starts to exist beyond the imagination. The mind is conscious of the real only through imagination, it is conscious of it only as it is self-conscious. Self-consciousness does not become a 'real' part of the world. If it did it would abolish its own need to be and we could not create a culture or go mad. The creator must be outside what he creates. We have no self, we seek a self. Imagination creates reality by investing it with Value and so with consequential meaning. Value does not exist in reality, only in imagination, but it is real because it is necessary to self-conscious apprehension and use of facts. Physical and instrumental systems have the meaning of their consequences, but Value gives meaning to consequences, not only as practical assessments but as judgements, structures in creativity. That is why unlike animals we may choose to act paradoxically and accept martyrdom, sacrifice, celibacy.

The child creates its world, its tragic and comic. Tragedy and comedy do not define themselves because pain and pleasure define themselves only in the trivial, in pinpricks not bayonet thrusts, jokes not the comic, sentimentality not the tragic. Story defines what is serious.

The sole precept of the monad's morality is 'I have a right to be in the world'. Its sole imperative is 'to make the world my home'. This is monolithic, elemental, cosmic, petty and egotistic. The monad dreads and needs the Tragic because it belongs to its ontological existence, is its *idea* of its existence, defines its self in its world. In the Tragic there is no guilt or blame. Instead there is the *idea* of the Tragic, the understanding that the Tragic *is* so that the child *is*. But the pre-real child's morality is atrocious. Like Yahweh the child accuses 'real' perpetrators of 'their' wrongs – it rages, punishes, destroys. God is angry but the devil is never angry because the devil has no guilt. A God needs a devil as apologist for his mistakes. The child has no devil, it seeks only justice and its rage is innocent. And so when a child is blamed for its anger it feels the rage of a guilty God. There is no other rage like this: it confronts the child with death and the child enters the charnel house. The biblical story clearly identifies sin with death, but the child is egotistical only because it has accepted responsibility for the world.

The child is conscious of its rage, the burden of justice shakes the child's imagination. And so it is tangled, turmoiled, in tragedy, in the search for justice. In this state it enters society. Society is unjust. It requires the child to pass from the elemental to the trivial, its morality to change from the traffic between the Tragic and comic to the business of management and administration. The child's morality is atrocious but so

also is society's because it is unjust – and, unlike the child, it does not
find meaning in the Tragic but seeks refuge in nihilism to justify its
injustice. From this comes the cosmic pettiness of human beings. The
child's innocence is radical because it relentlessly seeks justice. Its anger
is inconvenient to us but innocent to it. God was fortunate in having
enemies, the people who were not his chosen. The child must make its
enemies. It can make them only among those it turns to for justice. If a
God has an enemy, the enemy must win. The child must find that it is
not a God before it can become human or inhuman.

Aristotle's physics and theory of tragedy are both wrong but only the
physics have been discarded. The tragic theory is canonical. Unjust
society must misinterpret tragedy because it is threatened by it. In
Aristotle the 'tragic flaw' has the function of sin in Christianity and
purgation is redemption. The theory is part of the Greco-Romano-
Christian repression that has lasted for two and a half thousand years.
The tragic hero's 'flaw' is not hubris but innocence, he is without guilt.
If tragedy purged it would be only of the disquiet felt by innocence
when it is corrupted by injustice – and then tragedy would worsen
corruption. Tragedy belongs to imagination, and the *idea*, the meaning
of the Tragic is the human desire for justice. Innocence is made radical
when it confronts the Tragic. Our humanness comes from this. Why is it
that we are born innocent but everywhere are trivial and corrupt?
Imagination is always creative yet it may lead us into destruction. Story
is free *and* captive. Instinct determines animals but in humans the story
is determined *and* creative. Paradoxically it is because it is creative that
it is not always free. It is logical. Story cannot change its origins but it
may change their meaning. Instinct determines the instinctive through
its performance but story can choose – though not determine – its end.
Story is a dimension of our existence as much as are space and time.
Imagination must create a reality otherwise none can exist for us – it
would be as if imagination's time stopped and reality was a graveyard in
which no one was buried.

What follows from the inertia of imagination can be seen in those who
cannot imagine practical reality. Autistics cannot easily anthropomorphize reality and ascribe Value to it. A doctor asked an autistic child
visiting a hospital 'Give me your hand'. The child panicked. It
understood it was to take its hand from its arm and give it to the doctor.
Children anthropomorphize the world because it is their only way to
continue to be themselves.

A pre-real child does not 'own' its hand, it *is* its hand. But in the real
world everything is owned. Innocence did not own the world, it was

responsible for it – that it should be the good home of innocence. Ownership is not responsibility. In unjust society ownership is guilt and psychological repression. Adults do not own themselves – they are owned by the administration because as it owns the instrumental systems it owns the users of these systems. In unjust society everything is owned. The child learns to live in society. There 'Give me your hand' is not a literal request. But society may say 'Give me your life' in battle or in prison and in the more subtle metaphorical ways in which it destroys the self.

To be human the pre-real child makes reality a story. Society adopts the story and uses it to dehumanize the adult. Society does this – and is able to do it – because the child learnt to anthropomorphize. The child anthropomorphized the world to survive its dangers, society anthropomorphizes the world to use the dangers as threats: the child to be free, society to incarcerate. Society continues the story but changes the meaning: it transcendentalizes it. Transcendentalism is the anthropomorphizing of reality, it is parasitic on the child's mind, it reifies the irrationality in the child's mind, it corrupts innocence, it is the childhood of adults. Society instructs the child in God, devil, spirits, resurrection, reincarnation, ghosts, miracles, visions, telepathy, superstition, patriotism, nationalism, retribution, discipline, obedience, fortune telling, table-turning – down to the mental detritus of newspaper horoscopes. The same news broadcast reports a massacre in Africa and poltergeists in a vicarage. It is as if society were a vast monad enclosing all its members. What surrounds the monad is – to the sane mind – unknowable. In the neonate's monad all was immanence, but the adult's monad posits an external reality: a surrounding darkness. Society claims to have windows on to the darkness, to receive messages from it. The transcendental repeats the children's game of wood blocks which turns a thing into something else. Society uses this game to support its authority over life and death. The state controls the means of life and the institutions of punishment. Religion threatens with Hell and seduces with Heaven. This is the game of transcendentalism.

Society's story is its culture. It saturates reality with the unreal, the transcendental. Trees do not speak. Instead carpenters learn to make wood into tables and chairs. Administration uses its control of instrumental systems to enforce its culture and the transcendental, and uses these to enforce ownership of the instrumental systems. The division between material and transcendental is unclear. Although trees do not speak some trees are sacred, and the carpenter also makes cradles, coffins, scaffolds, stages, icons – these are self-names. It is as if in these things the transcendental were put into our hands. We live in illusion as fish live in sea.

If society were just, its transcendentalism would be harmless (and redundant). Children would enter Eden and grow to be adult: there we would be born, wounded and die, and plants would burgeon and wither. The Tragic would give these things meaning but it would not corrupt. We would be at home in Eden. Justice would be the daily common exchange. But society is unjust – this is obvious and need not be argued. It uses the transcendental to maintain injustice and make it acceptable. That is why the transcendental is claimed as the source of justice. Children must create their relationship to society. Even when they dislike their parents they accept their dictates as truth. It is the same with all authority. It is a matter of power. If the child believes the story, it lives – that is the point of every story, even if it is the short life created by suicide notes. The story explains but is also a mystery – every convincing story contains in it characters who do not believe in the story. Society uses the effort of belief to disguise the incredibility of what is believed.

Imagination creates reality – that is the source of our humanness and our human problem. The adult's pre-real world has the power of the real world, but through society's power to create culture and ideology the real world is dominated by imagination's power to create facts. The neonate does not actually have this power because it makes no distinction between imagination and facts. Imagination chooses its reality. Adults may see a table as an altar. When they do this the table *is* an altar, sacred in reality. Both carpentry and sacredness integrate society and change each other. Sacredness depends on carpentry but enters another system of relationships: an imaginary world with the real force of carpentry. If you take the wood-block car away from the child you have done more than take its car from it: you have taken it from the car. It is as if you had taken the child away from its mother. The wood-block car is the site of its creativity and so it is its world. If you insist to the child that the car is a block of wood you deny the child's creativity. Creativity is the right to be in the world. Without it the world is instantly mortal, the dreary plane of nihilism. God is the adults' wood block. He is dead but he may kill.

Pre-reality is not determined, necessary, because in it cause and effect are not connected determinedly. That is why simple societies perform rituals to ensure that spring follows winter. Complex societies build dams but still pray for rain in drought. It is still the game of the pre-real child's wood block, but it turns the child's creativity into destruction. The child's game created reality, the prayers seek escape from it. Only the Tragic can save us from this triviality and violence. David Hume accepted the unreality of reality in a philosophical autism: the philosophy of a sceptic taking part in a child's game. In response Kant said that the real was in effect founded in 'nothingness' because it is transcendental but unknowable: there is no window on it. Hume is in the pre-real but ignores the existential creativity of childhood in favour of the pragmatism of the Industrial Revolution. Kant is a seer trapped in the monad, a world dominated by cosmic, starry, existential imperative. Neither Hume nor Kant connects the monad and the pre-real world with their later consequences in the adult world. Philosophy is useful only when it is dangerous.

There is no reason why we should not gas Jews, gypsies, homosexuals and recidivists. There is no reason why homosexuals should not corrupt our manhood, gypsies steal our children, Jews take over the world and recidivists rob us. Gassing them might amuse us or satisfy our rage. Reason has nothing against either – unless it is the administrative difficulties of organizing it. We may imagine that a thing is right or that it is wrong and the motive for both judgements be equally innocent. The reason we massacre Jews is not that they take over the world but they take away our wood block. Then the world ceases to be our home, the good place in which we are good. We gas Jews to be good and no one could ever have another reason for doing it. If a Martian lately come to earth was told of a race which wished to take over the world, he would ask for a rational account of this. Being human, we may not. How can I ask for a rational account of why my wood block is a car? Humans may ponder long over trivialities but instantly make fatal decisions on the flimsiest evidence. Faced with a problem we regress to a self of the time when we first encountered the problem. The present problem may seem unlike the earlier problem, but the earlier problem will contain the core of the present problem in its elemental form.

There can be no gaps in the map, no end to the story. At times I am conscious but not self-conscious, but imagination is never absent. It interrogates and defines all things. The pre-real child anthropomorphizes the new into its fairy tale. For it all stories are autobiographies. It must account for everything. It is fiercely analytic but not scientific. Scientists are curious, pre-real children are creative. They do not say 'There is an X to be discovered'. For them X is already the dark place where the witch waits or the place where the princess sleeps. The child puts Value on what it finds, scientists find a use for what is there. In

Value there is no value or use (you cannot travel in the wood-block car), it only defines. As a child enters the real world it learns *use*, how a thing acts or is part of instrumental systems. Society owns use because it owns instrumental systems: this sort of use is value. A knife's value is that it cuts bread or kills. Its Value is that it is used to commit rights and wrongs. All Value comes from story, it cannot come from instrumental use – it would do that only if society were just and its purpose to make us human. Instead it is unjust and it sustains inhumanness. Human Value is made instrumental – *used* as value – when story is corrupt, as in religion and patriotism. Then imagination and self-consciousness are corrupt. Objects of value are given Value, as the tree is when it talks. This attaches Value to ownership – crudely, money talks. Unjust society replaces Value with value, the Tragic with nihilism. But even in the corrupt who act corruptly the Tragic may protect the memory of Value.

Unjust society is mad. It requires its members to behave in ways which – if the behaviour were private – it would regard as criminal and morally insane. All transcendence is mad and the source of social madness.

The difference between personal madness and social madness is power. Social madness has the power to insist that it is sane. The personally mad's imagination turns the wood block into what they desire or fear. The socially mad turn what they desire or fear into the wood block – they turn Value into value, use humans as things. Social madness is a form of alchemy which turns gold into dross. The 'social monad' is a vast madhouse.

Children are entered into society in three ways. First they learn the use and value of instrumental systems – how to achieve instrumental ends, to make, buy, sell, own. This is mechanical, largely – or sufficiently – a matter of facts. In this way the child acquires the skills, habits, customs, vices and uses of his society – *his* because the story is still patriarchal and *she* acquires *his* story of *her*.

Second, society adopts and extends the child's anthropomorphism. Land is not only earth to use but the fatherland or motherland. We must love it, its people and their ways. Anthropomorphism is usually generalized not detailed – details are too stubbornly close to facts. If the earth is mother how can I walk on her? Yet often in crisis details are given appalling and stunning power to authenticate generalizations: the newspaper photograph shows that the bomb threw earth into the dead soldier's mouth as if in death he kissed his mother.

The motherland has enemies. This is not the assertion of biological territorialism but the darkness of fairy tale. In society's structural processes metaphors are real. The profoundest metaphors originate in the monad, before the pre-real – they change not only sentiment but the appearances of things. Beauty is not restricted to biological origin. As with instinct, beauty derives from story. Tragedy is the *idea* of what makes possible the neonate's discomfort and disquiet. Beauty is the neonate's *idea* of harmony with itself. All beauty is the sign of nothingness, that is why it is desired. Nothingness is hidden behind beauty's mask. The neonate is threatened with nihilism and to survive it must approach it. It can do this only in the presence of the Tragic and its *idea*. The Tragic shelters the neonate in the presence of nothingness. The neonate's *idea* of this is beauty. Tragedy reconciles beauty with the earth. Injustice makes beauty transcendental, destroying its immanence: the ground plan of transcendence is death. The tragedy of war is that it is the least necessary thing we do.

The third way in which children enter society combines the first two ways into an immediate and potent power: the family. In large part the family is the child's first world outside the monad. The family is itself formed by society, but it is not exclusively an instrumental system because it has Value. Humanness originates in justice not love. Love is often a gesture of justice but love may be corrupted into hate and revenge. Love is blind because it wishes to be, justice because it must be. Love changes because it is psychological, justice is unchanging because it is an idea. Innocence remains even when it is the means to corruption. The vicissitudes of the world transmute love into tragedy. Justice enters our lives through the Tragic, not because of reality's harshness but through our confrontation with the Tragic.

Is my wickedness in my genes? Am I bad because I am a born sinner? These are explanations of intellectual turpitude. You cannot found a morality on immoral understanding. But reason alone cannot amend imagination because imagination's desire for reason is so strong that it creates the irrational. You cannot explain to the mad that they are mad or to the religious that there is no God. In time, religion came to dominate Western imagination.

Oedipus and Christ

The West's technological innovativeness became possible when the Greeks restructured the family as 'Innocence and Punishment'. Christianity debased this profundity into 'Crime and Punishment', which is an unwriteable story. This made complex administration possible. Christianity also had to make the story transcendental, the family divine.

Authority had to be beyond criticism or reproach. (The social father may be man, woman or group – but if it is the latter the child usually epitomizes the relationship into one with an individual in the group.)

Western religion is based on the pre-real. The religions of less technologically original societies are based on the monad's seeming permanency, the returning time cycles, the neonate's eternity. It is as if the neonate were released from its contingently tragic into nihilism. The social effect of this is to 'do less', the religious imperative is to 'do less but do it more'. Buddha was born in a king's house, Christ in a hovel, but the effect of both is the same. Buddha goes into the world, finds poverty and death and travels 'deeper' into nothingness. For Buddhists the world is illusion, as if they saw the working of imagination in reality but not that, by relating the human to the world, what imagination creates is real – so that our relationship to the world is either creative or destructive. Imagination creates the real not the illusionary, it exists in the real not in nothingness. Imagination itself – not what it creates – is often illusionary.

Christianity had already made religion worldly, political and adminis-trative. It is another patriarchs' story. To enter society a child must submit to violence and not be broken. It must integrate the power of violence into itself. It takes power from society in order to relate to society so that it may live and society may exist. Initially, rage speaks but violence acts. Later, violence may be corrupted into sadism as speech or in other ways. The Old Testament is set at the end of the monad and the beginning of the pre-real, when a child sees its father as a giant child, as a projection of itself – hence Yahweh's rage and atrocious morality. The New Testament is set in the child's *passing* from the pre-real into the real. It is the story of the crime of innocence.

Christianity takes the earthly family hostage by making it transcen-dent. The father becomes God, the mother the Virgin and the son Christ – son because Christianity is patriarchal. Christ is anti-patriarchal, sexless and precarious. In icons he has a beard and wears a dress, he teaches ambiguity and extremity. Crucifixion is a metaphor for castration and for its symbolization in circumcision. Christ embodies woman as an emasculate before the father. Antigone is also a Christ. She weakens the father by confronting him with the Tragic. Her punishment is to be buried before she dies. She is not resurrected (women, I notice, are not).

Religion precariously stabilizes society in the pre-real. To say God speaks is as unreal as saying trees speak. Religion is unstable because it is an ecstasy repressing a trauma. The crucifixion is intended to solve the problem of innocence, but saints must perform miracles which the resurrection should have made redundant. Miracles are like spells in fairy stories, there because the story itself is not a spell: description instead of enactment.

The child's story articulates the child's right to be in the world, to be creator of Value. That right cannot straightforwardly be turned into the right to be in the family. The family's tensions make it potentially unstable. In the monad the tensions that rise around the Tragic made it necessary for the neonate to create an *idea* of the Tragic – an understanding of it, an acceptance, an is. Later this becomes the way in which imagination resolves its existential conflicts. It is the structure of drama: *agon* (the conflict) and the *idea* (the meaning of agon, which goes towards making agon its own explanation and founds the human in the real).

Children cannot be terrorized into submission (they would become catatonic) or killed (they would then have ceremonial and sentimental value but little practical use). Instead a child is expected to use its power as impotence and *choose* to submit: to give birth to its death as before it gave birth to the world. God is death. The child must manage to achieve one moment when it confronts the threat and prevents death possessing all things – world, people, wood blocks, toys. It must steal life from the dead God. Society is a structure of impotence and power. If once there was a golden age we could not return to it. Rousseau said we could not return to the state of nature. We cannot return to the monad. Story begins in the realization of loss.

Christianity is the retelling of the story of Oedipus. Oedipus murdered his father and married his mother. Plague struck Oedipus's city: the personal has social consequences. The child must enter society or the world is ill. Christ enters his father's city on an ass, the clown's animal, to show his submission and impotence. Is the cause of Oedipus's crime sexual, alimentary, biological, psychological, political? The cause is not the point and knowing it does not resolve the human problem. If it did one revolution would solve the problem and it would necessarily succeed. The Oedipal effect is not restricted to one cause. It is total, inherent in the human situation: impotence desires power so that the just may live. Oedipus gains his father's power, goods and authority and the pleasures of the world. With them he gains the adult's responsibility: know yourself. The play is staged to help audiences know themselves. Only stories have access to the self's foundations, to the purposes of imagination. This makes stories real, just as when earth is made the fatherland real armies bleed on it. We know that Hamlet is not really killed. But at each performance of the play the audience's imagination must *really* kill him and be killed as him. Your life is a metaphor for all other lives. The difference between imagination and reality is often on the side of imagination – it has greater reality. We are the solution that produces the problem. That is why it is difficult to solve.

Drama, whether tragic or comic, has two ends: 'know yourself' and 'become yourself'. Not *be* yourself, because you must create yourself from what you are. The logic of imagination creates the self or submits to corruption. When Oedipus's drama was written it could not free society from plague, slavery and war. The gap between the real (the instrumental systems and the institutions of survival) and imagination (the story needed to survive) was too great. Oedipus's fate was decided by gods, a transcendental power beyond the social institutions. The gods required Oedipus's blinding (his social submission) but not the manumission of slaves. The Greeks were creative because they examined the ways in which we make ourselves human. Their answers were historically circumscribed. Slavery was an instrumental system necessary to society's survival – it helped to finance the theatre.

Both Oedipus's story and Christianity's use of it dramatize the child's passage from pre-real to adulthood. They are concerned with power and its entablature into social hierarchy. Drama represents to imagination core situations so that their *idea* – their meaning – may be changed. Oedipus defies the gods and is outside social law. His acts are not crimes, they come from the pre-social need to be at home in the world. To seek justice Oedipus murders his father and marries his mother. In the story of the Garden of Eden, Christ is the phallic serpent who seduces his mother (the virgin Eve) and in this way makes his father (God-in-Adam) conscious of his (God-in-Adam's) injustice. The son forces God-the-Father to make innocence tragic so that innocence may enter the world. (The earliest versions of stories are the extremest.) When Oedipus *commits* his crimes, peace comes to the city, because Oedipus, anticipating the future, answers the Sphinx's riddle: the definition of a human being. When Oedipus's story is known, his acts *become* crimes. Administration makes innocence criminal and uses the transcendental to make it a sin, an impurity. Administration requires people to live in the pre-real. It calls the Tragic guilt – every society is founded on the scene of a crime. The situations of the Greeks and Israelites were different. The Greeks enslaved, the Israelites had been released from slavery. God was on their side, he sent plagues to punish their enemies. But the Greeks and Israelites shared the same problem of power and impotence.

Drama's power comes from its interrelationships with society. Religions are plays which – it is claimed – are real. Such claims can be made only when the story's problem is already real in the imagination. Christianity redramatizes as real the problem of Oedipus. Oedipus's play presents to audiences a story already in their imaginations, created by every child in its passage from the pre-real to the real world. Society claims an imaginary story is real (as state religion, national epic, and so on) to use the story to structure its social control. Society solves the conflict in the original story and turns the power involved in the conflict into support for its solution: it turns the story into ideology. Religion secures administration's power over both the state and the self. Society's tensions – power and impotence, authority and defiance – are rearranged so that society may be administered and owned. Societies endure as long as they efficiently administer the instrumental systems and make ideology plausible by feeding imagination back to its own desire as fulfilment. This is also the way in which the mad try to control their world – but *their* story remains imaginary.

Religion sustains the problem's tensions in repression. It does not abolish the tensions but uses them to energize and administer society. Oedipus defied the gods and was punished with blindness (a metaphor for castration), but the tension was not used as administrative force – the Greeks did not claim reality for Oedipus. The tension cannot be balanced unless Oedipus – like Christ – becomes the father. It was necessary for Sophocles to write another play. In this Oedipus is an elderly Christ, an embittered old man, a sacred sufferer who curses his sons and dies to bless a surrogate, idealized son – Theseus – and his city Athens (the Jerusalem of Greece). The virgin who lives with Oedipus is his daughter-sister Antigone. The second play reverses the first play's plot and holds the tension in an even more contorted form. This wavering had to stop and the tension be reformed to make the story more creative and society more stable. Real gods do not die. Instead, the father now kills the son – Laius kill Oedipus, God kill Christ – and the son will submit to be killed. Submission replaces defiance and gains security: Oedipus is brought back from the dead and made one with the father. But the Holy Family must be a *ménage à trois* because it must include the mother. This is too provocative for the story. Neither man sleeps with the mother-wife. Instead she joins the Trinity as the Holy Spirit. The Holy Spirit is sexless but given what patriarchs regard as the sign of woman: the Holy Spirit has the gift of tongues – she talks.

Christ's story is Oedipal in all its details. Christ is bound to a phallic pillar and flogged. Flogging is a common sadomasochistic negotiation of an otherwise intractable relationship. He is crowned with thorns: the head of the phallus is circumcised. He is crowned, flogged and executed

by the state's soldiers: that is, by the father. The point of the story is that
the father is the state.

Christ must be innocent. But if the story is to evoke its tensions he
must be closely associated with guilt – prostitutes, outcasts and
criminals and be hanged among thieves. The robber Barabbas is guilty
but is pardoned and Christ dies in his stead. He is Christ's alter ego and
carries Christ's guilt – in this he is a pattern of all Christian believers.
Barabbas is the nails on the cross, the cement on the sepulchre. It is also
necessary to associate Christ with the state (its governor would not
condemn him, he consorts with tax collectors and soldiers) so the state
may be exonerated by its culpability.

Christ is to be sinless, cleared of Oedipus's guilt. If society abolished
guilt it would abolish the justification of its injustice. If Christ must be
innocent, his guilt is still needed to maintain the story's tensions. But
where will his guilt go? In the imagination the problem is as real as a
murderer's need to dispose of the body. The difficulty is that guilt must
always have a body to haunt (or to inhabit as illness), and here,
moreover, the problem has become how to dispose of the *murderer's*
body: so the dead Christ is buried under everyone's floorboards. If
Christ is to be sinless and die for the sins of the world, it is necessary for
the world to take on the sins of Christ – for all humankind to bear his
guilt. It is the purpose of Christianity to make the world guilty.
Imagination is not magic, its logic is realism. Whenever the real
appropriates the imagination, the result is paradox.

It follows that redemption cannot be a single event in history. Guilt
must always be present. The crucifixion must be repeatedly restaged in
the Mass. A ritual is a metaphor for which reality is claimed. But
however pressing the ideological, theological need, for legal reasons the
sinners at the Mass cannot be crucified. So the Mass is not an authentic
restaging: its power, its cathexis, is lost. A decathected ritual can be
recathected only by an earlier, more primitive version of itself. For that
reason, in a future crisis religion might have to return to human
sacrifice. Cult immolations make this more likely. The security we have
struggled to achieve in the present cannot protect us from the
superstition and violence of the past. (To anticipate the conclusion of
these notes: whatever is logical in the imagination is readily acceptable in
reality – that is why the unthinkable becomes the inevitable.) The earlier
ritual behind the Mass – behind the crucifixion itself – is cannibalism.
So the sinners at the Mass eat the host, Christ's body. In an earlier
version of the story the father (Saturn) ate his children. Cannibalism's
power comes from the neonate. For the neonate eating is elemental: it

eats in discourse with the Tragic. (It is difficult for us to understand the monad because in it all verbs turn to nouns.) What did the neonate eat? As the neonate is everything because there is nothing outside it, it eats itself – the world, God. It does not have the *idea* of these things, but later these things will bear the neonate's idea of itself: the power of its need. When the neonate ate itself it created justice as the future possibility of the world.

There is another consequence: the Mass is a ritual not of repletion but of starvation. It recreates its opposite because it represents the neonate's reality which is behind the administration's ritual and story. The neonate seeks justice – food, the manna of the self: it is its need for innocence. Seeking justice is the right to be. But the communicant is a sinner. God stole the sinner's innocence so that he, God, would be innocent before Christ. Seeking justice is the right to be at home in *this* world, but religion claims its justice is not of this world but of heaven. *This* world is a vale of sorrows – seek and ye shall not find. We cannot know ourselves here, we must wait till Judgement Day. This is the sinner's punishment: it represents the neonate reality but adulterated by administration, the authority of church-and-state, which of course is necessary – if the story's tension is to be maintained – to the conversion of the imperative to know (which is, finally, to know yourself) into the imperative to believe. Hell would be a cannibal feast in which you are eaten and eat but are not satisfied. We live the logic of our story. God and devil, justice and law, faith and fanaticism, the changes imagination makes to reality, the empowering of corruption by technology – if we trace the ramifications of these antinomies to our time we see that a consumer in a consuming society is the baby who devours its womb.

The execution of a man became a revolutionary religious story. On the mound at Golgotha were assembled all the elements of social, private, mental life at a time when enough history had been remembered to make it necessary to give it a radical new meaning. God was impotent before Caesar. Imagination needed to assert the power – and the authority of the *idea* – of justice over law. Otherwise imagination could not survive and the mind be coherent in the accumulating world – nor could ideology. Homer was distant enough for Greek dramatists to reuse his myths to examine their present: they created our heritage. By the time of Christ, the relation between power and impotence, administration and innocence, was so abrasive and volatile that it had to be turned into myth and made real. It is all so extravagant that it could never pass as fiction, anyway – it would only be credible as history. Christianity takes the main themes of Greek drama and turns them into reality – it abolishes theatre, turning 'use' (which is the only foundation of freedom) into theological dogma and administrative tyranny. The Christian story shows the desperation of imagination's search for justice in an unjust world, the imagination's immense power to create reality, the immensity of the struggle to be human – and the futility of trying to make the imaginary real. It solves nothing. It is religious dogma that one innocent son is killed by his father and the world is changed for ever. The problem of the self can be solved only by making society just, and this – and to make this understood – is the work of drama. To claim the imaginary as real merely rearranges the problem and delays the solution. At most it helps to prepare the means to solve the problem at another time. We are refugees from reality and build ourselves prisons to be free in. The freedom religion promised turned into its opposite – that is the paradox of making the imaginary real instead of making the real imaginary. The latter is the human purpose.

The Christian drama is psychologically and socially enormous. Yet it had to be constantly reinforced by miracles and martyrdom. Religion's instability is shown in the banality of its miracles – walking on water, curing lepers by touch, imprinting images on bits of cloth. It was also shown by the violence of martyrdoms – martyrs had to be atrociously punished by the reality they denied. Society became the Christian theatre in which the scaffold was the stage where real murders were committed and real suffering endured for imaginary reasons – as if all the violence crammed into a few centuries in the Colosseum was repeated and multiplied piecemeal for two millennia. Justice is not only a desire, it is also an *idea* awake in us even when we sleep: it is the need for the meaning of reality, to understand the social nature of our lives and deaths. Religion explains one thing at the cost of mystifying everything else. Greek audiences left the theatre knowing more of themselves (compare them to a modern audience leaving a 'musical'), but they could not turn their imagination's revelations into social institutions. Christianity was late enough to achieve social power. When congregations left church they took unreality out into society. But there is also wisdom in that. State religion repressed but also permitted – sometimes even forced – believers to seek justice, sometimes in defiance of the state. There may be a sort of happy folly, an ecstasy in faith. The elect believe they understand God and themselves. Not all madness is instantly malign, but in time it is. Religion is untrue, it is a form of social madness. When imagination seeks justice it must seek reality, and as in part it creates reality it must seek to know itself and what it does. When it cannot the gap between imagination and reality widens. Justice is not the seeking of comfort or even of happiness but of the real. We take this imperative from the monad – to seek justice, not delay it, to take responsibility for the world and not use it for our convenience because that leads to nihilism. Reality drifts from an untrue story. The story becomes fanatical and specious, and the flashes of righteous revenge meant to disguise its drifting opportunism drive it into nihilism. The gap widens into the Faustian Trap. In the end to believe the story costs the freedom the story once gave. As the Christian world became more unreal it became more dogmatic and narrow, the self-autonomy it had created turned into the rigid determinism of predestination and the forced labour of the Industrial Revolution. Experience teaches us that God compromises but the devil never does.

Unjust society maintains itself through law-and-order. In it there is no self-knowledge and so no sane community, only the community of the mob. Imagination is corrupted and its story distorted. Our lives become disciplined chaos. The fish are not caught in the net, the sea is. Unjust society builds prisons and even kills criminals. If it did not the chaos would be greater. But it is never sane to build prisons or just to kill. In the end it is not even expedient, it creates the conditions it seeks to prevent. But society tells its stories (of religion, patriotism, racism – the transcendental) in terms of the self's story, and this gives it the power of imagination and the force of self-consciousness – so its story is 'obvious'. The existential need for justice becomes the duty to be unjust.

Unjust society uses the transcendental to justify its story: 'God ordains this. Fate decrees that.' Atrocious morality is codified as law-and-order and crime becomes wickedness and sin. The system of money requires all money to be owned. When money is owned everything is owned because the power of money is owned. This is unjust. Fear and righteousness replace innocence. God has a guilty conscience: he always panics when faced with man – in God's defence it can be said that he is afraid of man because he sees the murder of anyone as the murder of himself. This is an echo from the infancy of God. From the monad. It echoes in us too. Each of us remains a semblance – a memory – of totality. And so when we see a murderer we see ourselves – but God does not, because in the Christian story he stole our innocence to hide his crime against Oedipus-Christ, so that we must bear the guilt of God. When God creates a world he builds a prison, humanness means escaping from it to the real. Prison is a common-sense place. No other state of mind is closer to madness than common sense. It has the least insight into the human paradox. It understands only the normal, and when that breaks down – as it must – common sense turns to violence.

Common sense is the philosophy of social madness – those cursed with it readily become barbarous not because they have no imagination but because their imagination is corrupt. We live on a boundary between the pre-real and the real. Many of our activities – work, science, recreation – are in the real world, but they are also in the metaphoric world of imagination. Science may become social madness. The irony of Frankenstein is that the monster is more profoundly human than the scientist who makes it. The monster's morality is atrocious but he is innocent and knows the Tragic. Yet (our mortal danger) it was when the scientist sought his own humanity that he made the monster. We must seek to be human or we become monsters, but seeking humanness may make us monstrous. The transcendental always produces monsters.

Imagination and Reason

To be human in the Technomachia we must understand imagination. Imagination is not mystical wisdom. It seeks to know the real. But unjust society owns the instrumental systems, the systems of manufacture and organization – and so it can 'prove' its fictions to be facts. Common sense and ideology are used to corrupt imagination. Punishment is made more draconian and surveillance more insidious. The more powerful social injustice is the more it corrupts the self. The transcendental is not wisdom but the debris of the most banal common sense. Our social and private behaviour is confused and paradoxical. Love becomes hate, anger reconciliation, sacred demonic, tyrants act for the people's good, the murderer obeys his heavenly voices, armies massacre for freedom, we are cruel to be kind – these paradoxes are not Manichean. If we are evil why do we pretend our acts are good? Why not boast of our evil? Why are we so modest about our barbarities? Acts are committed in situations that contain value and Value.

The human mind is not an object in the world, a thing like a table. Neither is it transcendental and outside the world of things. The mind *is* an object but *in* humanity. The mind seeks its sanity in coherence: the sane know a block of wood is not a car. The pre-real child creates the wood block as a *real* car – but the car puts wooden splinters in the child's hand. Few people act on what they know, but most people become their illusions. For our practical well-being and rational coherence we must seek justice – the world of things and organization, of instrumental systems, requires it of us if we are to live in safety. But society's story imposes injustice and the consequently irrational description of society and the world (in transcendentalism society is integral to the world, we are not free) and then imagination seeks the objectively unjust: injustice makes the world my good home. Minds corrupted in this way cannot know what they think or tell what they do. The mad take the normal to its limits. To the mad madness has the obviousness of common sense. The mad do not imagine they are mad, their imagination *is* mad. In the same way, because imagination's need for justice is so strong it may reason irrationally. It is normal – common sense – to talk of the blood of the fatherland: the mad see the earth bleed. It is normal to pray to God: God speaks to the mad. It is normal to say I am a sinner: the mad suffer the pangs of hell. Social madness provokes and justifies in the normal the behaviour and sufferings of the clinically mad – soldiers spill blood on the earth, the leader is the voice of destiny, bishops tell us what God is thinking. We make the world into what it is not. Adults who make guns are like children who make wood-block cars – but guns are toys that kill. Our daily life incorporates social madness into our use of the instrumental systems by which we live, so that living makes madness sane. Sometimes the socially mad are frenzied, at other times they fall into apathy and then their madness is a silent meditation on nothingness.

Unjust society imposes on the world ideological madness (religion, patriotism, militarism, the class system) and organization (prisons, schools, armies, stock exchanges, the economy). Ideology produces the society which justifies it but which destroys us. The economy is beyond our control. We do not arm with bows and arrows but with hydrogen weapons. Patriotism does not lead to drunken street-corner scuffles but to genocide. Our forebears tilled the earth, we pollute it as if it were already our grave. We lose our practical humanness and create a universal negative. In Hiroshima at the hour of the bomb a just act is not only Valueless – it is even valueless. Why should God come to Auschwitz? If he came he would be gassed. Our society makes decent acts indecent, they are like writing 'Showers' over the gas chamber. They stop people knowing their situation. A good act is like hanging pictures on the gas-chamber walls to comfort the dying. You might as well play cowbells in an abattoir or read poetry to an ape. The mad know one thing and it drives them mad because they know it with piercing insight: society is mad. Decent, law-abiding citizens are socially mad and, admittedly with occasional spasms of sentimentality, morally atrocious. Unlike the clinically mad they are not put away, they run society and make its laws.

People in unjust societies are in conflict in themselves and with each other. Why have we not destroyed ourselves? Till now we have had the will but not the means. Even the most elementary societies use the world's instrumental systems and relate to it through technology. When the harvest fails they pray for rain, only in the final desperation do they burn the withered crop in sacrifice to the rain god. Much the same is true of us. We go through life with the delusions of common sense. In crises we lash out in violence, build more prisons, go to war, kill each other. The greater our technological power, the more violent and extreme our outbursts. Everything changes – even God. The New Testament is a book of changes to The Old Testament. But institutions – administration – dislike change because it disturbs ownership. Unjust society is as monumental as a stone statue. It cannot change its expression or gesture, it changes through cracks. Truths of the past become lies of the present, and the effort to believe them is greater than the effort that would discover the truth. We are blind waving a torch over our heads to light the way.

What is humanness? Can we protect from corruption our need to be at home in a just world? – or must we shrivel as if we were imprisoned in our monad, adults still in the womb? The pre-real child's morality is atrocious and egotistical. It tolerates others only when it gets its way. The universal Kantian maxim is not love. Atrocities are committed in love's name, religion perverts it into love of God (martyrs' pyres, inquisitions, intolerance, anti-Semitism) or love of country (the same). The child's mind is finer. Its maxim is justice. It is egotistical for others – in a good world *all* should be at home. It knows the Tragic and transitory, the seconds which are eternity, nihilism – which is the act which has begun but has no end. The child's *idea* of justice is elemental, the subtlety of mourning, hope, compassion are not yet learnt, its egotism is total and untainted. It cannot compromise with decency and compassion – such things could become systems in the real world but as yet they are not. The child seeks a world that the Tragic should share but not overwhelm. But society takes even the Tragic from the child and debases it as right and wrong. Law cannot create justice, they are antithetical. The horror of the pre-real child is that it sees that the world is lost and weeps as God's cortège departs. 'Give me your hand'? – if the world can be taken away it is to be expected that bits of your body will be taken away: that is mortality. Justice and the Tragic are in union, but law unites with mortality.

Egotism is the only possible origin of altruism. The pre-real child's egotism is radical innocence, its self-consciousness is knowledge of its innocence. At first when society redescribes the world to it, it is bewildered – but then the world's corruption intrigues it. Might it be a game the giants play with the Tragic? It is then that the child gives birth to the world. This is its first act in the real – and later, altruism may come from the memory of it. The birth is not naive because by then innocence has understood the human abomination. Its imagination is in the real world not in the monad. Morality begins in egotism but may become altruism because *imagination* begins in altruism – it is shared as if external to the self. Before the pre-real child gives birth to the world it makes no distinction between reason and imagination, they are the same. When it gives birth to the world it must think of the world at the same time as the imagination imagines. The wood block (a piece of the world) can be a car (a piece of imagination). But though imagination begins in altruism, ideology may corrupt it to egotism. Imagination creates, ideology is learnt. The process is paradoxical: it is egotistical because it secures a person's place and role in society – so it is not personal but social (patriotism, racism, community of believers). Yet it is fanatically personal because it changes the person into another being reduced to two dimensions – imagination collapses into reason in the form of common sense and doctrine. The mind cannot question itself and so is as egotistical as a ghost. The mind loses its own imaginative logic and is possessed by ideology. It is a rigid, frangible state. Two-dimensional imagination is like a platform on which the images of ideology – saints, heroes, monarchs, criminals, warriors, ragged beggar girls, mythic people – ceremonially dance. Under the platform madness seethes – it is the shadow of the dancers but the shadow-dance is more complex, more vectored, a dance of the wounded and savaged. The pre-real child cannot pass into the real world because there is no real world – it still has to be created and entered. The crisis holds the possibilities of corruption or humanness.

Madness is not an external thing that displaces reason, it happens *in* reason, it distorts it but still uses it. It is the same with innocence: it is corrupted by learnt ways of reasoning. There are no reasons that can argue against these distortions – that would be like talking sanity to the insane. It is the same with imagination's altruism – ideology corrupts it and it consents through fear. But as imagination has logic but no rules its altruism cannot be completely lost – only displaced. It is preserved – kept in place – by what destroys it (and it destroys) as ground is protected and kept in place by the ruins which stand on it.

Egotism sustains its opposite and it may be recovered, but only through drama. The crises – dramas – of reality might also do it, but only at the risk of war and the certainty of damage, because reality's dramas are wars and disasters. Altruism (really, imagination itself) is recovered by drama in theatre when drama makes its stories apposite to what is in effect the drama of the self. Drama does not return to the pre-real because it cannot – if it could the effects would be infantile. It may deal with earlier stages – selves – as they appear changed as part of later situations: trauma repeats and attenuates itself in daily life in society and in its crises. Drama involves the symptoms of the crisis because it is not a medical disease to be cured but a problem in culture to be culturally recreated. Drama not punishment and the transcendental can release us from corruption and self-destruction. Only the mind can cure the mind.

A frightened child cannot create but begins to learn. It may turn fear into revenge. We punish others only when we have been prevented from being ourselves. We must be destroyed before we destroy. That is the aetiology of the good citizen. The child must acquiesce in society's injustice. Innocence knows that the demand for acquiescence – even as it succeeds – is society's injustice against its own innocence. As the child goes towards the world the gates close before it: it is our way of entering. There is no direct passage from egotism to altruism or from altruism to egotism – no isometric reflection. To survive we must be nursed by tragedy and glimpse the Tragic. But the Tragic has no place in the prison house – it is the ghost that haunts it in the prison's petty acts of cruelty and the prisoners' longings. There must be an apprenticeship of years before innocence can be performed as religion, racism, patriotism, exploitation, sentimentality, revenge, respectability, discipline, self-righteousness and corruption.

The consistencies of reality are the saving presence in chaos. We change as we learn to use the instrumental systems, to cultivate and manufacture. We are people of *this* world. The transcendental does not help us to live with the world of things. What use are prayers and magic to machines? God needs miracles – they are his *amour propre* – we do not. Only injustice and madness need the transcendental, reason does not. As our lives in the practical world become more rational, God becomes more vicious, sanctifying reaction (capital punishment, the wickedness of children, racial purity – fascists kneel at his altar) or is simply vulgar. When sixteen children aged five and six were massacred by a gunman in Scotland, a priest, dressed up in canonicals, told a congregation of children who had survived not to be afraid because God loved them. God is a model for all transcendental irresponsibility: wouldn't the bewildered children have wondered if God had loved the children who were killed? If churchmen, rulers, generals – all figures of authority – did not dress up in grotesque costumes like the mad in motley – and talk the wildest fantasies – then vulnerable people would not be driven out of their minds or support the blood-and-soil fantasies of extremists. They would not say that little children should be beaten – and in *that* world little children would not be shot. If you admit one jot of the transcendental the whole world is damned. Auschwitz, Hiroshima, Rwanda do not have their first origins in human depravity but in social respectability and social madness. When a bishop dresses up in his robes he is putting on a shroud that will be worn by his victims, little and great.

Administration combines organization and ownership. Things need not be unjustly owned but they must be used efficiently. Clearly society's story must always contain some reality, though not for the sake of plausibility: ideology flourishes on the incredible. In time all societies radically change. For a long while lies are on the side of truth. Lies make many truths work better. If they did not administration would not work. Fear or discipline would be so great that the mind would be incoherent and instrumental systems fail. Most people catch glimpses of the paradox of their lives, see each contradiction separately for what it is outside the social explanation. In time the efficiency of injustice runs out. Administration becomes so remote from the logic of things that it cannot cross the gap. We know things by their use. In time we see the emperor's old clothes are nakedness.

Changed sentiment will not create justice. Discontent must become knowledge and structure be changed. It is not enough to change effects, even when they are as extreme as starvation. Causes must be changed or they will continue to lead to disaster. The pre-real child's egotism is the imperative of the common need for justice. As the child enters the real world its egotism can become altruism. This possibility lies in reason and in imagination's altruism. Change is difficult. It must be from the transcendental to immanence. The neonate is immanent in its world and the pre-real child still has the possibility of immanence: when it creates the wood-block car the process is from imagination to the real world. But the process may be reversed, from the real world to the transcendental: man creates God. The child creates the world by its rational use of knowledge – society creates it irrationally. The child's egotistical seeking of justice is the rational use of what it knows, is prudential *and* existential. Egotism is its *idea* of justice. It is not an abstract idea because it is also behaviour. It is the child's innocence, its desire for justice not for self's sake but for the world's sake. When it finds that the world is different, that it is shared with others, that reality is not changed by magical anthropomorphizing – then its *idea* of the world changes. This is also its *idea* of its need for justice – so its need to seek justice changes to its need to seek to share the world. This becomes its egotistical imperative. The imperative changes with the child's situation. The need for justice is prior to the need for self, the latter is part of the former. Commonly we reverse this because we think justice is learnt, not created by existential need and coherence. Adults may separate the *idea* of the world from the *idea* of justice. This separation must be learnt. It is the origin of injustice.

Imagination is able to change and to know a new situation more quickly than reason can. Imagination is protean but logical, and justice does not temporize even when it is corrupt. Altruism cannot be imposed or learnt, it is created in imagination's desire for reason. Children pass through altruism before they are incorporated literally and metaphorically into society. If I want justice reason shows me I must share it. But society teaches us to obtain justice through power, violence and repression. So the child is faced with two choices. The first choice is to change justice into revenge – which is injustice in its state of madness. This itself has three stages. In crisis it is fascism, in times of change and apprehension it is reaction, and in the quiet times of the hegemony of common sense, it is conservatism. Conservatism is never at ease, it is a divided self papered-over (sometimes gift-wrapped) by complacency, diversion and entertainment. (To be at peace, a conservative should take up an absorbing but trivial hobby.) The second choice facing the child is rational altruism. In this imagination seeks to imagine the real. It is immanence, it observes the Tragic and creates. It is radical innocence.

It is an imperative of imagination to seek reason through experience. Radical altruism is not prudential or self-serving (which pre-real altruism unwittingly is) because it desires the just world. It is the human, existential imperative: in order to be others should *be*, and not as abstractions or in nature but in their social particularity. That is difficult. In the wilderness perhaps only the Tragic may keep us human. In unjust society our acts can be human only in intention – and even then only if the intention is radical. Otherwise they gloss and decorate the increasing human horror. Technology cannot save us, the machines have become the human irony. And transcendentalism no longer serves humanness. Religion is the effort made by the religious to change God's mind. Now he is dead. If he lived we could dismiss him, but his ghost haunts us and may still kill us.

Gandhi said that if his daughter were at risk of rape and he could not dissuade the rapist he would not kill him. He would kill his daughter to spare her shame. He was asked what he would do if he were in the plane flying the atom bomb to Hiroshima. He said he would look in the pilot's eyes. The question is a trick. Gandhi would not be in the plane. But his answer shows how his morality would work in extremity – and the coming Technomachia will be a time of extremity. Gandhi is radically innocent – but without reason. The *idea* of his innocence is transcendental. When we abandon reason imagination loses its logic.

Imagine we travel on a road and the road exists but we do not. We lie in pieces along the road as if dismembered, but as yet the pieces were never whole. The gaps between some of the pieces are long. As we go along the road we find pieces of ourself and assemble them. This image is imaginable but irrational. It is also rational but then unimaginable. That is the human paradox. There is a gap between the two understandings. The gap is the site of drama.

Drama

Drama is only initially concerned with the conflict between reason and imagination, society and justice – its deeper concern is why each is what it is, the logic of the interaction each imposes on the other. Their interaction impels the conflict into self and society. Imagination cannot lose the imperative for justice, it is the human mind's meaning – the logic of sanity *and* the logic of madness. If the mind loses this imperative it has no reason to be, consciousness loses its awareness. Imagination cannot lose its innocence even in corruption – that is why drama always invokes imagination, either in the ideology of, for example, war, or in theatre. To do this potently, impelled by innocence, theatre dramatizes situations critical to imagination's seeking for justice. It can do this without using the *idea*, the self-understanding, created by any particular imagination to *be* itself in the crisis which is dramatized. A play is specific in detail but general in import. Drama moves in the gap between reason and imagination, wood block and car. In art, imagination's intention is not to be itself but to understand reason. Reality is on neither side of the gap – it is the gap. As drama exists in the gap it is reality. In the gap the contingencies of reality, the difference between a king and an actor playing a king, have value but no Value. In – and in the relationships between – societies the two sides of the gap may be quiescent – then imagination randomly fantasizes or imagines itself in order to be untroubled by reason, and reason is fatigue, anomia, habit. When administration cannot maintain balance between the sides, each is disturbed. There is crisis – war, revolution, crime and panic too great for administration to use to its advantage.

Theatre need not necessarily (*by definition*) enter the gap. There may be theatre of fatigue, anomia, habit, diversion and static entertainment. But *by definition* theatre *may* intervene in the gap. It does so when impelled by the need for justice. Drama either changes the relation between reason and imagination in the audience's minds or confirms the relation. The response is from imagination (in its concern for justice) working through reason (its *idea* of justice). Theatre can make no direct appeal to reason – that would be like asking the mad to understand they are mad, as useful as asking the eyes to listen. But drama leaves no one indifferent, it either changes or confirms the audience's relation to justice or injustice. If it confirms a commitment to injustice it increases the self-repression needed to affirm the commitment – and this is movement towards crisis. Drama's effects on the audience become part of the conflict in society. Like matter, drama cannot disappear. Like water, it cannot be carved with a knife – cannot be shaped to dictate its effects. Drama is more a war than an execution.

Dramatic art relates imagination and reason not as abstractions but as two sources of knowledge, it relates the existing world and existential need. Simply, how we are in the world. Its imperative is imagination's need for justice. Unjust society coerces imagination into *use*, into mechanical reproduction and repetition. Drama incites freedom from this use, which imprisons individuals and reifies situations, but it can do this only by its own *use* of the individuals and situations in the drama. Drama is the logic of play. It is this logic – not the logic of reason – which frees the innocent and damns the reactionary. Art does not create freedom because we do not live in freedom, but it anticipates it. It can do this because the neonate structured in itself the logic of play when it created the world. It is logic because it observes the Tragic.

A wood block is made into a car, a car is not made into a wood block. That would be reductive and absurd – but it describes the process of fascism. Drama looks back in time, to when the self formed, in order to understand the future and enter it. What drama, any art, seeks to understand is not soul, psychosis, the transcendental, but the situation. Art is not eternal but *use*. What is seen as permanent in it is the foundation of the human situation: imagination and reason. If art were eternal its only use would be to coerce – that is, be God. People will always be individuals who react differently to a play because every imagination is different, but the need for justice is common to all people.

Drama cannot talk sanity to the mad. But it may detach reason and imagination from their bind in situations where there must be existential reason. This discloses the gap. In all daily life there is a difference between what we do and what we wrongly say and imagine we do. In all reality there is unreality. Reality is always temporary. To act we need expectation. Expectation is character. We are what we expect. But we also need a human image, not of an individual or even of a social being but of an existential expectation. It is not a static image but a process. Drama creates this image. Philosophy related the mind to the world, art creates the world – it is imagination trespassing on its own property, on its map. Instrumental reality – our dealings with the systems of things – approaches us as if all things sought to be works of art, they trespass on the habit of the self imposed on us by routine and administration.

A river reflects objects in light – an object reflected in another object. The human mind is not an object. Socialist-realism wrongly tries to use it as an object – and in that it shares an aim with religion. Religion sees people as God's objects, socialist-realism as history's objects. Instead, it is as if we were objects that seek their reflection in the gap – as if we had to seek it in darkness. The world's objects give pleasure or pain but do not satisfy our need for justice. In the gap we have one elemental activity – to seek justice. The rest is decency, sloth or barbarism. Seeking justice is not an objective consequence of our being (as a square's fourth side is of its) but the expression of our self. It divides us from all objects and pre-human minds. What are called the laws of nature and physics are only consistencies, the universe is a giant habit. A law must create danger. It must be possible for it to be broken. Physics cannot break its consistencies, a broken *thing* is another *thing*. We are made human by the only law that could be in this or any universe in which there were self-conscious beings: we must seek justice. This is not a psychological desire, it is structural in our situation: the mind cannot be coherent if imagination does not seek justice. And it is contingent on this that if we do not seek justice we will be destroyed in the Technomachia.

Observing the law means taking responsibility for the world. Only drama invokes the law. Without drama we cannot know if the law is observed and we are being human. Crises (wars, starvation, chaos in instrumental systems) lead only to defeat or survival. No crisis can of itself produce humanness. Humanness must be conscious of itself (it is experience, not innate being). In a crisis in unjust society there are always victims and victimizers (even if the victimizers seem remote from the crisis and the victims) and they give the crisis different meanings. The ordinary, the uneventful, automatically teaches us more than a crisis automatically, of itself, can teach us. We may learn more in a day in which nothing happens than a day in which everything happens. Crises confuse (the priest preached confusion to the children who survived the massacre) but the ordinary daily round turns to us in its hidden distress. Crises are the source of humanness only when imagination is itself dramatized as crisis. Otherwise crises do not happen in *reality*, the heaped bodies do not know they are dead and the victimizers do not know what they do to their victims. Drama deals with crises in order to change our daily life.

Drama must have a stage. Its stage is the gigantic habit of the universe on which people act. Drama is not transcendental because the universe is not transcendental: the edge of the universe is an ordinary place. If drama were transcendental it would be an instrument of violence. All transcendentalism is violence because whatever takes away responsibility from humans does violence to them. Religion, patriotism, racism – all transcendentalism seeks objects outside the world to govern the world. God is an object not a being because all self-conscious beings are subject to the law of drama: seek justice. Religion postulates a God prior to the law in order to create it. Otherwise God has no raison d'être (except efficiency). In religion justice is what God ordains – and so, strictly, religion is a bad habit, and habit is a form of violence.

Imagination is not of itself creative. Art does not express imagination, or imagination express justice – it seeks it. Imagination is not transcendental. Imagination also expresses triviality, destructiveness, genocide, serial killing, torture, cowardice, treachery, pettiness – imagination may be corrupt by ideology (the abuse of reason). In theatre sometimes things are justified as 'coming from the imagination'. The justification presupposes that art is the revelation of an immaculate presence, or the reflection of the mundane in the silver waters of Elysian streams. Performance art, happenings, ritual, mystic drama, primal screams, dream time, 'drama and the art of the warrior', the Absurd, theatre of cruelty, post-modern kitsch, the use of light, sound, music to produce 'concrete' effects from abstract causes, to use emotion in the place of reason instead of using reason (the meaning of the situation) to create emotion – such things have less to do with art than the honest band at Auschwitz. They fake transcendence and hidden meaning, their often frantic gyrations merely return imagination to the routine of habit. Art is *use*, imagination's engagement with reason, with instrumental systems, with the practical social. Art does not replace reason, it incites it. Art is not revelation, there is nothing to reveal, everything is already seen – what is missing is meaning. Imagination is often the resort of the overexcited, the mountebank, the incompetent – as useful as a palmist reading the palm of a corpse. Imagination is creative only when it expresses reason and its search for reason.

Transcendentalism derives from the child's pre-real world. Religion, patriotism, spiritualism, revenge, New Ageism are forms of childhood misbehaviour fossilized in adults. The child's tree spoke. In adult transcendentalism an object outside the world speaks: the object creates humankind by speaking to it. This repeats the creative pattern of the child's wood block: the child spoke and the wood block was a car. The adult's wood block is 'nothingness' – it is turned into God. The child created so as to expel nothingness from the world – adults bring nothingness into the world to control the world. In the gap the child plays with puppets and toys to humanize itself, create itself – adults put emptiness at the self's centre. This is the destructive isomorphism of violence and transcendence, sacred and satanic, mysticism and militarism. The child imitates the sound of the car wheels and horn. God is an imitation man: we alienate our fear and reify it as God's anger – it is more comfortable to fear God than to fear nothingness. The human transcendental haunts the gap: in it God's ghost builds prisons, executes, persecutes and acquires. All these things are the imitation of nothingness.

Our knowledge of reality is limited. We use its objects and systems before we understand it. But this ignorance is not our danger. We are mad – medically or socially – not because we seek knowledge but because we must seek justice and so reality. Society is a real system (carpentry) and a transcendentalism (Christ is a carpenter). Because it is also the latter, reality is used to enslave us. Ownership does not free us but integrates us into instrumental systems.

The neonate creates Value by observing the Tragic. Otherwise there would always be joy, and then there could be innocent joy in killing. Pre-real children find Value in all things. The instrumental systems of reality provide only value. The Value which imagination knows is mortal, but mortality is our means of existence and the use of value. Drama is necessary to the seeking of justice. The seeking must be imaged because the map is a plan – not a plan to locate place but to perform process. Even when it is reified by the social situation character is still expectation – and so imagination anticipates the past when, in the present, a past anticipation is proved false – so memory anticipates the future so that imagination may create a living praxis and a shape for drama. Hegel interprets this as the philosophy of the Spirit – but that is a slanted aspiration of the pre-real in which things are not created but are the poseurs of ideology. The owl of Minerva does not fly only at dusk. It flies up – startled – in the day and the sound of its wings are the death-rattle of history. The seeking of justice cannot be known if it is not dramatized, because justice is not a transcendence but is created as the child creates the world. In drama 'use' proves itself by recreating the radicalness of innocence and the burden of its responsibility – which even the unjust glimpse, if only in fear and anger. Hegelianism is, stubbornly, transcendence and it glimpses the owl in the light of the fire that consumes it. It is the same with the fire of revolutions – philosophical and political – which do not understand imagination's logic: they consume knowledge.

Creativity does not come from instrumental curiosity but from the need for justice. No curiosity is without that need. The need requires us to seek to understand reality and amend suffering. Because it is a need axiomatic to consciousness, 'moral feeling' is only a consequence. The need may be corrupted to consent to cruelty. In unjust society any need may invoke its opposite because the relation between reason and imagination, need and understanding, is volatile. Unjust society imposes corruption by law, ignorance by learning, tyranny by freedom. If authority were complete society would be like a stone statue which could put us in its pocket. In static societies of little technological innovation, authority is almost able to impose its story on creativity. But unjust society is unstable. Tyranny protects itself against its weakness by the chaos of discipline in which the living take on the malignancy of death. Mortality is my weakness. But if I am weak all things are weak and pass. But no unjust society can abolish the Tragic and its mortality, wounds and questions. At most it romanticizes it, but romanticism degenerates into farce. Even theocracy cannot administer death but only impose it. It must rebuild hell every day.

In unjust society you must know you are in prison before you can want to be free. If not you are content with revenge on the other prisoners. Worldly justice was imperfect, divine justice immaculate. The paradox is that justice is always innocent and so the desire for it always pure. Images of the crucifixion showed the state's soldiers as executioners and guards. The mourning sinners at the crucifixion were exonerated, the soldiers were not: they even gambled at the foot of the cross, and gambling, of course, is a serious moral peccadillo . . . The Renaissance could not convert the Church and administration to paganism. First it had to paganize the human image in Christian art. The new freedom was imaged in healthy bodies in place of the diseased, emaciated, mutilated bodies of the saints. Martyrs became athletes. The new human image was needed because people had to live robustly to use the new technology. This freedom made possible the predestination of the Industrial Revolution. The living were predestined to heaven or hell when they died, and to their social class while they lived. The desire for justice still haunted society, but the weak could not create it (they must submit to injustice to work and eat) and the strong dare not contemplate it. The impasse led to the determinism which served imperialism. Imperialism tries to convert the value of exploited labour into the Value of mortality. Take up the white man's burden, take up the cross, take up your bed and walk. The medieval malaise changed to modern robust barbarism.

The Technomachia

The story has become unstable. Till now technology has innovated slowly. But now technology is the Technomachia. It is as if the giant stepped out of the book and wrenched it from the reader's hands. In the past technology was a human benefit, now it begins to be a human danger. The Technomachia needs constant change, a market as innovative as modern warfare. It abolished seasons and the calendar of feast days and degrades geography and climate. The ancient justification of injustice was the administration needed to survive scarcity. Now injustice is justified by the benefits of prosperity: consumerism and law-and-order – but the latter only protects us from the chaos caused by injustice. Consumerism cannot spare us the terrors of innocence. We follow our fathers' footsteps and are lost. In the past natural disaster, climate, malnutrition, epidemics and the fanaticism caused by crisis threatened our survival. In the common struggle to survive ruled and rulers were tenuously united. They prayed to the same God if not in the same church. Their shared struggle created the image of Utopia in heaven or earth. You cannot have a private Utopia for the same reason that you cannot have a private God. You cannot have justice for yourself by taking it from others. In need, people united to secure need. Of course in unjust society the evil, the outsiders, would be kept outside Utopia. But the changing of egotism into the aspiration to altruism was profoundly implicit in the shared human image. Now it is not. Modern abundance produces the conditions of scarcity because technology increases only at the cost of producing the social and psychological consequences of scarcity. And because each consumer consumes privately altruism and Utopia are abolished.

When needs were not met the provider (God) was beseeched or the polluter (Oedipus, witches) was excised. Technology abolishes need and with it the justification for unjust ownership and administration. All needs could be met. What stands between us and our freedom? The

Technomachia. The Technomachia is created by the new technology
and the technological economy. The Technomachia is not a Wellsian war
between machines or machines and men. It is the combination of
technological giantism and the relentless activity of the economy. The
economy must expand to produce investment to save it from collapse.
The sheer weight of the Technomachia threatens and oppresses us. It is
a war in which the greatest danger would be peace, in which victory is
the administration of disaster. Peace is war: the Technomachia is our
way of life. In the bewildered imagination's existential metaphors,
investing money in the economy is the equivalent of libating sacrificial
blood. The imperative to consume – and expand – comes from the way
we own and use instrumental systems. But imagination requires its own
impulse to consume – fear is not enough because it may lead to stupor
and inactivity. In the past, need sustained the economy, but when there
is abundance new needs must be invented: these are wants. The old need
for the transcendental is gone, yet it was that need that also created
humanness, it was the crooked stick on which it was propped. But you
do not beseech God for a better computer. Structurally, *wants* cannot
function as *needs*. Wants invoke a new transcendental, not to reward the
good – technology does that – but to explain the bad and justify a
crusade against it. An American state governor was asked why thirteen
schoolchildren had been shot by two schoolboys who then shot
themselves. He said the two schoolboys were evil. Fine – you do not
have to look for a cause – in effect you blame it on God (though I do not
expect the governor to understand that). We no longer need to
understand ourselves, it is enough that we understand technology. To
survive we no longer need to be human. At the end of the
Enlightenment consumption replaces thought.

Technology will accommodate the ecological and human debris of our
injustice (the latter more successfully than the former). As the
Technomachia grows the tenates of reaction will become respectable.
Fascism will not need its old icons. Politically and morally it can appear
as democratic populism. It will be the story of the twenty-first century.
Western consumerism needs a philosophy of evil: its prisons are the
eating houses where it consumes its enemies – in consumerism
everything is a metaphor of consumption. If humanness were a matter of
genetically secured instinct (or even if humanness were genetically
contested) survival would be easier. But humanness is a story,
imagination understanding itself in its place in reality and so creating
reality. It *was* a communal purpose, we were social beings. Consumerism
isolates us. Others are to consume not so that their needs may be satisfied

but to sustain the economy so that my wants may be met. Consumer democracy is a crowd in which no one looks into another's face.

We cannot choose wants because they are not existential desires. Wants are manufactured in mass by the Technomachia. Need created images of a future Utopia – and this was part of the way present needs were met. Imagination created humanness out of the suffering and waste of scarcity, and out of this the transcendental was created. It was not a quirk of fancy or an evolutionary accident, it was part of the deliberate creation of culture. Even destitute communities celebrated festivals, dressed and decorated the living and the dead and created art. These rituals created the 'self' and anticipated the ideal. Culture grew from the way we met our basic needs. Increasingly the Technomachia makes images out of images, tenuating their meaning till they are foam without waves. Now we need wants but do not want them – really our wants are our machines' needs. We are being integrated into the process by which the ancient impulse that created humanness is now put to the making of perfect machines. The discipline of evolution is needs not wants. Now we *need* wants to help us forget the terrors of innocence, the knowledge of the suffering our injustice brings to others. Now we need to be human because we want to be neurotic.

Imperial Rome took work away from its workers. Instead of farming corn in Italy, it imported it from African colonies and distributed it to the workless. People did not need a God to save them from harvest blight and scarcity and in doing so integrate their work and life into the seeking of justice. Instead image became spectacle, a distraction without human purpose: the Roman games. Utopia had come down to earth, so it was administratively necessary for the Caesers to become Gods (and most of them had the courtesy also to be mad). Heaven has no use for innocence, but it must have a hell and this turns innocence's fear into revenge and cruelty. The Christian hell was in the imagination – but Rome had power and so the Roman hell, like its heaven, must be on earth: the Colosseum. The relationship between imagination and reason had changed, innocence could not seek justice as part of the way needs were met. Justice cannot be sought abstractly or even in practical activity, such as prison reform, devoted to it – it must be part of the whole of human life. In Rome it was as if the empire became a human machine, masses of people functioning without a human purpose. Christianity was said to be a religion of slaves. It became a religion of emperors when administration could not maintain itself through bread, spectacles and army but needed the iron fist of the transcendental God.

The Technomachia invents wants to stimulate dissatisfactions. Our needs are limited and the more profound they are the more limited. But we must want and consume to sustain the economy's proliferation. Technology could abolish need but does not because it does not create justice. Wants give us a new bizarre purity, a mechanical perfection, almost a symptom of the machines' satisfaction with us. The Technomachia is the new father and we are its obedient children.

The imperative to consume makes us our machines' domestic slaves. Because wants are stimulated by images and spectacles, in place of the human image we have images which machines – if they had imaginations – would imagine for themselves. We are what machines 'imagine' us to be, what they need us to be. We are their reality. We imagine on their behalf, it is a service we provide for them. Instead of imaginations they have mechanical catalogues of eternity, sites for the Technomachia to invade and occupy. The line – the chain – of consumption runs mechanically and administratively from machines to humans, and the line of imagination is the reverse: from humans it is transmitted mechanically to machines. As machines have no imaginations but create our 'lifestyles', we become our machines' fictions or the dreams the dead have. To have their own imaginations machines would have to pass through the stages of neonate, pre-real childhood and so on. But a living brain and its memory installed in a machine would together be a human being – perhaps disabled but not schizophrenic. Humanness comes from imagination not the body. The humanizing line – the line along which our humanness evolved – runs from consumption, through imagination to humanness. The Technomachia reverses the line's direction and so it cannot produce justice, instead it evolutionarily opposes the totality of 'people and objects' to justice – the evolutionary line which produced our humanity has now been parasitized by machinery to perfect itself. We are our machines' raw material, their evolutionary environment. We deceive ourselves if we think an act of will could reverse the line again: its logic is anchored in the foundations from which it starts.

Reality has become artificial. We are at the mercy of the arbitrary. The logic of the arbitrary is that it has memory but no past. It is as if the mirage created the desert around it. Justice must always be refined as its situation changes. Law is not refined but multiplied, or distilled to be more vicious. We will live in prisons or affluent ghettos and seek to avoid all semblance of life: it will be too painful to be human.

Justice exists because of the practical in life and its instrumental systems. Wants do not invoke this practicality, only the permanent busyness of machines. When people were still at the mercy of the real they prayed to God the Rain Maker for rain. Technology destroys the

relationship between prayer and God because technology is now the rain maker. Now prayer does not make us human and practical but dangerous and bizarre. Technology solves its problems with more technology. In the Technomachia we must submit to this imperative. By living for wants we create a universal negative transcendence. We consume 'nothingness' and are addicted to it.

We do not live now but pass through 'lifestyles'. These are manipulated and changed to provoke wants. Their dynamic is that each should be remote from at least those others immediately preceding it. We do not have lifestyles, they have us and turn us into their puppets. Lifestyles do not embody the logic of the need for justice. Images of justice embody newness and innocence not novelty. Styles used to come from the process of life and expressed historic humanness. Lifestyles do not come from our life and embody stages in humanness, instead they are imposed on it and exhibit stages in technology. We are adverts for our machines. Yet we cling to lifestyles as if they were our 'self'. Justice was not simply the means by which in time all needs would be met, it defined the Tragic. Why do we *want* to be happy, not *want* to die, *want* community? Instinct cannot provide these wants, they are part of story – not inert motive but reason. The Greeks said 'It is better not to be born. But should this calamity befall you it is better to die quickly.' That is a tragic irony. There can be only one response to it: we do not *want* to live – we *need* to live, and that must mean that we need to be human, need justice, need community, and that these needs go beyond all wants and the trivialities of life and death. There is one law: seek justice – and only one need: to be human. To need is human, to want is to be lost. To need justice (not *want* justice for *me*) means I need the world to be just even when I am dead – especially *then*. How else can I bear to live now?

In the past administration was stable and sustained its story for centuries. The story fostered our relationship to the unchanging natural world. The first story was the pre-real fable of the magic time. People believed seers spoke to trees and animals. The second story came from the real world. It was epic and combined history and myth to span the values of time with timeless Value. The third story was religion. The fourth story is ours. If it were stable it would use technology to force us into the fanaticism of clinging to the past and there would be intensity without development. But our 'story' is not a story. Instead there must be constant stochastic change – a story with no structure except the ability to change. It is without meaning, even without the symmetry of paradox. There is cacophony instead of coherence. It will create in us a profound need for our situation to become worse. We cannot be satisfied with the cheap trickery of devil-worship, the squalid, superficial games of injustice – we desire to confront the Tragic. But we have nothing to offer it. We cannot offer it our humanness because we have lost it. If we have nothing to offer Tragedy we *are* nothing. We will go tearlessly weeping into the desert and the sand will turn to glass at our presence.

Humanness

We learn from history but the wrong lessons. We learn to avoid the dangers that will not be ours. In future there will be no structural need for rabid anti-Semitism, the immolation of heretics and witches. Deviations of thought do not matter when no one thinks, you cannot offend against an idea when there is no orthodoxy. Freedom of speech is anodyne when speech is logorrhoea. For centuries society feared the anarchy of mind that led to mobs' violence and administration's cruelty. Now it begins to seek these things. Social mores that seemed as lasting as if carved in granite, as unchangeable as if our forebears' gravestones foretold our future, now change as if written on water. Marriage, parental authority, organization of work, sartorial class codes, personal identities, sexual customs – all change, not because reason replaces them with its ways and ideas but because we have forgotten why we needed them.

In unjust society deviance has a positive function. To enter such a society innocence must be corrupted. Corrupted innocence's chosen victims are the deviant – society kept its outcasts at its centre because by persecuting them it made itself legitimate. Imagination fulfils its corruption in revenge. But all corruption is self-alienation – we are all deviants at heart. In unjust society deviance is the practice of freedom. The Technomachia still structurally needs deviance. In injustice, the meaning self-consciousness gives to its acts is always the opposite of the motive for which they were done, because repression creates what is repressed: innocence and its anger. So revenge is called justice, the cruelty of racism, love of country, and so on. The human being must change places with his deepest desire in order to keep some respect for our present way of living. And yet this is a profound debasement. But we almost need this debasement to take place – only a sliver of our humanity is still left to stand between self and that need. But the need is strong because we wish to be decent and human in community with others, and so we cling to the travesty which passes for decency and humanness in our society. It is as if it were a need to change places with oneself, to become corrupt not out of fear but out of the need to be human. Perhaps that will be all that is left to us.

All revenge is revenge against the self. In imagination the victimizer changes places with the victim. Hence the victimizer's insatiable rage. You can only totally destroy the victim by destroying your need for him or her – that is, by destroying yourself. Revenge is insatiable not because it provokes the cycle of revenge but because no act of revenge is radical enough. In its raging – but passing – atrocious morality the pre-real child would, if it could, destroy the world. It cannot – but the Technomachia gives us the means to destroy it. Injustice is radical when it is not restricted by need. It is not only an administrative contrivance for sustaining communal inequalities. It is radical because imagination expresses it, and imagination has no natural reason and so no limit. Its fanaticism is in its search for reason. But society is now irrational. We lose the (partial) rationality of transcendence, but have not learnt the total rationality of immanence. Medieval popes or heretics armed as we are would have destroyed the world – it would have been their transcendental duty to do so to save heresy from itself. Our nihilism is as dangerous as their faith. Mental structures are founded on the repression of their opposites. The energy to repress comes from the energy of the repressed, so that what comes to be socially obligatory is what is privately forbidden. Our acts are haunted by their opposites. The more we repress the more we create the need to repress, because repression creates what is repressed: innocence and its anger at being repressed. In this way innocence is transferred to society as social madness. Social madness makes possible – and often obligatory – what society forbids in the individual. This is why people change and suddenly are bewildered by what they find themselves doing. Technomachia makes the whole social and personal structure more volatile. In future people will not be astonished at what they have done, it will be as if they do not notice what they are doing.

In unjust society the need for justice becomes the dogmatic and belligerent commitment to injustice, and the need for injustice becomes revenge. All punishment is revenge. The unjust require a victim. As the victim is also the self, the victim should be as innocent as possible. This allows the victimizer to identify with the victim and, because the identification is denied, makes the lust for revenge ruthless in order to try unsuccessfully to enforce the denial. In Christian societies anti-Semitism was the ideal revenge. The Jews were guilty of killing God, yet the victims chosen were obviously innocent of this. In the sixteenth and seventeenth centuries witches were the ideal victims. Technology and science provided the new energy of the Industrial Revolution. This destabilized society but at the same time made it possible to strengthen its injustices and put new classes of people into the niches of its social structures. The administration had to understand and control the new scientific power, but witchcraft was an individual power, scientifically unknowable and administratively uncontrollable. It led to the anarchy and licentiousness that were already feared as a consequence of the impact of the new scientific power. Witches' power made them guilty, and as almost all of them were frail old women or children they had the necessary innocence. They were the perfect victims – that is why the witch-hunt was so ferocious. In one day a hundred witches were burnt in a German town square. At the end of the day the surrounding houses were covered in human grease.

For the Nazis the appropriate victims were again the Jews. Nazism is parasitic on the past and its pagan transcendence. Capitalism destroys the past, Nazism tries to restore the past. It can do this only by using the power of the modern world. It wants union with capitalism but also revenge on it. Jews may be seen as arch-capitalists, so they are guilty – but most of them, especially in the East, were poor – so they had the necessary innocence. Persecutions and pogroms seem to come from nowhere but really they come from every pore of the body politic. Auschwitz is a logically impossible place. In this sense there was no holocaust. There could never be a reason for it. It is too wicked for humans to do. Yet it took place in history because it was the logic of imagination that it should. Auschwitz was the Tragic of human innocence: the innocent killed by the innocent but socially mad.

Deviance protects the social structure. This is not an administrative conspiracy, it is the psyche's need. The psyche is the interrelated structure of reason and imagination, how we live the human paradox and create and survive chaos. Catastrophe comes not from instinctual or theological wickedness but from good intentions. Anti-Semitism, witch-hunting, capitalist wars – *all* are still imaginable but they are not our danger. They no longer have structural use and they would hinder consumption. The ideal victims for consumer democracy are criminals.

In unjust society crime is the criminal's way of acting justly, of practising innocence. The motive for all crimes (as laws define them) is innocence. A crime has two meanings. First, a criminal understands crime in terms of value – he steals a victim's property. When he attacks the victim what he attacks is the victim's power to consume and own – even if the victim is a tramp. In consumer society everything is understood in terms of consuming and owning (the power to consume) –

this is the meaning in consumer society of 'human rights'. Criminals often consent to be punished because their crimes are against value. Many criminals passionately support law-and-order, capital punishment, flogging and imprisonment. This support has the psychological advantage of freeing the criminal from needing to understand his crime – guilt is easier to bear than understanding. But there is a second meaning to crime: it is an assertion of Value, of the criminal's right to be at home in a just world. Property is theft. In unjust society the owner steals from those who do not own and are therefore owned. This creates the confusion that leads to chaos and violence: property is murder. Crime is the criminal's way of punishing the unjust society for stealing from him. But the criminal's violence is impotent. It is meant to achieve a practical end – theft – but also a metaphorical end, to take possession of the metaphorical: Value. But it can only possess the practical, the property: value. To possess the metaphorical – the power to redescribe what is done – ideological power is needed – and this is the prerogative of administration, laws and the transcendental: for instance, the state might order the criminal to attack its enemy because that is God's will. Another way to possess the power of the metaphorical, the power to redescribe, is radical innocence's occasional power to change the real, to redramatize it – but unjust society restricts this. Because the criminal *acts* metaphorically but without ideological power, he is the story's villain. It is the difference – in another situation – between the one who confesses and the priest with the power to exonerate. At least religion dabbles in tragedy, but law is pure melodrama.

Confounded by common sense and transcendentalism, and his own confused promptings, the criminal moves between the two meanings of crime. We must accept responsibility for our acts – but also for their meaning. Society's meaning is given by injustice not by its law. Really the criminal is as innocent and corrupt as the judge, jury and law that try him: they are all bound together in ignorance of the human condition. When understanding is trapped in story, when common sense displaces imagination, when social madness dominates consciousness – how can the situation be explained? The sea is the net the fish are in. Society's injustice comes closest to being justified not because we are instinctively violent and devious but because – given the two meanings of crime – the result is the same: chaos. Only a fool would open the prisons tomorrow but reform or a revolution that changes the legal definition of value but does not embody Value in the rest of its acts – fails.

Crime is the criminal's appeal to the innocence lost by the righteously corrupt. Witch-hunters and anti-Semites took revenge on their own longing for the innocence they had fled out of fear and prudence. As compensation for their efforts – and to put them in its power – administration gave them the power and authority to persecute innocence. Imagination is its own betrayer – the righteous corrupt are paranoid about themselves, the mad cannot trust themselves. Practically, the criminal is socially reactionary – metaphorically, he is incorruptible, inviolable in his innocence. The law-abiding take revenge on this incorruptibility.

Law and prison are straightforward street-corner common sense. That is, they are socially mad. They – not crime – will destroy us. In America, two decades ago there were under two million prisoners. Now there are over six million. More than three thousand prisoners are waiting to be executed. Recently a prisoner was executed for murdering his parents when he was sixteen. His other relatives pleaded that he should not be pardoned. They watched his execution. One complained that the method did not cause the prisoner to suffer enough. When President Clinton was a state governor he said he 'always went home for an execution'. It is not what the child meant when it asked for justice to make the world its home. If we understood the meaning of what the president said, or of putting on make-up and choosing what to wear for an execution and afterwards celebrating it in a restaurant – we would understand social madness and its corruption.

Great persecutions have small beginnings. A witch cures warts, a Jew lends his neighbour a few coins. Then a woman comes to the witch to be cured of barrenness and a sovereign asks a Jew for a loan. Imagination must radically redramatize reality before there can be pogroms. The enlightenment's science and technology depended on reason, but the witch-hunters were as irrational as they claimed their victims to be. Fascism intended to do what it said its victims intended to do: take over the world. The victim owns – through unjust society – what the criminal intended to own. In unjust society there is a practical difference between blackmail-money and a salary, large or small, but metaphorically there is no difference. The combination of practical and metaphorical, act and its meanings, cause our problem. In morality the metaphor is real, the practical imaginary, and we live metaphorically, even when the immediate cause is practical. A starving man practically steals to eat, metaphorically he steals for justice.

The distance between innocence and throwing a brick through a Jewish shopkeeper's window (or any immigrant's window) is vast – the whole human problem is in it: the fear and loneliness of innocence, the relentless effort needed to corrupt it, the conviviality of the corrupt, the dogmatism of the transcendental. The difference between breaking the window and the ovens and heaped bodies of the Holocaust is small – a matter of administration's fidgeting with lists and forms. Disasters come unawares. One day we dress up to watch an execution, one day the houses in the town square are coated in human grease, one day the air is so full of ash the camp guard must cover his cup with his hand to protect his coffee, and one day we realize that the ash from a holocaust would make a good fertilizer and provide a reasonable profit for the small effort required. One day we may wake up and ask why.

Drama concerns objects and our relation to them. They are parts of the instrumental systems of the world in which imagination seeks its home. To this extent a tree is not nearer to nature, more natural, than a cup. All objects have value and Value, practical use and metaphor. The bones of soldiers killed in Napoleonic wars were dug up, shipped to England, ground in mills and scattered as fertilizer on the fields of the new Model Agriculture created in the Industrial Revolution. The bone fertilizer had value. As bones that came from a life of crawling, growing, labouring, playing, begetting, enlisting, fighting, killing, dying – belonging to human, mortal life – they had Value. Breaking the bones by cannon shot and grinding them down in mills increased their value. But Value is not destroyed by value. When the bones are reduced to value, their Value increases. It is increased by the enemy who breaks them, the iron masters who make cannon to break them, peasants who dig them up, merchants who buy them at knock-down prices, mill masters who grind them, and labourers who scatter them on the fields and harvest the crops to serve on their children's plates. Immanence multiples Value. What happens has Value because it is told as story by imagination. In this story of bones and fertilizer, there is the structure of all drama and art: the seeking of Value in value, of justice in immanence.

In the Second World War some Japanese wished to treat prisoners of war as objects – human encumbrances to be used. They called them 'wood blocks'. That is not the absence of imagination but its corruption, imagination in the state of ownership. Eventually reality forces humanness on self-conscious minds or destroys them. The destruction follows from the breaking of the one law – it is the inevitable verdict of any universe in which there are material objects and self-consciousness. That is the granite law of justice and no judge may rescind it.

Future catastrophe will not begin in social breakdown. It will come from whatever is needed to keep society running in an orderly way. We will not be led into catastrophe by charistmatics or by demogogues shouting on balconies. They belong to the past. The Technomachia is faceless. Communities will be divided. People will live in rich ghettos or prisons, both as big as cities. They will be administered efficiently. The violence needed will pass as normal. Wars will not be between nations. Each nation will wage the Technomachia against itself. Fighting will be formalized into execution. The consumer economy has no structural need of justice and as long as it can administer crime efficiently society has no need of humanness.

It will be enough if we forget our humanity for a little while – a few days – in fact we need only be distracted for a moment – and we live in an age of distractions. We will not try to return to it or look for it, we will have forgotten it. Its last remains will be taken from us as a common-sense measure of administrative convenience, as simply as waiters brush crumbs from a table. We will not wake up in ruins, there will be none. The ghettos and prisons will be well maintained. We will not concern ourselves with how we lost our humanness. We will not know we have lost it. When humanness goes it is not missed. Only humanness could miss humanness. We will be like those who dress up to see an execution. How can you tell those who willingly watch someone being killed they are corrupt?

In the past transcendentalism reminded us of our humanness. We were God's children, children of the motherland, the people of the sea or mountains or plains. Now we are the people of the market. The market's dynamic is not the search for humanness – it is the imperative to consume. We must submit to this imperative not in order to live but to survive – living is a luxury the affluent cannot afford. Now we have no structural reason to be human. This seems an exaggeration. The disasters of the last hundred years seem an exaggeration. But history never exaggerates. Who imagined the ashes of Auschwitz or the brick wastelands of Hiroshima and Nagasaki? Wait a little while and the unthinkable becomes inevitable, the impossible becomes commonplace. Do not imagine we could not walk home from Shopping City and calmly pass the blockhouse and pit. It would be a matter of lifestyle.

Drama involves the audience's imagination and reason in story. It can make the story objective for the audience, give them unavoidable responsibility and choice. But now the institutions of drama are corrupt. The market almost monopolizes drama. It saturates daily life with the brutality of common sense and the metaphysics of corruption. It does not ask what justice is but obsessively repeats the law. Its concern is the certainty of guilt not the paradox of innocence. It is the drama of social madness, less intelligent than child's play. The market requires the abolition of the human image and the humanizing process. The child would not give up its hand, we give up our humanness because we do not know what it is. Everything changes. The Technomachia does not create the ruins and graves of past wars. Instead it creates ghosts who have not even had the dignity of dying. Our death will be taken from us and we will be required to live. The heaps of bodies will come later, of course, but they will be refuse to clean away. The Tragic would vanish into God's grave. The human would end.

Everything changes except the newborn child. It lies protected in its citadel of ignorance. The unjust cannot reach it to turn its innocence into error. But perhaps it will be possible to change the human genotype. That would be the triumph of the Technomachia. A new eugenics, the manufacture of the genetically-modified human being: the GMH. It would be the crime of the twenty-first century.

We can remain human only by being radical. The child's radicalism enables it to create the world. 'Turn the other cheek.' This is not radical enough. The contradictory sadomasochism of the New Testament will not help us. There is no God to think on our behalf. There is only the market. We must combine radical imagination with reason. We could understand innocence and corruption and not be bound together in social madness. We could see the emptiness of the transcendental. Imagination could make materialism immanent. We could come closer to the world. We could recreate ourselves. It is not the creator's – the writer's – job to compromise, that is the job of manufacturers. We must be more radical. When manufacturers compromise, they change our dreams. When creators do not compromise they change reality.

(1998)

Lear War

As I lay dying on the wooden floor of the station waiting room
I understood again
Sun shone in the grit in the peasants' footprints in the dust on the boards
Trains passed
In the corner of the window a spider jerked like a stone trapped in a catapult
And I understood that the rails came from nowhere and go nowhere
And there is no victory in war

I am dead but the good clay does not cover me
My grave is an open wound
They bring children to its side
I reach out of the grave and sprinkle them with earth
They call it baptism

Once when the old were dead they dreamed no more
When the flesh had rotted from bone they felt no pain
I am dead – I dream – my bones bleed
I am the afterbirth of death
Anger is a fever that keeps me alive
The serpent's fang burns in its mouth
I am angry at their crimes and follies
When will they learn that war has no victory?
They weave a garment around a stain

Once I was killed in battle
I ran between the divided guns and tanks
I pleaded for peace – my shirt and trousers fluttered like ragged flags
The giant butchers came and torched the stumps of the legless man
I lay on the field
My body was black with anger
When the war-dogs found me they would not eat
They slunk away howling like men

At another time I gathered berries from trees in an orchard
I put them in a basket of woven rush
A madman sprang up in a thicket

Gaunt as a burnt-out truck
His hair was a wire mop
He grinned and cut his throat with a knife
No no I cried
Blood ran down the grass blades and in the rims of his toenails
His mouth was an iron girder twisting in fire

At another place I met a woman sitting beside a ditch
By her feet a great bundle of linen as if she were washerwoman to a city
Her fingers knotted and knotted her hair
Knotted and knotted
Her fingers were white and on them she wore a ring made of a hoop of hair
Her hair was black and wet with ditch water
And shone like the eyes of men staring behind a blindfold
Tied to a stake

When will they learn that war has no victory?
Their enemy's death is not victory
Nor his ruined house – nor his wasted fields – nor his looted store
The fire-scorched mattress
The broken chair
The roofless walls
These are the victors' spoils
And the parade when they march to the beat of crutches striking on coffins
Lunatics' music

They weave a garment around a stain
They are the enemy who lays waste their city – who cuts off their limbs
Neighbour deals unjustly with neighbour
There are rich and poor
One is better fed than another
And one wears rags and his head is haunted by holy tunes
They search for reasons
Split matter in cells – raise up gases and search in them for phantoms
But the map of war is on their streets
It is the rags – the empty tins held out for coins on the steps of the subway
The abandoned lot behind hoardings where drunks sleep their faces made
    foul by spittle
The leering young – the frightened old
They do not see it
Yet at their approach birds scavenging offal fly up and flutter about their

heads red–clawed and screaming oracles
War will follow war
There will be no peace till they live justly
They search but God himself could not tell them more than the beggar they
  passed today in the street has told them

Now the children who came to bury me are old
Wizened – grey – crouched with heads on knees as still as stones in a desert
Spiders spin on their faces
They did not play
And the lessons they wrote in the dust have been blown away into blind
  men's eyes

Those who make weapons are not fit to have care of children
They do not know that war has no victory
They weave a garment around a stain
I am tired of anger
I will go and they will be madmen naked within and cold
I will not curse their children
I will take them to the shore
I will lead them into the water that plays there
They will laugh and shriek
And I will sleep under the ocean
And the rise and fall of my breath will be the swell of the water

When will they learn that war has no victory?
They weave a garment around a stain
The spoils of war are the fire-scorched mattress
The broken chair
The roofless walls
They weave a garment around a stain

(1993)

Notes on *Coffee* for Le Théâtre National de la Colline

Coffee is in two parts. The first seems set in the 'imagination'. People appear and things change as if by magic. The second is set in 'reality' – in fact, what happens in it happened in the real world. Yet it is the real event which should be beyond all imagining. Why did it happen?

Soldiers massacred innocents at Babi Yar. They thought they had finished for the day. They relaxed and brewed coffee. A last band of stragglers were herded in to be shot. A soldier was so upset at having to work overtime that in disgust he threw away his coffee – the gesture of a sulking child refusing food. The gesture images the last century and the dangers that threaten this century.

Evil is not banal but it makes everything else banal – our homes, society, politics, lives. Evil is throwing away the coffee. We live in the age of banality. The problem is not why soldiers killed at Babi Yar. The problem is how was Babi Yar – and Auschwitz – ever possible. The historical and social explanations do not explain, they ascribe causes that might have had other effects. Auschwitz has no history. It is always in the present. Auschwitz is the cradle in which we rock our children – that is the gift of our banality.

How does the play's first part relate to its second part? It is said that human infants are animals that must be socialized. They are without human minds and human concerns. Hitler and Freud agreed on this. They were wrong. The human mind is an impenetrable barrier between animal and human. All human experience is part of the post-animal mind. We cannot be reduced to socio-biological animals. Animal vocalizations are not elementary language. But humans do not even have to wait for language before they enter the social, symbolic order. From birth we communicate by signs, expressions, gestures. If we stroke or strike an infant there is mutual communication of *meaning*. If we do the same to animals no *meaning* is communicated.

Infants have only one purpose: to be at home in the world. It is a rational purpose. An infant must try to change the world to make it its home. When the world will not bend to its will it may rage and wish to destroy – but only to make the world its home, a human place to be human in. The wish to make the world human is axiomatic to the child's existence. But the child has to discourse with reality before it has learnt how reality discourses with itself. Yet in its small world the desire to be human is total and will never be greater. It seems that in the great world of adults the desire is easily lost. This is the passage from innocence to corruption. The child has no guide to being human. It is Dante without Virgil. The world cannot understand or cope with the child's clamorous desire for humanness. Instead it punishes it. So by demanding that the world be human, the child turns the world into its hell. Hell is the place that is outraged by innocence. Society is the trauma of childhood.

The child's innocence is radical because it does not seek to be good. Within its knowledge of itself as a child, it *is* good and can no more be evil than a God could be. It strives to make a world in which it may act innocently and not be punished for it. However distorted or corrupt his desire may later become, it remains the desire for innocence. History is the labyrinth of this paradox. When the child grows and enters the adult world, its existential need to be at home in the world becomes the desire for justice. But the world is unjust. In the past 'sages' have withdrawn from the world to seek the lost world of childhood innocence.

When the growing child finds itself in the 'real' world its increased understanding ought to show it that there can be justice only when it is shared. If we had to relate only to a natural order it would be easy to be just, but we have to relate to other people. Our existence depends on it. To become members of society we adopt its injustices. If we judged the child by its relation to the 'real' world, the child is mad. Adulthood should do away with madness. Instead, because society inducts us into its injustice, we become *socially* mad – that is, decent law-abiding citizens, religious believers, patriots, money-earners. These things are the institutions of social madness.

Madness is a matter of beliefs not opinions, because all madness is founded in the child's consuming existential need for innocence and later the adult's need for justice. So the labyrinth twists. Social madness makes the desire for justice the practice of injustice, the desire for innocence the obsession with corruption, the desire for reason the habits of madness, the desire for love the lust of hate. Our social order is chaos, we live in a death culture. Evil is our attempt to be at home in this world – to earn our coffee and drink it in peace.

We live in two worlds. Both are real. Human reality is the interaction between the two. But because we are socially mad the motive that produced innocence in the child's world, primarily the world of imagination, is the same motive that produces corruption in the other, material, world. The two worlds are not distinct. If they were there would be no problem, we could always know which world we were in.

But the imagination can understand itself only in terms of the material world, and our material world exists only by depending on the imagination. We never meet ourself. We live in the gap between the two worlds and struggle to draw them closer. We are not like a blind man tapping the pavement with his white stick to find where he is in the world. Our state is stranger. It is as if the blind man tapped us to find what world *he* was in – and that was the only way we had of knowing what world *we* are in.

We cannot say the imagination is childlike and the material world adult. Or that the imagination is the world of 'art' and the material world the world of 'technology'. We live in the material world only by being in the imagination world, and in the imagination world only by being in the material world. What the clifftop soldiers call their guns are their toys and killing is the game they call Duty. They are socially mad.

I have been told that *Coffee* is like the world of Plato's cave, where shadows pass for reality. But we must not understand this as Plato would. There is no transcendental world of justice. Instead we have the existential need to create justice – and if we do not we must turn the whole world into Babi Yar. No compromise between destruction and creativity is now possible. In the past our technology's strength made us more human, it forced us into a greater understanding of the material world. But we survived only because of our technology's weakness – it limited the power of social madness. The clifftop soldiers were armed with puny weapons. Now we arm social madness with technology that can destroy the world in war or peace.

These are the two worlds of *Coffee*. But how is it that a man is older in the first world than he is in the second? Or another man good in the first world and suddenly bad in the second? Why is the process of change not shown? How may a girl be dead in the first world and alive again in the second? We live in both worlds at once and in each as if we were in the other. Our cultural and social ideologies are parasitic on these dualities. They turn them into confusions. We howl their credos in the labyrinth. That is why innocence may be corruption, and why corruption may even be radiant with innocence – as it often is in the pathetic tatters of civilization we cling to.

Waiting for Godot is a play of *fin-de-siècle* degeneracy because implicitly it is set in the imagination world but interprets it in terms of the material world. The play waits for Satan, to confirm imagination as material and proffer evil as an excuse. It seeks to lave our banality with the placebo of misery. Really the play has no imagination because it has no material world.

Coffee is set in the two worlds. But we cannot show people in two worlds at once. It would be aestheticism. *Coffee* shows people in the material world. But the imagination world irrupts into the 'Second House' and haunts the 'Big Ditch', the other 'Houses' and their characters. When they are in the ravine the characters are still also in the 'Second House'. They do not know it. It is as if they tried to remember it to understand what they were doing in the ravine – or turned away from it in fear. Later, as they approach the catastrophe in which the two worlds collide, it is even as if the imagination world strove to remember *this*, the material world – to irrupt into it again. It is then that the characters talk of visions, other places, spaces, worlds. But all visions are written in the dust of this world until we are human.

The self – the mind – is a story. The story has the logic of imagination. Imagination is more logical than pure reason because it is embodied: it does not need proof. The logic of imagination is what the Greeks called Fate or Fortune. But the imagination has no past, it has only the present. The past is in it not as memory but as part of the present. Because imagination has no past we need not be imprisoned by the past. The past cannot deliver us to fate. The Greeks thought otherwise because they still saw the material world as children see it – Fate was a God in the material world. We may understand the material world and its relation to imagination differently.

The mind is a story – a drama – in which the tensions holding the two worlds together are the dramatic structure. The privilege of the stage is that it is in neither world. It is in the gap between them. That is why the mind must create drama. Art is the mind's memory of the present. Each mind is its own story. Drama's generalizations relate each of us to the particularities of our own story, its origins and logic. Drama is not a revelation of truth, it reveals a question: 'Why?' Not why do these characters act as they do, but why do you act as you do – are your acts innocent – do they seek justice – who are you? If drama does this it has no need of answers. The answers at Delphi were always questions.

We cannot speak sanely to the socially mad. But drama allows the self to escape from its present so that for that moment we become ourself in both worlds. What would it be like if everything in the material world stopped, caught in one instant? We would be imprisoned in it. But the imagination is always caught in the present, stopped, trapped. We are imprisoned in the imagination. Yet it is the source of our humanness – and to create our humanness we must be free. So we must secure an exit from our imagination: we do this by putting it on the stage. We cannot endure this for long. In our present wounded state it is exhausting to be human. But we may endure it long enough to appear to ourself in the gap. That is why we need tragedy.

In theatre the usual process of being is reversed. Usually we see ourselves in the material world but are also in the imagination world. In the theatre we see the imagination world on the stage, and therefore actually in the material world. How to describe this! It is as if we had eyes in the back of our head, or time and space and events were released from their prison and made mutable. It is because of this that in drama we meet ourself for the first time – it is always for the first time because we are always changed as the relationship between the two worlds changes. Yet at the same time the stage shows us in the process of creating the relationship between the two worlds – we are not in fantasy but in the logic of imagination. The logic is written on our mortality. The Greeks knew more clearly than we do that humans live in this relationship: it is not surprising that they regarded performance as sacred. *Coffee* is overtly concerned with seeing this relationship. In this it is like Velázquez's *Las Meninas* and Plato's image of the cave. It is concerned with the morality of seeing. In it we see our prison from the outside.

We must trust theatre again. Brecht's Aristotelian account of tragedy ought to be a scandal. Aristotle's catharsis is the purging of pity and fear after the act, Brecht's alienation effect is the – prescriptive – purging of pity and fear before the act. To say that empathy is all is foolish, but it is as foolish to say that we need no empathy. The soldiers shot the Jews at Babi Yar – the Nazis gassed the Jews at Auschwitz – because they had no empathy with them. Auschwitz is The Theatre of the A-effect – so are the Gulag and Babi Yar. Brechtism is cultural Stalinism. It has no use in the modern world. It is the irrelevance of mandarin intellectuals. Brecht was too good a writer to be a Brechtian.

Justice is created by material acts not by desires in the imagination. Imagination seeks reason and understanding. This makes it vulnerable to social madness. It also means that it must seek to understand the materiality of others, their being, presence, in the material world. How could we recognize this presence if we met it? How could the Nazi recognize the material – not the imagined – Jew? How may Nold recognize his victims? You may recognize others only when you can recognize yourself. In drama this is possible – in drama we may meet and recognize ourselves in the gap. There is no certainty of this. Art is not transcendental – nothing is. If art is to free some, it must be possible for it to drive others deeper into corruption. Our present media are the sewers of consumerism, an entertainment offered to our banality. All we can do is seek to know ourselves. Drama helps us to do this when it deals with the extreme, because there the questions that define us are found. They were the questions of the Greek and Jacobean theatres.

All of us – even those born later – are survivors of Babi Yar and Auschwitz and Hiroshima. It is not certain that anyone will survive *this* century, that humanness will survive violence or banality. We must create a new theatre. It will be unlike the theatres of the Greeks and Jacobeans but it will serve the same purpose: to create the human image. That is why we must learn to trust theatre again.

(2000)

Letter on Brecht

Rudolf Rach
Paris

18 March 00

Dear Rudolf

You know that I regard Brecht as an influence and of course I shall continue to be influenced by him. But it is an influence about which I have always felt – and stated – unease. He is a major playwright and about this I have no unease.

Like Brecht I have spent my middle years in exile. Because of you I have seen in France some of my major plays in good productions. I have also seen them in France in marred productions. Some directors did not understand the problems of my plays, some understood them but the solutions were destructive. In particular the production of War Plays at Nanterre – which was often magnificent – was damaged by a litter of Brechtisms.

I called the theatre of the A-effect the Theatre of Auschwitz. Obviously I do not mean this in a simple sense. In a simple sense it is the opposite of true. The Nazis at Auschwitz would have exterminated Brecht not staged him. Brecht spent his energies and life trying to make hell-holes such as Auschwitz – or the Gulag – impossible. Nothing more serious could be said about Brecht than what I have said in the 'Notes on *Coffee*' (for the Théâtre de la Colline). It is in the spirit that I called the play *Coffee* and not *Blood*.

Really I need to talk about the whole of human life if I am to explain my remark about Brecht. I try to do that in 'The Reason for Theatre'. 'Reason' is a Brecht word. But I describe and establish the nature of reason differently. This means saying what a human being is. And this – and its consequences – are the whole of my difference with Brecht.

I have a strong sense of being at the start of an epoch. In this I suppose I feel not unlike Brecht's Galileo – at a new beginning. It is a feeling captured in the drawings of the moon that Galileo included in *Sidereus Nuncius* and in his description of his puzzlement over his observations – beginning on 7 January 1610 – of the moons of Jupiter and of how they slowly reshaped the whole universe and the relations of humans to it. A sense of a confusion which slowly resolves itself. I feel that as a writer I have also moved towards this moment. I also feel that if Brecht were alive he would have come to it – or have become the Inquisitor. As to Galileo, it is not quite like seeing what is physically there – because humanness is created and so one must read the observer not the observed. The writer must *create* the observed. The writer arrives at this by comparing what has been written and recorded of the past with the maelstrom of the present. You are part of the maelstrom but are guided by the past. The past is the shore – and for dramatists that is Chekhov, Ibsen, Strindberg, Brecht. A modern writer needs those writers and many more – and many painters, musicians and novelists. *But they are not in the maelstrom with you.* There has to be a new beginning. It is new not as a matter of literary fashion. That is why I am criticizing not Brecht but a whole civilization.

A writer abides by certain values and these identify him and – if they are human – justify what he writes. This is true of Ibsen and Brecht (and the other writers I mentioned). We can ask how well they understood their contemporary situation, the repressions and creative resistance. This would make them better or worse writers because of their ability to describe their times. Writers must do more, they must have a sense of history. Within that sense they may be like the astronomers who constantly complicated and complicated the cycles of the stars and planets in order to reconcile observation with theory. Galileo does something different: he changes the whole argument. We need a new paradigm of knowledge. We think moralistically – we see literature as part of the Manichean struggle of the good and the bad – this struggle is an intellectual and moral framework which has aesthetic consequences – aesthetics is the way we accommodate the truth (not the truth itself). Thus styles and forms change. There is no way in which astronomers can reconcile astronomical cycles unless they abandon geocentrism: the adjustments – the purported improvements – simply compound errors. And so it is as if instead of a Manichean struggle between right and wrong, each epoch of knowledge has to exhaust its errors until there can be a movement into a new paradigm of knowledge. We live in an age of exhaustion. For astronomers after Galileo there are still the stars and planets – but there are more of them, there is more to be included in the theory – and a new universe is revealed to be lived in.

Brecht's Galileo says something to the effect that a new world is dawning and it cannot be prevented. I believe this is happening now. The changes of the last hundred years have been revolutionary in almost all respects except in the human image – and in that the change has been one of decay. The aporias of Brecht and his position can no longer be reconciled any more than the pre-Galilean model of space could be reconciled with observation. This matters particularly for me because I am sometimes compared to Brecht. It is necessary for me to elucidate why I am not Brechtian – and cannot be if I am to write of my times. And so I have to make clear why I cannot be: and that means not dismissing Brecht but arguing that he belongs to a now redundant paradigm of knowledge. I take alienation from within the act – I do not apply it. I do not have to alienate *Coffee* – from within the centre of the drama the alienation may be made to reveal itself as fact – the coffee cup (and so I have had to create the TE). I achieve 'specification' – I specify what is happening – so that it cannot be ideologically cloaked (without a deliberate effort of denial by the audience).

We have to begin to think in epochs of understanding – in waves of newness – when arguments within the old paradigm are no longer real, actual, have meaning. We are trapped in our knowledge. There would be a way out of this – it is the whole argument of radical innocence, of the 'Notes on Imagination'. It means the abolition of all ideology. We can do this only by understanding how innocence is corrupted and how reason relates to imagination. I think that when Galileo counted the moons of Jupiter Auschwitz was inevitable. This is not a deterministic theory because I think that new paradigms of knowledge are possible. But you cannot move directly from ancient human sacrifice to twenty-first-century consumer democracy. What I think now becomes possible is a new understanding of how human understanding progresses – and so the captive paradigms of the past, which were inevitable, are so no longer. But for that to be so, the processes in which people recreate themselves – the stage and the media – must be different. I think so many strands of theatre seek this: Artaud and his outrage, Brecht and his (*soi-disant*) reason, the concern with individual psychology, Beckett and his map of despair: all these lack a total theatre which can describe our lives and take us into the act of self-creation.

The problem is connected with Sarah Kane. Her suicide has to be understood. She was the most gifted dramatist of her generation. It is said that she killed herself because she was clinically depressed. What does that mean of a writer? Not that her death had a cause, but that her life had no inducement. She saw no future for theatre and so none for herself. But it is possible to see a future for theatre. Her plays present the need for such a theatre. She was as remote from Brecht as I am.

The ironies in all this are many: Brecht, me, Galileo, the Inquisition, a cup of coffee. But they go to the centre of things.

Best wishes

Edward

The Seventh of January
Sixteen Hundred and Ten

Our understanding of the material world is ideological. We use the material world but much of it is beyond our control and use. For both these reasons the material world is able to impose itself on ideology. Our understanding of the material world is also the foundation of our understanding of ourselves. We are less able than the material world to defend ourselves against ideology. Ideology distorts our self-understanding. If the lords of creation cannot solve this problem they will become its victims.

The mind cannot describe itself objectively. The description combines ideology and practical knowledge of the self and the material world. We fit into the world – eat, procreate – but also into society. We do the latter not as matches fit into a box. We become part of society and it part of us. Society is unequal, unjust. It may be believed that the inequality is inevitable, necessary, unnecessary, unjust. Whichever *is* true will be part of our 'being', but so also will our belief as to which is true. The belief will be part of ideology. Ideology is the meaning society gives to itself, reality and so to 'being'. Ideology is the justification of injustice. Injustice may produce mutability, rigidity, creativity, destructiveness – *which* depends on the meaning 'being' has to itself. But all injustice degrades behaviour. Injustice finally destroys because it makes the relationship between us and reality irrational. Ideology is historically determined by our social and technological relation to nature – but this imposes the necessity of choice and the possibility of freedom on 'being'.

Ideology organizes society to maintain our lives. Historically the organization depends on ownership. Ideology resists change, either as formal conservatism or as reaction against 'change in change' – that is, the corruption of revolution and liberalism. Liberalism's corruption is less spectacular than revolution's but much more enduring, because liberalism is corrupted by common sense.

Human 'being' is critically tense because it is on the border between ideology and practical knowledge of reality. This border is like the meeting of tectonic plates. As they move they cause perturbations and earthquakes. 'Being' is where the plates meet. On one side there is material reality and its consistencies, on the other society and ideology.

'Being' is the gap between – the site of self-consciousness, imagination, reason. The boundary is not neutral but existentially critical because it involves security, food, sex, parenthood, class, sickness, the psychosomatic and so on. These are on the social side and determined by ideology. But there is no neutral, mechanical reality on the other side because it is imbued with ideology – ownership, culture, the sacred, and so on. Nature returns to us in the personification of ourselves – if it were otherwise we could not image a God to create it. Nature is defined by our practical and ideological uses of it. (To say a God walked on water does not change God but changes the water.) Ultimately society submits to nature's domination, the transcendental to the material, the intellectual to the mechanical. Our body exists on both sides of the boundary, as a socialized self (a worker in a workshop, a soldier on the battlefield) and as a natural object (a foetus in the womb, the dead on the battlefield). The living and the dead are part of nature and part of ideology.

The boundary between these (metaphoric) plates is the gap. The gap cannot be closed, self and ideology are never secure, never at home in the world. The gap is the site of the meaning we give to reality and our self: it is our understanding of the totality of things. This meaning is our 'being' (and the meaning of our 'being'). We are the gap, it is our consciousness and self-consciousness because 'being' is its meaning to us. Natural reality cannot exist apart from ideology, even though it finally dominates ideology – nor can natural objects (such as knives and tables), which have utility and also symbolic power.

The gap, its factors and vicissitudes are our consciousness and self-consciousness. Imagination and self-consciousness are aspects of each other. The gap is in tension because of the relationship between the real and the ideological, and this is the tension of 'being'. The gap is also the site of our individual story, which is partly our specific biography and partly the events in ideology. 'Being' is not isolated in its body – the gap is a commonality and this is part of our 'being'. The gap's tensions are partly personal (mortality, profession) and partly in common: no mind is an island complete unto itself, every mind is part of the gap, rent by its tensions and healed only by the reconciliations of the commonality in the gap.

Personal tensions take their meaning from common tensions. I am not my own 'being'. All I have is my own death – of the rest I can choose to have everything or nothing. Mortality is not a tension when it becomes Tragic knowledge. All other tensions are caused by social injustice and its ideology and by nature's power and indifference. Notwithstanding ideology's practical justifications and historically its part-promotion of humanness, it is created by social injustice and authority's ownership of reality. Reality is imagined in the gap – there, image has power over physical reality, but reality must 'consent'. Ideology must integrate practical knowledge into itself or it is finally destroyed by reality. Then society becomes more just or more chaotic. We bring our existential needs to the gap, but society has existential advantage over us because ideology uses knowledge as ignorance. The mind is more important than the body to humanness, so injustice's greatest offence is to the human image.

Reality is material not transcendental. Ultimately mechanics dominate intellectuals. Galileo and Newton discovered the mechanical consistencies of nature. The modern age began. The great iron machines of the Industrial Revolution seemed to be nodding in agreement with Newton. Work, city construction, travel, punishment, war, finance, trade – society changed. Most people survived more easily but over time our security does not depend on consumption. It depends on the meaning we give to ourselves, which is our 'being'. In Galileo's drama there were two sets of instruments: Galileo's telescopes and the Inquisition's instruments of torture. There was a new paradigm of knowledge but not a new form of 'being'. The new knowledge made us ignorant because it was trapped inside the old ideology. Society did not become more just. That is why, when on 7 January 1610 Galileo saw through his telescope the three moons of Jupiter, Auschwitz became inevitable.

What Galileo saw changed the meaning of reality, but ideology changed only enough to stay the same. A paradox, but that is how injustice maintains itself. Until Galileo ideology described society as a reflection of the sacred universe. When knowledge of the universe changed society had to change. The new knowledge was refracted and diffused into society in distortions. Society no longer reflected any sacred order, it was like a reflection in a broken mirror. Ideology imposed the transcendental on society although its practical relation to reality had changed: those who own the earth own the heavens. The stress of holding to old beliefs and living in old social structures became greater, relations between owner and owned, citizen and law were no longer sacred. Dogma became rigid, ideology claimed the infallibility which science – practical and pragmatitic – did not. God was in favour of injustice. And so the new technology was corrupted and used to accommodate the new effects of injustice. This was done to hold society together. Society fell apart.

All this is possible only because we exist in the gap. We are part of, and relate to, material reality, but not as material objects, subject to immediate cause and effect. We act through 'being' in the gap, we are the meaning desire gives to itself in the face of necessity. We cannot remain in the 'being' of the past because reality does not 'consent' (we could not live practically). As ideology withdraws further from reality, from practical understanding, the gap becomes paranoid. All ideology is held together by existential force, the need to survive, but under threat existential force becomes ideological violence. Fragments of ideology, old forms of 'being', break off and become monstrous – the fragment grows to be the whole, dwarfishness nurtured by malice takes on the power of the giant. Faith is the belief that something which cannot be true is true. Reality is powerless before faith. When the ideological meaning of self and society is no longer plausible or practical, even to a jackass, faith turns into fanaticism. There are new creeds – Christian, pagan, hedonistic, ascetic, mystic, instrumentally rational. Ideology loses its human aspect and becomes fascistic. Inevitably in time the new technology became the gas chambers and crematoria of the Auschwitz industrial conveyor belt, and the new science became the medical experiments of Dr Mengele. Scientists practised the arts of the Inquisition. The hydrogen bomb was made.

If it was inevitable, then resistance had been empty. But resistance is human, without it there is no humanness in the gap. There are many forms of resistance. The Enlightenment replaced revenge with moderation and lessened the flowing back of rage into the psycho-social system, the exploited organized to free themselves from poverty and sickness, there was the cultural resistance of philosophy, theatre and art. Finally there was military resistance. The three world wars of the twentieth century were all internecine within ideology – even the third, cold war. They did not bring peace. The world is now more unjust and technology produces in peace time the devastations of war. We destroy the earth.

We have to understand the nature of 'being' – the social and material consequences of being in the gap. Otherwise resistance is remedial, a constant coping with symptoms. Neither action within the self nor solely in society removes injustice. Ideology constantly reforms itself to contain change. It is protean, and armed with modern technology nihilistic. Human 'being' depends on meaning. Meaning is not 'about' but 'in' existence. Reason alone cannot change the meaning of 'being', because 'being' is itself the means of thought. To change the means of thought, 'being' requires a new way of 'being' itself. It cannot do this by rearranging the existing determinants of 'being' to meet a changed situation. What initially disturbs 'being' is change in the meaning of the universe and its practical consequences in our use of reality. When

Galileo looked through a telescope it was as if the universe looked at us differently and used us differently. We cannot resist change – or the need to change – because the universe is (as far as we yet know) too consistent to be resisted: that is why we must talk of determinism *and* freedom. Technology rapidly recreates its own image through its use and practical aesthetics. The train does not require a man waving a red flag to preceed it. But 'being' cannot so easily free itself from its past. It is as if a man with a red flag wanders and marches – as ideologically appropriate – in our 'being'. It is not that the need to survive existentially pressures us, because we may sacrifice survival on the altars and battlefields of ideology. It is a cognitive problem. We do not directly relate to reality but create reality in the gap. The inertia of ideology is existential and psychological. It is not as if we had to use letters to make new words but new letters.

Reason alone cannot help us to understand our situation humanly, or even use ideology against ideology. That would be possible only if thought could detach itself from the ideological infestation of the gap in order to reflect on itself. We could do that only if we were 'calculating matter' and not 'being'. Then there would be no problem because we would not be human – but there would be no imagination, creativity, Tragic or meaning. We fear others because we think we know ourselves – but what we know is the ideological image created in the gap. We know ourselves to be reactionary, atavistic and primitive, in need of reason to restrain us. As that is our meaning, it is our 'being' and becomes the way we act: this confirms the meaning. The 'self' is the image created by ideology in the gap: its origin is in injustice. We need to understand the drama of 'being'.

We cannot rationally justify an action by its results because any action however inhuman may be justified: whatever is logical in the imagination becomes inevitable in reality. Imagination's logic does not come from an atavistic 'essence' but from the relationship of imagination and reality – which is the meaning of reality in imagination-self-consciousness. Reality does not impose its meaning on imagination-self-consciousness. Meaning is the use 'being' makes of reality. That is why imagination cannot be taught but may learn. We learn by 'being' in reality, but that is not what is called experience. It would be as true to say that (over time) we are the experience reality has. Reality experiences us not through our actions (interventions and responses) in reality, but in *our* apprehensions of reality. This is obviously so in the neonate (which is a monad) but remains true throughout life. Imagination has a 'here' but no 'there'. Usually such considerations are unnecessary because we act *in* reality and not *in* our imagination. They are necessary when we seek to understand ourselves.

'Being' changes only when drama (in reality or theatre) enters the site where imagination forms its relation to reality. This is the site of situations. Theatre drama returns to originating (not original) situations. This is not psychoanalysis because the situations are in the gap's commonality, common to everyone. But they are not archetypes because the situations are in reality, not in 'being'. In these situations, 'being' creates a module which is the way it receives the world, a habitualness which is not psychological but cognitive. The psychological is a reaction to cognized reality (so that even the nature of physical stimuli may be changed). We do not know what knocks on the side of the early monad, nor can the monad know – the 'what' is established (created) by its reaction. Nor need we know what form reality takes at these founding moments, it is relevant only that it occurs and establishes a relationship to the world beyond. A mouse may be afraid of an elephant, an elephant may be afraid of a mouse. A cat may look at a queen, a queen may look at a cat. 'Being' achieves a self through the chances of necessity. Only 'being' exists in the gap. If we had no imagination ideology would be impossible, there would be only action. But imagination and self-consciousness are one. That is why 'being' must have meaning, innocent or ideologized. We are faced with drama or death.

'Being' creates its module which is its means of being in reality and which makes possible the meaning which is given to reality. Socially it appears as something like character or mindset, but it is more basic because it is cognitive. Though unreflective it would, if it were reflective, know more about the individual than the individual knows about it: it is the consciousness which preceeds self-consciousness. It is 'being's' method of being and the way it attaches itself to what is not itself. It is prior to appetite. It exists because of 'being' and is created (and has no other being) through 'being' realizing reality and its autonomy. It is not an 'unconscious' because it is 'being's' means of maintaining reality – the module relates to reality and not itself. The closeness to identity of the relationship is important because it is what makes drama dramatic and not merely tense, emotional or physical: drama tears at 'being'. At this level, 'being' is not open to discursive thought. It is a relationship described in Oedipus's story (but the description is not the enactment): if Oedipus would see again he must stab out his eyes.

Module – or better, modularity – is in effect 'being' in situation. It is an existential relationship to the world, but in origin it is radical innocence relating to the world, the monad's primary self-cognition. The module is not radical innocence but is radical innocence's means of entering into 'being' in the fullness of the world. The module is cognitive and evaluative – it is a relation between reason and imagination. Ideology may corrupt 'being' – ideology practises itself through the module and attaches 'being' to social injustice and ideologizes thought. In this way imagination may be corrupted *in practice* – but only in this way. The module is a relation of imagination to reason. Reason may be corrupted but imagination cannot be because it has no ideas – and so drama may directly confront imagination without the distortions of corrupted self-consciousness (and reason in its service). That is the power of drama.

Radical innocence has no situation (other than totality), it is only the need to be at home in the world and so desire justice. The desire may be expressed only through the module because that is its way of cognizing – interpreting – the world. Ideology's power of manipulating reality gives it access to the module. It may *in practice* corrupt imagination – but radical innocence is uncorrupted because it is prior to imagination. So corruption is ever only a practice. Radical innocence is uncorruptible, it is the source of value. The origin of humanness is radical innocence's need for justice. But radical innocence has no situation, its situations come from being in the world as it is apprehended through the module: the way of seeing, of interpreting the world, which is pre-empted by 'being'. In corruption we are made our own prison. The importance of drama is that it may directly confront radical innocence and the need for humanness. It may do this by dividing the module, separating imagination from reasoning. Real events (in war, sickness, triumph) may also confront the relationship between imagination and reason, but reality tends to be subordinated to ideology, because ideology can manipulate the existential necessities of reality. Drama is the means 'being' has created to circumvent this, to release itself from the tensions in ideology and between ideology and its need for justice: drama uses these tensions.

The module is existential but abstract because it relates to all situations, events and objects which can be described in social, psychological or natural terms – and ultimately all terms are social because ideology polarizes the meaning of nature and reality. Drama presents situations to the module. The module cannot be indifferent because it is 'being's' means of consciousness. The module must constantly iterate itself by reproducing objectivity. 'Being' is drama, it dramatizes and is dramatized. Drama is ultimately the way society coheres. The subjects of drama are instances of this way and may potentially exemplify the whole. There is the drama of real life and the drama of theatre. The first is social reality (politics, work, family) and is ideological or in the social tensions within ideology. In theatre, drama is whatever ideology deems drama (and which it can authenticate in terms of its own relation to reality) or the tensions between ideology and reality. These are drama's subjects. Its methods come from the relationship between 'being' and ideology – because all 'being' and drama is in the gap.

To subvert ideology so that 'being' and society may be changed, drama must directly confront imagination. Brechtism seeks to reverse this process. It deals with judgements, assessments, made by value. But value is structured in the module (in the relationship between imagination and thought in self-consciousness). If 'being' is innocent, discursive thought (at that level) is irrelevant. If 'being' is ideologized, discursive thought is corrupt. Brechtism seeks to use the module to initiate social change, but the module is neutral and merely monitors. It stands between radical innocence and ideology – but also between radical innocence and 'being', so it monitors 'being' to its own self. If 'being' is corrupted (ideologized through fear and confirmed in ideology through revenge) the module interprets the world corruptly. The point is that in the module reason and imagination are combined – reason-and-imagination may be corrupt but imagination itself cannot be. Brechtism appeals directly to reason and cannot subvert corruption. Drama must directly confront imagination so that corrupt thought cannot occlude it. Drama's story need not be overtly accusatory but imagination will discern in it whatever is inhuman and thwarts radical innocence's desire to be at home in the world. Of course, imagination may find itself innocent before the story.

Brechtism's error lies in its historical origins. Nazism aestheticized politics. It stimulated 'being' by creating real hells, by the rituals of performance arts, by stereotypical imagery – the swastika ('the crippled sprinter') – drums, rhythmic calisthenics and marches, torch parades – by the stichomythia of its torture chambers and the blood of its axe-executions. Brecht could meet the 'stage' drama in the reality of the naked corruption of the streets. Alienation is a devise against realist-melodrama. Now ideology is again hidden in common sense, law and order, anomie and respectable conduct.

Both Greek epic poetry and Greek drama used the same subjects. Epic poetry was written for a settled, pastoral, aristocratic society and was discursive. Drama was written in a time of defeat and social collapse, it belonged to the city, its audience was proto-democratic. Ideology is less beneficent in Greek drama than in Greek epic poetry. In drama humans created meaning in despite of the gods and their meaninglessness. In epic poetry the Gods thought for humans and gave meaning. The beneficent deity of Brechtism's epic theatre is practical Marxism: Marx-*ism* as God – the module not sited in the vicissitudes of 'being' but objective and secure in the world. (It has been said that self-consciousness had not evolved by the age of epic poetry.) This is now a problem. If Marxism is the politics of justice we live in a time of its impracticability. Seeking justice is replaced by consumerism: the beneficent deity behind consumer-media and the aestheticization of modern life. Mass consumption is a new stage in history. It is as if humanness were abolished or become a habit.

Brechtism depends on the rationality of Marxism as an objectification of justice in unjust society. But justice is still only its promise. It is as if Brechtism used sign language but expected to be heard. It gives an unjustified sense of security, not just of something to do but also of something done. But we no longer have the security of three world wars, Auschwitz and Hiroshima. Brechtism is committed to social change and even armed struggle. But it does not address our audience's situation and this makes its strenuousness superficial. Why is this not true in the same way with Chekhov and Ibsen – or Rembrandt and Bach? Because as a technician Brecht claims to be a scientist and not an artist. Brechtism abandons 'being' to discursive reason, but that cannot disturb faith or even opinion. Meaning is changed only when value is related to a new idea, a new understanding: when imagination has a new meaning (meaning is our 'being'). Rationality, the negotiation of ideas (in human not technical matters) is spurious. Starting from the same premise reason may lead to emancipation or repression: whatever is logical in imagination becomes rational in thought. You could not usefully apply alienation to theatre such as Shaw's. As a rationalist Shaw argued for the extermination of all recidivists (burglars, arsonists, shoplifters), painlessly and if possible without foreknowledge. Imagine the fear and rumours in such a society. The rest of society could not be completely rational (Shavian) because if it were there would be no offenders to exterminate. So extermination would have to be kept secret from relatives and friends and then – obviously – from society at large. The consequences would ramify everywhere. It is the society of Nazism and Stalinism. Shaw thought of Stalinism as an 'experiment' to watch with interest.

But Brecht is primarily a poet. He uses dramatic poetry in language, music and situation to invoke value. When it has been invoked it is abolished by alienation. Discursive reason replaces value. The self – not the situation – is alienated. The solution is presented before the problem is shown. Audiences assent if they have already agreed. Brechtism is far removed from Nazi folk-mysticism and *blut-und-boden* melodrama. But Nazism was also a technology. It put value at its base, it wanted people to 'feel' not think. But it administered society with the rationalist calculation of its bureaux and murder squads. It invented a socially mad, galvanizing (liberating and condemning) division between emotional indulgence and alienated action. Its Utopia – the site of its value – was the heroic past. Brechtism's Utopia – the site of its value – is in the future. Brechtism: 'Do not feel when you think' – as if action could be pure thought. This is the cause of Brechtism's reversals, recantations, contradictions. They are not expediency but attempts to find a value to act on instead of one to reach for. They are unlike Nazism's contradictions (consistent only in death), which come from its irrationalism. Brechtism's come from the rationalism of its method. Neither Utopia (Nazism's or Brechtism's) has any reality. Marx decried the notion of Utopia: a politician must. A dramatist or poet cannot. Utopia must be implicit and implicitly practical in the work of art, just as in any act of honesty the whole of justice is implicit (though to be made practical). That is the difference between art and morality: art is implicitly optimistic because it uses imagination as it directly expresses radical innocence. A work of art is not a description of justice (though its subject may be) but an enactment: the reality of justice is implicit in the work which creates the work of art (individually or communally) because it performs the originating act of humanness: it imposes value on reality, to change reality by giving it meaning. This encompasses the child's destructive rampage when it puts its rage at the world's 'injustice' into objects by damaging or destroying them. Destruction and creation are not one (except in the limitations of the possible: a child has few possibilities) because imagination seeks reason. Reactionary art turns its rage into the discipline needed to achieve smooth conformity: the undisturbed line of drawing, the unparadoxical line of text. Academic art is a form of revenge.

Brechtism is trapped in the ideology Galileo implicitly refutes: the old ideology revitalized by the corruption of new knowledge. Brechtism opposes that ideology but its method derives from it. Like the Inquisition it sees 'being' as lost without the saving power of reason. The Church sees reason as transcendental grace, Brechtism sees it as immanent – but it also sees 'being' as lost. Brechtism was influenced by contemporary pessimism. We were supposed to be atavistic and pre-intellectual, art was reactionary and elitist, imagery came from the huge world of Freud. Brechtism arrives at the Church's position by a different route. Brechtism's method uses reason instrumentally. In this Brecht was influenced by Piscator (a theatrical idiot).

Ideology is most repressive in critical situations. These situations become calcified into the scars of corruption. They bind the module to ideology. Drama must break this bind. It can do this only by directly confronting imagination. Otherwise change cannot be initiated. Drama should not seek reason – it should seek imagination knowing that imagination seeks reason and is the only possible subversion of ideology. To do this drama does not gesture towards reality but imitates it. Its imitation enters the present tense of imagination, its 'here' – and this is the reality of drama. It enters the site of meaning, which is our 'being'. At this level there is no difference between the imagined and the real, imagination has the reality of the mind when it created itself. Only drama can recreate this concentration: then to 'being' it is as if the whole world came to watch. It is the way in which responsibility for the world may be accepted. Imagination must seek reason in the critical situation. The monad cannot – unnoticed – impose corrupt reason. The relationship to reality is changed – either innocence asserts itself in new meaning or corruption asserts itself by fanaticizing ideology and in this way driving it closer to destruction in its war against humanness. The situation is radicalized.

In stable unjust society ideology owns imagery (the means by which situations are known) through its relation with reason. It gives imagery ideological meaning. Discursive reason cannot displace this meaning. If the image is alienated drama itself has no 'being' and cannot enter human 'being' in the real and social world. This makes the audience's 'being' a petit-catatonia, a de-empathized state which can be humanized only by empathy. It is intended that this should be restored by Marxism. But Marxism is a science – not aesthetics or poetics. Marx favoured bourgeois novelists over socialist novelists not because the former had solutions (they did not) but because they had greater understanding of the human paradox. Marx did not explain why this was so, his book on aesthetics was unwritten.

Imitating reality does not reproduce it. Art is memory and because its situations present the logic of imagination it is also the logic of history and so the memory of the future. This is part of drama's existential power to create meaning. Drama enacts a situation in which imagination has to confront itself. It cannot seek refuge in existing meaning – but must seek reason again. The dramatist's skill is not in imitating dramatic forms but enacting situations which are critical to 'being'. These situations are secured by violence: the TE is an aggro-effect. The violence may be physical, intellectual, comic, ironic. The violence disturbs ideology at the points which hold it together. As daily life is saturated with ideology, a cup or coat may be used to show the total human meaning. Ideology's grandiosity must be reduced to immanence. This is not alienation because the detail is used to have the effect of the whole.

When imagination is confronted in this way the audience are forced to be creators not discursive thinkers. Whatever response is given, because the module is cognitive thought must be more radical than it would be if imagination were alienated. Unalienated drama forces the self to recreate itself. The effect need not be conventionally 'theatrical' – it may be reflective, amused, intellectual. It may also be anger or fake-indifference. But the effect is permanent. Imagination has howled. The self has witnessed itself.

Social justice would rid us of social madness but not of other forms of madness and despair. Our needs of justice are too manifold and various for the administration of things to accommodate them. Living would have to be a school of justice. All our needs are social but society cannot meet all of them. Humanness must respond to all the demands made on it in the gap. When imagination is not corrupted in the module, its logic is severe. We have Tragic and hedonic needs that society cannot accommodate without life being made a hobby. We must accommodate them ourselves for the sake of society. We are not human without Tragic knowledge.

Drama is about the attachment of self to society – not, directly, of society to self because finally that is always a process of instrumental reason, even in ideology's rituals, pageants and stories. That is the cruelty of ideology. Existentially we depend on society and find our humanness in it. But unjust society is parasitic on us because ideology has no mind.

Consumer democracy aestheticizes consumption. All that can be met on its streets are ghosts – only with crime is it otherwise, because that is innocence objectified as revenge against injustice. Post-Brechtism drama must confront ideology in the corruptions it produces. When the confrontation is specific and clear it cannot be ignored. Brechtism gives us reason to act but not to live. Temporarily that may have been enough. Now it is not. We become pawns in the Technomachia. We cannot rely on our humanness, there is no permanent humanness to fall back on. It is not secured in reason. Each of us must create it. If that is not understood our situation is hopeless. Like the Greeks we must confront the origin of our 'being'. Brechtism avoids our most important question: not, what shall we do? – but, first, who are we? The media dress us in the death mask of the future. Brechtism leaves us prey to their manipulations: the sustained use of the violent image to enforce ideology by invoking fear, and of sentimentality to compensate for the absence of humanness. It leaves us prey to the rituals of performance art and other reactionary theatrics which remove reason from imagination, to kitsch and – in post-modernism – the consolations of triviality.

Brechtism lays claims to the highest function of drama. It must be judged on those terms. It patronizes its audience, is locked into an old paradigm of knowledge and hinders the creation of a modern theatre. Alienation is the Theatre of Auschwitz.

Quantum mechanics have replaced Newtonian mechanics. They show the greater subtlety of being, the unfixed relativity of reality, the power of the self to be the self. All this knowledge is used to strengthen the old ideology. There is a new paradigm of knowledge but not a new paradigm of humanness. A new theatre could create it. It would be closer to Greek drama than to Greek epic poetry but unlike either. It would create a new image of humanness. To do that we must learn to trust theatre again.

(2000)

People Saturated with the Universe
(Notes on *The Crime of the Twenty-first Century* for Le Théâtre National de la Colline)

I wish to say nothing about *The Crime of the Twenty-first Century*. It is written. It can speak for itself. But I will *try* to say something. At the end of the century will the world be as it is shown in the play? How could it happen? Not by sudden catastrophe but slowly inch by inch. The play is a parable of swiftness and slowness.

The world is unstable. We sustain our lives by four structures, each with its own dynamic and unbreakable laws. These structures are nature, society, technology and the economy. They are now in mutual conflict. It is as if the limbs of a body tore the body apart.

The economy must expand to sustain itself. To expand it must use technology. Technology increasingly destroys the natural world. Once, nations warred to occupy each other's land. Now the economy and technology occupy the land and increasingly they lay it to waste. The devastations of peace are greater than the devastations of war. We destroy the world.

We also destroy society. The economy depends on consumption. Consumption no longer depends on natural appetite but on inequality. Without inequality there is no incentive to work and consume to sustain the economy. Inequality is not limited to the market. It creates poverty that penetrates the whole society. There is no longer a solidarity of poverty. Instead there is depression, narcotics, crime, racism, social unrest, city decay, apathy, revenge, reaction. The ancient symptoms of poverty become the modern symptoms of affluence. Our solution is to increase consumption and production but these are the causes of our problem. Once it was thought that 'abundance' would end human conflict. Human beings are more complicated than that. They must have justice. Democracy can no longer create justice – justice is incompatible with what we must do to sustain the economy and everything based on it. The markets are free, we are not.

We cannot understand ourselves. We live in the fantasies of the past – religion, patriotism, racism, original sin, innate aggression, the soul. We are socially mad. Culture is dead. The causes of our problems are rationally understandable but our explanations and solutions are irrational. When the mad are frustrated they become violent. A dictator could not create the world of *The Crime of the Twenty-first Century*. There would be a counter-revolution. But little by little democracy can create it. As society disintegrates authority will become more controlling and repressive. There will be no social protest because whatever authority does will be done to protect possessions and consumption and punish the anti-social. Even the victims will accept this as morally necessary. Democracy will destroy itself in the name of democracy. When it is destroyed the ability to see the destruction will itself have been destroyed.

Ivan Karamazov said there could be no God because a God could not endure – and so would not allow – the suffering of one little child. Then what of the human suffering of the last century? If we were human could we endure it? Do we allow it only because we have no power to prevent it? No, the power to *do* it is simply the power to *prevent* it misused. God is dead, humankind is still not born. We are not human because we are socially mad.

There is no residual humanness, no inner law, we may fall back on in barbarous times. All things living and unliving exist in relation to an environment. The animals' environment is the natural world. It changes slowly and so they change slowly. The environment for humans is their 'situation'. Compared to animals' environment the human situation changes rapidly and so our 'nature' changes rapidly in relation to it. The change is so rapid it is as if we could not see our new changed self in a mirror – the mirror *becomes* our situation, and we *become* what *it* sees. There is no time for a space between us and our situation to come into being.

We create the power of abundance but suffer the impotence of poverty, we have the power of reason but are socially mad. We use reason in the service of the irrational. We build our madness into our weapons and our machines. We misuse the machines that could help us and so even they destroy us. The human situation is a paradox. The only alternative to understanding the human paradox is violence.

The future does not depend on our individual acts of kindness and integrity. They are just tears shed over our impotence. The future depends on how our culture understands itself, on the public understanding of the individual, on the human image – the image we paint on the mirror so that we may know ourselves. Theatre is a necessary part of that understanding.

Auden said that all the poetry in the world did not stop one murder at

Auschwitz. *Nothing* stopped the murder at Auschwitz, and the liberation of Auschwitz came too late. When people start to fight against the world of *The Crime of the Twenty-first Century* it will already be even later. The dynamic of technology-and-culture will have created a world of self-genocide. We are playing Russian roulette. Social madness drives us to survive by taking increasing risks with chance. One by one we fill the pistol's chambers with bullets. When all the chambers are full we will hold the pistol to our head and hope the trigger will jam.

The world of *The Crime of the Twenty-first Century* is unthinkable. But history shows that the unthinkable always happens – that it becomes the inevitable. But what is unthinkable is not unimaginable. One of the functions of imagination is to imagine the unthinkable. Imagination is not arbitrary fantasy but logic. Imagination has only one tense: the present. It is always in the present and so it has no future, past, subjunctive, no 'mights'. Because it is in the present, it may – *in the present* – already live through the future effects of present conditions. That is why behind all the gaiety, speed, noise and lights of post-modernity there is a huge foreboding.

In 1900 people imagined the disasters of the twentieth century. They were mistaken. They foresaw invasions from space and wars between worlds. They did not foresee the three world wars or genocide or Gulags. Because the socially mad are unable to understand their present situation, they are unable to project it into the future and understand that accurately. Instead they fantasize their forebodings into fictions. To know the future we must combine reason and imagination. It is what drama may do.

Each of us acts out – in the drama of our imagination – our existence in terms of the whole of reality. Because imagination has only one tense – the present – it is not confined to one place, the self, but contains 'everywhere'. It is as if one grain of sand could soak up all the oceans of the world. The human drama is vast because it relates to everything else. The meaning we give to the world is the meaning we give to ourselves. In drama imagination seeks the extreme situations which will take us to the limits of meaning which is where humanness is defined. It takes us into the extremity of the self. It seeks to show how people must finally come to the extreme situations in which they lose every illusion about themselves yet hold on to their humanness or suffer what follows when they know they have lost it *because* that is the only way they can hold on to it. The characters in the play – the actors and the audience – define themselves in their reactions to these extreme situations. It is only in this extremity that the radical need to be human is found and humanness created. In drama imagination strives to clothe itself in reality so that it might become itself. Imagination must seek knowledge, and so drama must be relentless in its search – because finally there is no difference between the stage and the plate on which you eat. Finally imagination and reality are one: and we have created many hells but no heaven. Finally, our imagination is not our own – it is the human visitor who comes to our house. We go to the theatre because we are people saturated with the universe.

Drama cannot be judged by anything other than itself. Reason and morality cannot judge it because drama is the self – in each actor and spectator – creating morality and reason out of the debris, the bric-a-brac of their individual lives. Out of their personal chaos we create the image of the human. Not, of course, the image of the tailor's pattern-book or the state's ideal citizen – but of the desire in each of us to be innocent before justice. It is the 'Greek sense', the human obligation to confront the gods. It is the need to travel to the extreme situation and return from it human. Because all the time we run away from this need we become monstrous, little by little the socially mad put themselves into the hands of the clinically mad and though we are born innocent everywhere we commit crime. But in us there is a spark the giant cannot stamp on. Theatre has to confront us with our innocence. It can do it only by making us responsible for our crimes. Tragedy is the search for innocence.

Drama may lie. Most modern entertainments – films, TV, news programmes (now part of the entertainment industry) – degrade the human image. So does 'high art' – the empty rationality of Brechtian theatre, the impoverishing impotence of Beckettian theatre, the 'Theatre of Symptoms' of the new young playwrights. The human image is exploited and sold and integrated into the dynamic of the economy. The advantage of imaging humans as animals is that animals will always consume. But we are not inhuman because we are animals, we are inhuman because we seek to be human in inhuman societies. Social madness cannot understand this paradox.

There are two elements in *The Crime of the Twenty-first Century*. The first element is the real world created by the economy, technology and the administration. They have turned the world into a wilderness and society into a desert. As society collapsed the administration reorganized it to make it easier to control. It put everyone into prisons and ghettos, the counterparts of our camps and Gulags. The administration and the soldiers are everywhere, they parade in the sky but they are never seen. All of this happens in the future. The play's other element is in the present because it is already in our imaginations. Four people in the wilderness act out their individual drama in universal terms. This is in our present because when we are apprehensive and afraid of the future, the future itself becomes a real, objective burden on our present. We break under a burden we do not yet carry – we break under the terror of it – we break ourselves in order to find ourselves. It is the hidden drama that takes place in our imaginations now – already its symptoms appear in our daily and social life. Theatre finds images to reveal this hidden drama so that its reality may not drive us into extinction.

A Norse saga describes a human lifetime as the swift passage of a sparrow as it enters the Great Hall by a window at one end and passes out of the window at the other end. Imagine that all human beings had destroyed each other, that one day a sparrow found a scrap of rag that had been woven by human hands, that it flew with it in its beak to build it into its nest – and that at this all creation shuddered. Poets cannot tell this story. The remnant of the rag has become possible and we have already made creation shudder with our bombs. We should be afraid of the future – we have been there before.

(2000)